WHOM

SHALL WE

SEND?

Understanding the Essentials of Sending Missionaries

Joel Sutton, Editor

Contributing Editor and Compiler - Joel Sutton

General Editor - Sheryl Hash

Theological Editor - Chuck Lawless

Cover Design - Mona Hewitt

Proofreader - Melissa Martin

Contributing Authors

Caleb Crider	Eric King
Areba Houston*	Chuck Lawless
Ken Eells	Randy Rains
Brett Freemon	Jim Riddell
Alan Garnett	Joel Sutton
Larry Gay	Andy Tuttle
Susan Gay	Carlton Vandagriff*
Duane Hammack	Mark Whitworth
Van Williams	

Cover photo: ©iStockphoto.com/Beboy_ltd

* Throughout the book, an asterisk indicates the name has been changed

All scripture references are from the New King James Version

CONTENTS

Prologue: Why Selecting/Sending the Right People is Important   4

Chapter 1 – A Theology of Missions   9

Chapter 2 – Biblical Precedents for Sending and Selecting
     Missionaries   24

Chapter 3 – The Five Components of an Applicant's Life   38

Chapter 4 – Evaluating a Person's Spiritual Maturity   49

Chapter 5 – Facets of a Call to Missions   57

Chapter 6 – Missionary Competencies and Qualifications   74

Chapter 7 – Qualifications that Match the Assignment   85

Chapter 8 – Assessing Physical Health   101

Chapter 9 – Emotional and Psychological Health   113

Chapter 10– The Necessity of Marital Wellness   132

Chapter 11– Educational and Developmental Screening
     of Children   151

Chapter 12– Minor Details are Important   159

Chapter 13– Right Person, Right Place, Right Time,
     Right Assignment   168

Chapter 14– Interviews and Techniques   190

Chapter 15– Personnel Assessment as a Tool in God's Hands   209

Chapter 16– Discipling a Congregation to be "Missionary
     Material"   223

Chapter 17– Developing a Sending Church   239

Chapter 18– Ongoing Relationships on the Mission Field   253

PROLOGUE

At the dawn of the Christian era, the gospel spread rapidly through the efforts of Jesus' apostles, including Paul. According to the church historian Eusebius, the disciples divided the task of evangelizing the world, each one adopting a specific region (Blocher and Blandenier, p. 9). After sowing gospel seeds in the major centers of commerce, Christians in each area proceeded to focus on smaller cities and villages. The early Catholic Church became the vehicle for many of these missionary efforts.

As men proved themselves spiritually—even attaining the status of monkhood or the priesthood—they set out for unknown lands in order to share the good news of Jesus and plant new churches. Unfortunately, paganism was not eradicated in most areas and the gospel's impact appeared to recede. During the ensuing years, the world experienced the rise and spread of Islam, a religion based on good works and rules that were adopted as a quick antidote to people's problems; however, it did not address the need for salvation. Added to that was the augmenting corruption of the institutional church, resulting in a dilution of the evangelistic message.

When the church returned to its biblical roots during the Reformation era, the Anabaptists, among others, pointed back to the Great Commission of Christ. They underscored the need for missionaries to renew their efforts in spreading the unadulterated gospel message to the nations and peoples who did not know God. As European nations began exploring and colonizing other areas of the world, they took with them that commitment to plant the truth of God in foreign soil.

This caused many Protestant believers to form missionary societies, groups that would support those men and women who were consecrated to sharing the gospel among unreached peoples. From then until now, we have seen untold thousands of believers, chosen with care by churches and mission agencies, sent out across the globe with the gospel.

Sending missionaries has always been a hallmark of worldwide evangelization at the heart of the mission of the evangelical church. This has included the careful selection of missionaries, since they are the trusted emissaries sent to the ends of the earth to share the good news of Jesus and to start churches in places where there are none. Even going back to the first missionaries of the Christian era, Paul and Barnabas, we find they were called by the Holy Spirit, with that calling confirmed by the leaders of the Antioch church (Acts 13).

Those who followed in their footsteps and felt called by God to share the gospel in unknown lands were evaluated as to their spiritual maturity, the depth of their foundation in theology, and their readiness to undertake an arduous task. Paul and others like him mentored them so they could not only assist in the ministry of evangelization but also lead the effort in new locales (2 Timothy 2:2).

The need remains for today's churches and mission agencies to exercise care in selecting missionaries they hope to send. Just as Paul modeled in the New Testament, we are to identify and prepare those who are willing to respond to God's call. Not only is there the biblical precedent, there also is the need for these groups to be good stewards of their limited resources. The body of Christ can ill afford to squander members' tithes and offerings by sending out personnel who are not likely to succeed. We have personally witnessed fledgling missionaries who abandoned their post, even before completing language studies.

It's also not fair to prospective personnel to send them out merely based on their personal claim to be called and prepared. Churches and agencies owe these workers a discipleship process that helps them determine if they are mentally, emotionally, physically, and spiritually ready for the rigors and demands of cross-cultural life and ministry. This deep discipleship can help candidates confirm and clarify their calling as well as discover where that calling can best be fulfilled in the missions setting.

The result is the sending of the right people to the right place at the right time in the right assignment. We want to send the right people, those called by God just like Paul and Barnabas in Acts 13. But we also need to know them well enough to confirm the right place—the location and assignment where their gifts and competencies can be best utilized to meet unique local needs.

Perhaps most importantly, the discipleship process takes into account the right timing for deployment, both for the missionary candidate family and the field location. This process is more than simple checklists, although guidelines and procedures play a critical role. It also is a process of spiritual discernment, where the calling in the life of individuals is affirmed by those around them. This is the responsibility of both their local church and the mission-sending agency who work together to confirm the work of the Holy Spirit in their lives.

Margie* is a good example of someone who was eager but not physically ready for living overseas. Margie sensed a deep burden to carry the gospel to unreached peoples and places. But as she went through the selection process, she was newly diagnosed with multiple sclerosis. Since that is a progressive disease, we knew that she would not be able to carry out her tasks in the coming years.

When she was declined for missionary appointment, she was deeply disappointed. However, three years later she sent us a thank you card. Because she remained in the U.S., God had blessed her with a husband and two children. She was so grateful that we had made that difficult decision to not send her to the mission field. She felt that she was truly on the pathway that God had envisioned for her.

Sometimes the decision on whether or not to send someone overseas is not a simple "yes" or "no." It can be a matter of timing. When Stan* and Cara* presented themselves as candidates for missionary service, there were concerns about her episodes with depression as well as his lackluster personality. Undeterred by the delay, this couple proceeded to move to East Asia and work directly with an international school.

While teaching for two years, they demonstrated their heart for evangelism and Cara's ability to function in another culture without falling into depression. It was a time of growth for Stan and Cara, and they were thankful for that interim phase. They were subsequently

6

commissioned as full-time personnel, and they are now serving effectively.

To the casual observer, one might think that those who assess potential personnel simply look at objective data and make decisions based on probable outcome. Actually, the opposite is true. Just as in Acts 13, selecting missionaries is a process guided by the Holy Spirit and fueled by prayer. Mark* and Linda* were interviewed by their mission agency, and nothing suggested they were capable of being effective bearers of the gospel. However, there were glimmers of potential. After much prayer, their interviewer decided that God wanted this couple on the mission field.

Mark and Linda had several obstacles to overcome such as substantial debt and a lack of theological education. But these folks were persistent. With God's help, they removed the debt load and gained the tools they needed for being effective in another culture. Now they've been on the field for eight years. They've seen people come to Christ in an antagonistic culture, and the gospel is making progress in a spiritually dry area.

The vision behind this book is to gather in one place a cumulative wisdom on how to best prepare and select missionaries. Past publications about missionary selection have generally focused on one or two aspects of an assessment process. This volume takes advantage of multiple authors who have a combined total of more than 400 years of experience with missionaries and life on the mission field. Their expertise covers the full spectrum of the missionary's life.

Each author was allowed to voice his or her own perspective on their assigned topic, which implies that not all the writers would necessarily share the same opinions or views. Also, all of these authors were writing out of their experiences with one agency, the International Mission Board (SBC). Each chapter is designed not to be an academic study of a topic, but to reflect the extensive personal experience of the author.

While fund-raising is a common element in the process of sending out missionaries, that particular element does not lie within the scope of this book. Rather, our desire is to share best practices for evaluating potential personnel in every sphere of their lives.

We trust that this book will be a blessing and a resource for all those who bear the responsibility of sending the right people to the right place at the right time—for the purpose of spreading the gospel into all the world.

Carlton Vandagriff, Joel Sutton

1

A Theology of Missions
Why We Must Send Missionaries
by Chuck Lawless

"Theology."

For some hearers, the word itself is not a positive one. I have heard it from students, missionary candidates, and church members alike. "Sometimes theology is just boring." "Why do we need to spend time studying these things? I just want to go to the field and tell others about Jesus." "Theology can be so divisive. I'd rather avoid controversial topics."

I understand these responses. Theology *can* be boring when presented in a dull way. Some of the topics of theology are, in fact, controversial. And for the passionate missionary-to-be, anything that slows the process of getting to the field seems to be an unnecessary obstacle. Zeal for the task sometimes seemingly eclipses the need for training.

This chapter really does matter, however. This book is a book about missions preparation. In it you will learn about the process of missionary sending—from the selection method to member care. This process is an important one, as it is about spreading the greatest news ever heard to people who need to know Jesus. The missionary-sending process is a life-changing one, both for the ones sent and the ones who will hear the gospel.

This chapter is about *why* we send missionaries. It is our theology— that is, the study of God or, by application, the study of doctrine related to God—that drives us to do what we do. Were it not for our theology, the need for this book would not exist. Because we believe what we believe about God, humanity, lostness, and salvation, we know we must send men and women to those who have never heard about Jesus.

Our theology is both the message we proclaim and a motivation for proclaiming it. This chapter will examine that theology in terms of the love of a seeking God, the grace of a suffering God, the mandate of a sending God, and the worship of a saving God. †

The Love of a Seeking God

The God of the Bible is far beyond our comprehension. He always has been, is today, and always will be; He is God from everlasting to everlasting (Psalm 90:1-2). He knows all things (Psalm 147:5; 1 John 3:20), has all power (Jeremiah 32:27; Revelation 19:6), and is present everywhere (Psalm 139:7-10; Proverbs 15:3). He is the source, the sustainer, and the goal of all things (John 1:1-3; Colossians 1:15-17; Revelation 22:13). This God is the One who created the world and Who will bring its history to His appointed conclusion (Genesis 1:1, Revelation 20:11-22:5).

At the apex of His creating the world, God fashioned Adam from the dust of the earth and created Eve from the rib of the man (Genesis 2:7, 21-23). He created them "in His image" (Genesis 1:26-27) and for His glory (Isaiah 42:7). While the text does not tell us specifically what "in His image" means, we can assume that His image was in some way their capacity to be in relationship with the Creator. As God's image bearers, Adam and Eve were to subdue the earth and rule over it as God's representatives (Genesis 1:26). Through the human beings created in His likeness, God would extend His rule over the earth.

All of us are created in God's image, thus affirming the value of all human beings. Even after sin corrupts our being and distorts the image of God within us, still we bear His image in some fashion (Genesis 9:6; James 3:9)—and we matter to Him. Thus, my African friend who sacrifices animals to his perceived gods matters to the only true God. My Muslim friend striving to do enough good works to outweigh the bad at her judgment likewise matters to Him. My Buddhist friend who spins a prayer wheel and my Hindu friend who chants a mantra matter to Him. My European friend denies the existence of a personal God, but even he matters to the God of the Bible. Created in His image, every human being on the earth—even in his/her state apart from God—has intrinsic value and dignity.

Nevertheless, the first human beings listened to the lies of the crafty serpent in the Garden of Eden, followed his enticements, and ignored the word of God (Genesis 3:1-6). Tragically, they rejected the One who had created them in His image and instead idolized their own wishes over the commands of God. They committed sin by crossing the boundary God had established, failing "to live up to the glory of that image (God's) and to give God the glory that naturally belongs to him" (Ashford, Kindle Locations 1298-1300).

The results were both devastating and far-reaching (Genesis 3:7-24). Alienation set in as Adam and Eve were distanced from their Creator, from one another, from creation, and from self. They attempted to hide from His presence, as if that seclusion were even possible. The marriage relationship, childbirth, and physical labor changed. The fall affected even creation, now longing to be freed from the curse brought about by human sin (Romans 8:18-22). God's good creation became a place of catastrophe and chaos.

More specifically, God exacted judgment on sinful humanity by demanding death as the penalty for sin (Genesis 2:16-17, 3:19). Adam and Eve died spiritually immediately, and physical death would occur in years to come. Today, graves around the globe are reminders of the continuing effect of the disaster in the Garden of Eden. As a descendant of Adam, every human being in the world is by nature a child of wrath who does what sinners do: sin (Romans 5:18-19; Ephesians 2:1-3). It is in fact the case that "There is none righteous, no, not one; There is none who understands; There is none who seeks after God. They have all turned aside …" (Romans 3:10-12a).

This story of the Garden of Eden, if it had ended here, would be nothing less than tragedy. What began as a story of intimate relationship and life became an account of separation and death. We, too, live that story. Dead in our sins (Ephesians 2:1), we can do nothing to fix this problem apart from the grace of God.

11

The story was not over, however. God already had a plan by which He would redeem fallen human beings and restore broken creation. In Genesis 3:15, God declared that someone from the seed of the woman would someday crush the head of the serpent, even as the one from the woman would be wounded in the process. Considered to be the *protoevangelium* (that is, the first reference to the gospel), this text foreshadows the triumph of Christ at the cross—a triumph that paradoxically comes through death. Thus, Genesis 3:15 records much more than an announcement of judgment on the serpent; it records ultimately a pre-victory cry from the Creator-Redeemer who would crush the serpent (cf. Romans 16:20).

That this story in the Garden also remains both intimate and personal is evident in Genesis 3:9, where God seeks Adam as the first man hides in his sin. Knowing exactly where Adam was, God nevertheless sought him out and called him to face his wrong. The problem was not fully resolved in that dialogue (Adam and Eve both blamed others for their sin), but a clear biblical pattern was established here: God takes the first step toward sinners who have rejected Him. He is the initiator who seeks those who are running from Him.

Indeed, this theme echoes throughout the Bible. God provided a skin covering for Adam and Eve even as they dealt with their shame (Genesis 3:21). He called out a people in Abraham, through whom the nations of the world would be blessed (Genesis 12:1-3). At His initiative He redeemed His people from slavery in Egypt, illustrating in the process that redemption demands the shedding of blood (Exodus 12:1-13; Hebrews 9:22).

His people often rebelled against Him and followed other gods, but still God remained faithful to His promises to them. Via descendants of Abraham like Joseph, Moses, Joshua, and David, He preserved a remnant of His people and paved the way for the coming of the One first prophesied in Genesis 3:15—Jesus Christ. Through Him would come redemption for a people from every tribe, tongue, and nation in the world (Revelation 7:9-10).

It is for His glory (Habakkuk 2:14; John 12:27-28) and because of His love (John 3:16; Ephesians 1:4-6) that God calls sinners to follow Him.

As we will see in this chapter, His love for a fallen world is so deep that He initiated sending His Son to pay the price for our sin. His love also is so broad that it covers the nations (Genesis 12:1-3, 22:18; Psalm 2, 22, 67, 145; Isaiah 49:6, 52:10; Jonah 1-4; Micah 4:1-2; Habakkuk 2:14; Matthew 28:18-20; Revelation 21:22-26, 22:1-2). Through the story line of creation, fall, redemption, and restoration, the mission of God (*missio dei*) will be completed: all the earth will be filled with the knowledge of His glory (Habakkuk 2:14).

We who are being conformed to the image of God's Son (Romans 8:29) must not ignore our responsibility to take this good news to those among the nations who do not know Jesus. This God of love is still in the process of seeking and saving those who are lost (Luke 19:10).

The Grace of a Suffering God

"Tell me about this man," I said to the caretakers of the burial shrine of a Muslim holy man. Hearing his story, it made sense to me that others might consider him holy. When I asked if that man was in heaven, though, the caretakers' answer was telling: "We hope so, but we can't know for certain." At least they were honest with me—they understood that their faith has no answer for the sin problem all of us face.

Christianity has that answer. At God's appointed time, Jesus took on flesh while maintaining His divinity (Philippians 2:6-11). He was tempted like we are, yet without sinning (Hebrews 4:15). No one taught as authoritatively as He taught (Matthew 7:28-29). He was the Master over nature, demons, sickness, and death (Mark 4:35-5:43). Over against the railings of his opponents, He forgave sin (Mark 2:1-12). So mighty was He that the Gospel writers recognized Him as the Son of God (Mark 1:1), the Father identified Him as such (Mark 1:11), and even the demons recognized His deity (Mark 1:23-24).

Jesus was, as John the Baptist declared, "the Lamb of God who takes away the sin of the world" (John 1:29). When we found ourselves utterly helpless—blinded by the enemy (2 Corinthians 4:3-4), in the domain of darkness (Colossians 1:13), and dead in our trespasses

(Ephesians 2:1)—Jesus died in our place. As the divine sacrifice, He bore the wrath of God we deserved for our sin (1 John 4:10). In the cross He disarmed the powers and broke the back of the serpent of Genesis 3 (Colossians 2:15). Apart from His death there is no salvation (Hebrews 9:11-26), but through His death come reconciliation and redemption (2 Corinthians 5:18-19; Mark 10:45).

Through His resurrection Jesus then broke the power of death (1 Corinthians 15:54-57) and gave believers a living hope (1 Peter 1:3). As the King of kings and Lord of lords who will someday return in power and glory (Revelation 17:14, 19:16; Matthew 24:30), Jesus is indeed the answer to the sin problem for those who turn to Him in repentance and belief (Mark 1:15).

The implications of this truth are several. First, salvation is by grace. While every human being is created in God's image and thus has intrinsic worth, no human being can earn his or her own salvation. No works, regardless of their number or value in the eyes of the world, can bridge the gap our sin has created. Salvation is instead "not of yourselves; it is the gift of God, not of works, lest anyone should boast" (Ephesians 2:8-9). We are God's children solely because of God's unmerited favor, not because of our earned approval.

Second, salvation is costly. Nothing less than the atoning death of Jesus was necessary for men and women to be saved (Luke 24:25-26). Jesus paid the penalty for our sin as He suffered the physical agony of the cross, "bore our sins in his own body" (1 Peter 2:24), and received the wrath of God against our wrongs. His cry of "My God, my God, why have You forsaken Me?" (Matthew 27:46) gives us only a glimpse into the sense of isolation and abandonment He must have felt in that moment. Yet, He so loved the nations that Jesus had already chosen to do the Father's will—regardless of the cost (Matthew 26:42).

Third, Jesus must be central to the message we proclaim to the nations. From Genesis to Revelation, He is the focus of the Bible. He is the prophet who reveals the Father (Hebrews 1:2), the priest who offers Himself as the sacrifice (Hebrews 2:9), and the king who has abolished death (2 Timothy 1:10). Unique to Christianity is the belief that this Jesus—the Son of God—died for us "while we were still sinners" (Romans 5:8); that is, at His initiative He loved us, came to us, and suffered for us despite our unworthiness.

Not only is He central to the message, but He also is the one who gave us the command known as the "Great Commission" to proclaim that message to all nations (Matthew 28:18-20). The one through whom all things were created (John 1:3) and in whom "dwells all the fullness of the Godhead bodily" (Colossians. 2:9) spoke these words. If we perceive Him as less than the Son of God before whom all will be judged (2 Corinthians 5:10), His words will lose their force; a low Christology will lead to a diminished Great Commission focus. On the other hand, truly knowing the majesty and power of the Son should lead to a deep desire to proclaim His name—and consequently, an uncompromised obedience to His commands.

Fourth, there is no salvation apart from conscious faith in Jesus; that is, people must hear the gospel and respond to it in faith and repentance to be saved. No one ever comes to God except through Jesus (John 14:6). As Peter proclaimed, "Nor is there salvation in any other, for there is no other name under heaven given among men by which we must be saved" (Acts 4:12). More specifically, the apostle Paul stated clearly that "whoever calls on the name of the Lord shall be saved" (Romans 10:13)—thus necessitating that others know about the one on whom they may call. Indeed, God sends proclaimers to announce the good news because non-believers cannot be saved apart from the gospel of a suffering Messiah (Romans 10:14-15).

Several years ago, I had the privilege of proclaiming this good news in West Africa. Traveling with a team of students, we journeyed by car to a missionary clinic several hours from any city. There we met missionary doctors and the nationals they were serving that day. It was my responsibility to begin the day with a devotion for the dozens of Africans waiting for treatment. At the end of the teaching, several followed my translator into a side room, where God used him to lead these folks to follow Christ.

Later that night, I quietly reflected on the grace evident that day. I was a seminary professor, but I was not worthy for God to use. The doctors were brilliant men and women who were serving God in a distant land, but they were still sinners. The locals were beautiful people, but their kindness and warmth could not secure their salvation. All who were believers that day were so solely because of the grace of God. Jesus had willingly suffered centuries before because He loved us and did not want us to perish (2 Peter 3:9). That story of grace really is amazing.

The Mandate of a Sending God

As noted earlier, Jesus gave us the Great Commission. Spoken at least four times from the lips of the Son of God (Matthew 28:18-20; Mark 16:15; Luke 24:45-47; John 20:21; Acts 1:8), the Great Commission clearly matters to God. Matthew's expression of the Commission is perhaps the most familiar one:

> Jesus came and spoke to them, saying, "All authority has been given to Me in heaven and on earth. Go therefore and make disciples of all the nations, baptizing them in the name of the Father and of the Son and of the Holy Spirit, teaching them to observe all things that I have commanded you; and lo, I am with you always, even to the end of the age."

This singular plan God has given us assumes a *message*, *messengers*, and *hearers*. The *message*, of course, is the gospel: Christ died for our sins, was buried, and was then raised again the third day (1 Corinthians 15:3-4). His followers were to proclaim repentance and forgiveness of sins in His name to all nations (Luke 24:47); His death was the means by which forgiveness of sins would be offered, and repentance would be a necessary step in gaining that pardon. In a first-century world haunted by unresolved guilt over wrong—and in our world—the forgiveness Jesus offered was surely a welcomed answer to some.

The message includes more than simply sharing the gospel with non-believers, however. The task is not finished with evangelism. "Make disciples" (Matthew 28:19) is an equally non-negotiable element of the Great Commission. Indeed, the disciple-making process includes everything from leading a non-believer to trust in Christ and repent from sin to directing that new Christian in the lifelong task of walking with Christ in obedience. The former is marked by baptism (Matthew 28:19), and the latter is accomplished through teaching (Matthew 28:20).

The goal is that those who follow Christ will live like Him and lead others to do the same. Hence, a process of making disciples that ends with only the conversion of the evangelized is incomplete at best, disobedient at worst. To be frank, the results of this omission can be disastrous. Untaught believers are ill equipped to face trials, untrained to recognize false teachings, and unprepared to teach others. They quickly become easy prey for an enemy who seeks to devour them (1 Peter 5:8). We must, therefore, do the entirety of the Great Commission.

Jesus' followers, including we who are believers today, are the *messengers* who tell the story. In God's amazing plan of grace, He not only saves unworthy people, but He also gives us the privilege of spreading His good news so others might know Him. God takes imperfect people, sends us, and works through our spreading the Word so other imperfect people might follow Him—and then they, too, might lead even more people to trust Him.

It is through the power of the Spirit that we do our work as God's messengers. Knowing that doing the Great Commission was beyond His disciples' ability, Jesus commanded them to wait for the coming of the Spirit prior to beginning their ministry in Jerusalem (Luke 24:49). He also promised them His continual presence (Matthew 28:20); He was, and is, Immanuel ("God with us;" Matthew 1:23). Today, the Holy Spirit empowers us (Acts 1:8), gifts us (1 Corinthians 12:4-11), convicts the world (John 16:7-11), and grants new life (John 3:1-8). Hence, we never do the Great Commission alone.

I wish I could introduce you to some of God's messengers who are serving around the world in the power of God's Spirit: D, who is striving to reach Hindus in South Asia; K and L, who are trying to influence a major South American city for Christ; M, whose family follows Jesus in a war-torn part of the world; A, a North American local church pastor who leads short-term teams to Africa as often as possible; and M, a lay leader whom God has deeply burdened for

Eastern Europe. Each of these messengers would confess an inability to do the Great Commission, but each is a believer filled with the Holy Spirit. Sent by God in that power, all are making an eternal difference.

If the message is the gospel and we are the messengers, who then are the *hearers*? A review of Great Commission passages makes it clear that Jesus intended His followers to carry the good news to the entire world:

> Matthew 28:19—"Go therefore and make disciples of *all the nations.*"
> Mark 16:15—"Go into *all the world* and preach the gospel *to every creature.*"
> Luke 24:47—"repentance and remission of sins should be preached in His name to *all nations.*"
> Acts 1:8—". . . and to *the end of the earth.*"

Though scholars have understood the term "nations" (Matthew 28:19; Luke 24:45) in different ways, it is likely the phrase refers to "peoples" or "ethnic groups." Accordingly, many missionaries today focus on reaching people groups, defined as "an ethno linguistic group with a common self-identity that is shared by the various members" (Web, IMB). With thousands of people groups who still have little or no access to the gospel, the task of fulfilling God's Great Commission mandate remains. The peoples of the world die daily, eternally lost apart from the gospel.

How then do believers make a difference? First, we must accept our responsibility to go to the nations. The God who ordered us to make disciples of all the nations is by nature a sending God who loves the world (John 3:16). The Father sent the Son in "the fullness of the time" (Galatians 4:4). The Son sent His disciples to proclaim the Word (Mark 3:14; John 17:18, 20:21). The Father and the Son sent the Spirit who empowers believers and convicts the world (Acts 1:8; John 16:7-11). Now, this same God sends His followers to the nations with the charge of sharing the gospel. As the Father sent Jesus, so Jesus now sends us (John 20:21).

God does this sending through His church, modeled in the first-century Antioch church's sending out missionaries Paul and Barnabas (Acts 13:1-3). The church is both a partner and a goal in the missionary-sending task: a local congregation affirms, commissions, and prayerfully supports missionaries who seek to plant new churches to the ends of the earth. Those new congregations then become sending units themselves as they in turn raise up and deploy missionaries. Hence, for both the missionary and the locals, the body of Christ is essential to the task of the Great Commission.

Second, we must never fail to proclaim the message of the gospel. Without question, proclamation—that is, verbally speaking the message—is essential to doing the Great Commission. That should not be surprising, if indeed we believe Romans 10:14—"How then shall they call on Him in whom they have not believed? And how shall they believe in Him of whom they have not heard? And how shall they hear without a preacher?"

Apart from hearing the gospel, no person in any people group of the world can be saved; thus, proclaiming the Word is imperative. For this purpose, God sends us to the world—"And how shall they preach unless they are sent?" (Romans 10:15)

Reaching the world will necessitate that many believers cross cultural and linguistic barriers so others might be saved; in fact, this cross-cultural work is the essence of missions. Some go on short-term assignments, and others go under a life calling from God—but all must go out of a sense of "sentness." When we follow the mandate of this sending God, He graciously uses us to draw the nations to Him.

The Worship of a Saving God

Most stories have a beginning, a climax, and conclusion. In some ways, however, the gospel story has no ending. Actually, there can be no ending when the story leads to eternity. The story that began in a garden disrupted by sin will eventually lead to a garden city where sin and death will reign no more (Revelation 21:27). The glory of God will be its light, and the nations will walk in that light (Revelation 21:24). Around the throne of the Lamb will be the global community redeemed through Christ's shed blood:

> After these things I looked, and behold, a great multitude which no one could number, of all nations, tribes, peoples, and tongues, standing before the throne and before the Lamb, clothed with white robes, with palm branches in their hands, and crying out with a loud voice, saying, "Salvation belongs to our God who sits on the throne, and to the Lamb!" (Revelation 7:9-10)

Believers from every nation, tribe, people, and language worshipping the Lord are the glorious picture of the fulfillment of God's plotline of creation, fall, redemption, and restoration. Honoring God around His throne are the nations, recipients of the blessing promised through Abraham (Genesis 12:1-3; Galatians 3:8). They are the fruit of the redemptive work of the Lamb, to whom the worshippers also addressed their adoration in Revelation 5:9-10—"…You were slain, and have redeemed us to God by Your blood out of every tribe and tongue and people and nation, and have made us kings and priests to our God; and we shall reign on the earth." The sheep from all people groups of the world will then be gathered to the Great Shepherd.

These dramatic images of the consummation must be more than words on the page to us. They must be motivators to participate in the mission of God. These images, in fact, give significance to our lives today. We live in the light of eternity, waiting for "the city which has foundations, whose builder and maker is God" (Hebrews 11:10), but we are called to be God's witnesses *today*.

That assignment has eternal consequences: in response to the gospel, some will find forgiveness through faith and repentance, but others will remain unforgiven in rebellion (John 20:23). In either case, we are undeservedly privileged to be God's instruments in kingdom work much bigger than ourselves. Consequently, this Great Commission task ought to humble us.

I have been blessed to preach the gospel and worship with believers around the globe. One worship service in Russia was a formal gathering in a church building with a choir singing hymns. In the Philippines, I worshipped with hundreds of local pastors as they raised their hands in exaltation. In Africa the believers danced and jumped as they honored God in their mud-hut church structure.

The worship location in East Asia was a hidden one, but still the Christ-followers sang so loudly that their praises echoed off the walls. We worshipped in various locations in different languages, but all of us will one day gather and worship God together—because somebody shared the gospel with us, and God saved us. Others will also someday join the worship because God uses us to tell them that same story. That's humbling.

Our desire for others to be among that throng should produce urgency in our work. While these worship images in the book of Revelation are glorious, we must not forget the equally biblical images of judgment for the unforgiven. Ultimately, God will justly condemn non-believers to hell, a place of unquenchable fire and eternal torment (Mark 9:43; Rev. 14:11, 20:10). Our demonic enemy will do all he can do to distract our attention from this teaching, but we must not abandon its truth.

This gripping reality of judgment ought to produce in us a grief that drives us to the task of missions. Jesus agonized over the state of Jerusalem when that city rejected Him (Matthew 23:37-38). Paul considered the lost condition of the Jews with "great sorrow and continual grief" (Romans 9:2). He was, in fact, even willing to be accursed himself in order to save his kinsmen if that were possible (Romans 9:3). God finds no pleasure in the death of the wicked (Ezekiel 33:11), and nor should we. The reality of hell must lead us to evangelistic action among the nations.

Finally, the promise of worship described in the book of Revelation should give us confidence in doing the Great Commission. The world may see evangelism as politically incorrect and intolerant, but gospel work goes on. The evil one sows his tares in the church (Matthew 13:24-30, 36-43), but God will judge rightly in the end. The righteous will suffer persecution (John 15:20), but death for the believer has lost its sting (1 Corinthians 15:55-56). The enemy seeks to keep non-believers blinded to the gospel (2 Corinthians 4:3-4), but God will ultimately save and gather His own around His throne.

We go, then, to the nations not only in the confidence that the gospel will be proclaimed (Matthew 24:14), but also in the assurance that the gospel will save (Romans 1:16). We go in His strength (Ephesians 6:10). We march forward wearing His armor (Ephesians 6:10-17), proclaiming His Word, and trusting His Spirit to change lives. We go knowing that the church of Jesus Christ stands behind us. The work of the cross will be effective, and our efforts will not be in vain. The redeemed from all the nations *will* worship Him.

With that confidence, we can go wherever God calls us to go without regard for sacrifice. In that same assurance, we can send others. Should any of us die in the task, we will simply join in the eternal worship of a missionary God.

Conclusion

I assume you are reading this book because you have interest in recruiting and sending missionaries. If I were to ask you why you have this interest, I suspect your answer would be related to your theology. A loving God suffered for our sins, seeks and saves us, and will gather His own around the throne in eternity. We proclaim this word to the nations not only because He mandated us to do so, but also because the message is a message of life and death. We go, and we send missionaries because of what we believe. It's really that simple.

So, I challenge you to rehearse this story of the gospel over and over again. Love it. Believe it. Follow it. Tell it to others. And then send others to the nations to do the same.

<u>**Works Cited**</u>

Zane Pratt, "The Heart of Mission: Redemption," in Bruce Ashford (2011-09-01), *Theology and Practice of Mission: God, the Church, and the Nations* (Kindle Locations 1298-1300). B&H Publishing. Kindle Edition.
http://public.imb.org/globalresearch/Pages/default.aspx

† Some portions of this article were first published in "To All the Nations," *The Southern Baptist Journal of Theology,* vol. 15 no. 2 (Summer 2011): 16-27.

About the Author

Dr. Lawless currently serves as Professor of Evangelism and Missions, Dean of Graduate Studies, and Vice-President for Graduate Studies and Ministry Centers at Southeastern Seminary in NC. In addition, he serves as Global Theological Education Consultant for the International Mission Board. He is a graduate of the University of the Cumberlands (BSEd) and The Southern Baptist Theological Seminary (M.Div., Ph.D). He and his wife, Pam, reside in Wake Forest, NC.

2

Biblical Precedents for Sending
and Selecting Missionaries
by Jim Riddell

In October 1944 my parents, Gerald and Virgie Riddell, arrived in Richmond, Virginia, for a week of meetings with the staff of the then Foreign Mission Board (now International Mission Board). During the following week, they participated in a series of interviews and other meetings hoping that it would result in their appointment as Southern Baptist missionaries.

After writing an account of the history of their lives, they received a medical exam and had interviews with a psychiatrist. They attended a variety of other meetings until Friday when they were appointed as overseas missionaries. They went on to serve for 36 years sharing the good news and planting churches in Colombia and Chile.

In those days the corresponding secretary of the Foreign Mission Board and his assistant were responsible for evaluating candidates for missionary service. The use of doctors and psychiatrists was one part of the board's evaluation process for many years. They also used tools such as interviews and written documents, including a personal testimony, a statement of call to missionary service, references, financial profile, doctrinal statements, medical history, and a personal history including family dynamics and marital adjustments.

The evaluation process has always been an attempt to "send the missionaries who are called and otherwise qualified" (IMB public minutes, October 1990, February 1992). But many have said, "If a person is called to be a missionary, then why should all these other aspects of their lives be examined?" That is an excellent question, and it demands a scriptural response. Are there biblical precedents for delving into a missionary applicant's personal life, family dynamics, and emotional well-being?

In the following sections, I will point to numerous principles found in scripture that support the evaluation and assessment process required of prospective missionaries. There are biblical precedents that can instruct any organization or church that proposes to send missionaries overseas.

Responsibilities of the Senders

Let's begin by reflecting on the connection between the sending body and those who actually go out to share the gospel. The primary New Testament example would be the relationship between the church in Antioch and the men who were sent out from that congregation: Paul, Barnabas, and John Mark.

> Now in the church that was at Antioch there were certain prophets and teachers: Barnabas, Simeon who was called Niger, Lucius of Cyrene, Manaen who had been brought up with Herod the tetrarch, and Saul. As they ministered to the Lord and fasted, the Holy Spirit said, "Now separate to Me Barnabas and Saul for the work to which I have called them." Then, having fasted and prayed, and laid hands on them, they sent them away (Acts 13:1-3).

The Holy Spirit took the initiative and led the church to set apart Barnabas and Saul. The congregation was obedient to the Holy Spirit and in so doing became the human agents for setting them apart. The laying on of hands simply affirmed the congregation's blessing and endorsement on their call. When the church took the initiative to set apart these men as missionaries, the congregation and its leaders took on a variety of responsibilities and roles.

1. Nurturing

One of the church's greatest privileges is found in nurturing and challenging its own to be a part of the great missionary enterprise. As mentioned above, the church at Antioch separated Barnabas and Saul

25

for the missionary task. That was preceded by a transformation in the church where Gentiles were first accepted as true believers. The movement of the spirit was so powerful that the people in the city started calling them "Christians." It was a church environment that spiritually nurtured its members to the point they were ready to leave and share the gospel.

Another example of a church sending out its own was the church in Lystra where Timothy had grown up. That congregation had nurtured him for many years, shaping him into a mature believer. That's why "he was well spoken of by the brethren who were at Lystra and Iconium" (Acts 16:2).

A pastor's wife recently recounted her struggle with being called to missions. The church she and her husband attended was actively involved in volunteer projects in the country where they would ultimately serve. She said that during a women's prayer group, the women were praying that someone in their church would be called to missions. Yet in her heart, she was saying "Shut up, that's my life you are talking about" (Creswell, p. 39). It was the church's nurturing environment that allowed her to wrestle with her call to the mission field.

Drew and Cassie Roberts* described how their church provided the environment that nurtured them as they recognized their call. Drew said that while growing up in the church, he participated in several mission trips in the U.S. When the church developed a ministry in Honduras, Drew went there six times as a part of that effort. Then they went on their first trip as a couple. That experience, along with the encouragement of their pastoral staff and the support of their small group, enabled them to explore their call and find affirmation through fellow believers. Their church knew them well and had nurtured their growing interest in missions.

2. Authority

Barnabas and Saul did not make the decision to undertake a new ministry on their own. Even as they traveled, they were not functioning as individuals but as representatives of the church in

Antioch. Yes, the church respected Barnabas and Saul because they had been critical in the development of the church, and because they knew that God had set them aside for service. But the church was the source of authority for those early missionaries. Barnabas and Saul respected the church and relied on that body to provide direction, to offer prayer support, and to serve as a home base.

When we look at the first-century church, the strategic decisions about where to serve appear to have been made by the missionaries themselves. In addition, the church did not dictate the means or methods they were to use. But when there was a decision about key doctrinal issues or areas where there was conflict, the church as a whole did exercise its authority.

For example, when a dispute arose about Gentiles becoming a part of the church, the conflict required an authoritative word. That was a decision that Paul could not make on his own. Even the sending church in Antioch would not make that decision but instead sent the men on to Jerusalem. And that was the setting for the first church conference, the Jerusalem Council, described in Acts 15. In that instance, we see Paul, Barnabas, and the Judaizers accepting the authority of the church and the decision they reached.

3. Validating the Missionary Call

Before considering the sending body's responsibility to validate a person's call to missions, we must first discuss the biblical concept of such a specific direction and vocation. Throughout the Old and New Testaments, God has called His people to proclaim His Word to the whole world, and He has been calling and sending individuals to proclaim the kingdom of God throughout history.

Abram is introduced to us in Genesis with a statement of call. God's instructions required him to leave his home and his roots and go to a distant land. It also carried the promise that through him the whole world would be blessed.

> Get out of your country, from your family and from your father's house, to a land that I will show you. I will make you

a great nation; I will bless you and make your name great; and you shall be a blessing. I will bless those who bless you, and I will curse him who curses you; and in you all the families of the earth shall be blessed (Genesis 12:1-3).

Isaiah later described for us an event that took place in the context of a worship experience in the temple. After undergoing a cleansing from sin, he heard the voice of God saying, "Whom shall I send and who will go for us?" to which Isaiah quickly responded, "Here am I! Send me!" (Isaiah 6:8). Note the profound effect of the experience on Isaiah. His enthusiastic response stands in contrast to Moses who was so reluctant to respond to God's call on his life (Exodus 3). Isaiah volunteered to go without even knowing the task that would be required.

Jonah is usually thought of as the prophet who ran from God's call. But in looking carefully at where God sent him, it was a specific call to Nineveh, the capital of the despised Assyrian Empire that ultimately defeated the northern kingdom of Israel (Jonah 1-4).

The prophet Jeremiah also described a powerful sense of call from God. The Lord said "Before I formed you in the womb I knew you; before you were born I sanctified you; I ordained you a prophet to the nations" (Jeremiah 1:5). Jeremiah was designated as a prophet even before he was formed in the womb. That call demonstrates a powerful sense of divine selection, an appointment to a specific assignment.

A quick look at the New Testament shows us that the concept of being called to service ultimately has worldwide implications. The Gospel of Matthew demonstrates the concept of a progressive call. Chapter 4:18-22 is the account of Jesus calling James, John, Peter, and Andrew to follow Him. They had already been His followers (John 1:35-42), but He would now make them "fishers of men," which can be seen as a call to be disciples.

Then in Matthew 10 He sends them on a preaching mission to proclaim "the kingdom of heaven is at hand." On this occasion He sends them with instructions to only go "to the lost sheep of the house of Israel." But ultimately, the gospel ends with the Great Commission

(Matthew 28:18-20), which has clear implications for the church but can be understood and applied in a personal way.

Paul's call was specifically to serve as a missionary to the Gentiles. In his letter to the Galatians (1:15-16), Paul talks about being set apart from birth, attesting to a powerful sense of destiny and mission. He also speaks of this call in his testimony described in Acts: "Depart, for I will send you far from here to the Gentiles" (Acts 22:21).

Throughout the scriptures, God calls individuals specifically to "go to the nations." That call literally transforms their life and identity from that point forward. It also gives the individual a sense of destiny and purpose.

Let's return to the story of my parents and see what led to their appointment as missionaries. Both of them experienced a call to ministry while they were in college. They met and married while they were students in seminary. Sometime during their first year of marriage there was a chapel service where a well-known local pastor was speaking. This pastor had recently been appointed as a missionary.

When they went to bed that night, my parents couldn't sleep. After several hours, my dad told my mother that he believed that he had been called to missions. My mother replied, "I have been lying here trying to figure out how I could tell you the same thing." The events of that day were so compelling that it set the course for their ministry and their sense of identity for the rest of their lives.

Another missionary described his call to missions while serving as a pastor. This church had everything—a healthy budget, progressive people, and an average age around 30. Houses were going up in the area, and it was an exciting time for the congregation. Still he wasn't as happy as he expected to be.

"It was exactly what I wanted, but still there was not that contentment," he recalls. In the back of his mind, the thought of international missions kept returning (Creswell, pp. 41-42). It was in that context that the pastor was able to sense God's call to leave his home culture and share the gospel with those who had no opportunity to hear about Jesus.

Cassie Roberts, the missionary mentioned earlier, describes how her call was the result of trips to Peru.

"On the first trip, God overcame some barriers, making it possible for us to go. During that time, God really touched my heart. But on the second trip, I was in the kitchen most of the time cooking with Marujah. I was frustrated that I could not share deeply with her. I did not speak any Spanish and she did not speak any English, but we got along very well. Then it came time to leave and I did not want to. I began feeling that I could live here."

So is it necessary for a church to validate and verify that someone has truly been called by God to serve overseas? Yes, that is a responsibility revealed in Acts 13. Imagine if a person has been caught up in the excitement of a mission trip or has had a powerful spiritual experience. He or she believes that they're definitely called to go share the gospel overseas. But fellow church members may have some concerns. Perhaps they perceive potential difficulties in relationships, or they question the person's ability to survive long term in an overseas assignment.

One pastor I knew was an effective preacher, an enthusiastic evangelist, and he had participated in several mission projects overseas. It seemed like he would have made an excellent missionary. But as we continued to talk, there were some things that caused us to question whether his ministry would be better at home or overseas. We spent a lot of time talking, but in the end we did not recommend him and his wife for missionary service.

They were understandably disappointed and a bit angry. But years later, this pastor wrote a book. In the acknowledgements section, he thanked me for preventing him from making the biggest mistake of his life. In time, it became obvious that God had a different ministry in mind for him (Roberts, p. 9).

We've already seen there is ample biblical precedent for the sending body to look carefully at a person's statement of call to missions. It is their responsibility to sense God's leadership in validating that call. There may be times when a church cannot affirm a person's desire to serve, but a closed door to serving overseas is simply an indication to look for the open door of opportunity that God is providing.

4. Stewardship

In Luke14:27-33, Jesus gives two parables that speak to the issue of counting the cost before making a commitment. The first is about a man who plans to build a tower, and the second refers to a king who is preparing for war and must decide if they should go into battle. Using that same wisdom, God's people can also be good managers of the resources they have at their disposal, whether human or financial. A sending body must exercise caution before sending out missionaries. They should count the cost of supporting the missionary on the field and providing resources for living and doing ministry. That includes, in today's society, the cost of transportation, medical expenses, children's education, housing, and other obligations that are a part of daily living. The sending body must consider two things: a) whether they can afford to send this individual to the field, and b) whether there is a high probability that this person will be effective in service.

In this same vein, missionaries must also be good stewards of the resources being invested. They need to count the cost of living in a foreign country, consider the separation from family and friends, think through the dynamics of raising a family in an international culture, and weigh the risks that are a part of living overseas.

In talking to candidates who were applying for service, I would often challenge them to make sure that when they go, they will stay for their designated term. We discussed the investment our agency and denomination were making in their preparation, training, transportation, language learning, and salary. If they were to resign after a few months on the field, then that investment would represent a loss—a loss for the sending group, for their financial supporters, and for the field personnel who expected them to make a significant contribution to the ministry.

5. Assessment of Timing

Some have assumed that since God has called, one must go immediately to the place of assignment. But if we look at Jeremiah, we note that he was called before he was born. He obviously had to wait years until he grew up and was mature enough to handle the ministry to which he had been called.

Another example is seen in Paul's ministry. In the testimonies he gives in Acts 22:1-21 and 26:1-23, Paul indicates that his call to the Gentiles came quite early in his Christian experience. Galatians 1:11-24 tells us that soon after he gave his life to the Lord, he went into the Arabian Desert for three years. Then he went to Jerusalem and presented himself to the church and started preaching. Paul ran into opposition, was secretly taken to Caesarea, and then went back to Tarsus, his hometown (Acts 9:26-29).

We do not know how long he was in Tarsus, but it is estimated that it could have been as long as nine years or more. Then Barnabas came to Tarsus and invited him to come and help him in the Antioch church (Acts 11:25-26). What happened during those in-between years? He likely spent the time reflecting on his theology and rethinking it in terms of his newfound Christian faith.

In addition, he needed to spend time separating himself from his reputation as a persecutor of the faith. This occurred while he most likely practiced ministry on a local level. It was on that first mission trip with Barnabas, after they completed the ministry in Cyprus, that Saul was finally ready to become Paul and assume leadership of the mission team.

Frequently, we may find that people sense a call to missions but are not yet ready. They may need to complete their education, spend time getting some ministry experience, work through personal issues that need to be resolved, etc. The sending body must determine the right time for someone to leave family and home in order to share the gospel in another part of the world.

6. Selection

Should a church or missionary agency simply send anyone who states that he or she has been called to serve as missionaries? What is the responsibility of the body to evaluate and select those whom they will send?

In Acts 13, there was no apparent elaborate system for evaluating people who would follow the call to serve in the missionary enterprise. But as mentioned earlier, Barnabas and Saul did not make this decision by themselves. The church knew them and had watched them function in life and in Christian service. Many of them had likely been discipled by Barnabas or Saul. Their Christian maturity was evident to the congregation.

Another example of selection can be seen in Acts 15:36-37 where Paul and Barnabas are contemplating their next missionary journey. In that discussion, Barnabas wanted to take John Mark along. But Paul "insisted that they should not take with them the one who had departed from them in Pamphylia, and had not gone with them to the work" (Acts 15:38). On the first missionary journey, John Mark had accompanied the team through Cyprus but left them once they arrived in Pamphylia.

We do not know why he left the team. Perhaps he lacked the emotional and spiritual stamina necessary to stay the course. So Paul questioned the wisdom of taking Mark a second time based on his previous experience. In this case, it was Paul's assessment that Mark should not go rather than the church's. It should be noted that in spite of Paul's assessment, Mark did accompany Barnabas to Cyprus and he did have a significant ministry, which Paul noted years later in 2 Timothy 4:11. Why did Barnabas affirm John Mark? Probably because he knew the young man better than Paul. After all, they were close relatives (see Colossians 4:10).

Character Qualities of the Sent Ones

1 Timothy 3:1-13 and Titus 1:5-9 both outline the qualifications that churches should use to evaluate prospective elders and deacons. Is it valid to apply these qualifications to missionary applicants? Commentators on both passages state that the qualifications are not limited to Christian leaders, but they represent "sensible traits that would aid in any job performance" (Lea and Griffin, p. 107). Another states that the character traits would encompass any position, secular or ecclesiastical, where oversight is necessary (Guthrie, p. 79).

Following that line of reasoning, it would be appropriate to evaluate prospective missionaries in light of the qualifications listed in 1Timothy and Titus. In addition, if we consider that the primary task of missionaries is to be witnesses to the ends of the earth, it seems reasonable to expect them to live up to the standards required of elders and deacons.

The length of service and the type of ministry could define the degree to which these areas are evaluated. For example, if a person were going on a short-term mission trip with a group from his or her church, not all of these characteristics would need careful scrutiny. However, if the person is looking at an assignment that will be several months or more and he or she will spend considerable time ministering alone, then these traits would need to be considered more carefully.

These personal qualities can be summarized in the following positive character traits:
- Above reproach
- A faithful spouse
- Temperate
- Self-controlled
- Respectable
- Hospitable
- Gentle
- A good reputation with outsiders
- Upright, a solid teacher able to teach sound doctrine

There also are some negative character traits to be avoided:

- Given to drunkenness
- Violent
- Quarrelsome

- A lover of money
- Greedy for gain
- An immature believer

Missionary personnel are called to go and serve all over the world as "ambassadors for Christ" (2 Corinthians 5:20). They are asked to live in societies that may be antagonistic to the gospel. Yet they also are required to relate to people in a warm and engaging manner that gives them the opportunity to share the good news. The positive characteristics mentioned above are essential to that task. At the same time, missionary personnel are constantly under scrutiny. Any negative behavior has the potential for canceling the person's effective testimony.

The life of a missionary is not an easy one. Learning a language and living cross-culturally are stressful. In that environment, temptation is very real and the missionary must be well defended against Satan's schemes to undermine his or her testimony. A careful review of the missionary candidate's emotional life, marital adjustments, and struggles with morality is mandatory. These personal qualities will demonstrate to the sending body whether or not that person is ready to engage in cross-cultural life and ministry.

Summary

Whatever happened to Drew and Cassie Roberts? I had the privilege of traveling with them on their two church-sponsored trips to Peru. During those trips, I observed their quick adaptation to the field, their servant spirit, and their ability to work in a cross-cultural setting without any language preparation. In addition, they seemed to exhibit the character traits that have already been mentioned.

At the end of the second trip, we were sitting in the departure lounge shortly after midnight, ready to board the flight back home. By that time I was convinced that they would make great missionaries, so I asked them if they had ever considered serving on a long-term basis.

They smiled and said that their missions pastor had talked to them about the same thing. I simply affirmed to them the qualities we had seen and encouraged them to pray about future opportunities.

After returning home, they did pray. They also sought out their small group in church and shared their interest. Many of their fellow believers affirmed them, saying "We wondered when you would realize that call." One day, Cassie was looking at potential assignments on a mission agency's website and she found a request that "seemed to be written with them in mind." So they started the application process. After writing their lengthy personal history, filling out medical questionnaires, preparing doctrinal statements, submitting references and attending an interview conference, they finally yielded to that compelling sense that God was calling them.

The agency carefully reviewed their documents, looking for evidence of the character traits that we have already mentioned. The assessing team was able to affirm what their church had seen, and they were approved for service within months after returning from that mission trip.

The Robertses were selected to be missionaries following the biblical model outlined above.

1. The church nurtured this couple and helped them grow spiritually.
2. They submitted to the authority of their church's sending body.
3. Their church and its sending body took the time necessary to validate their sense of call to missions.
4. In light of stewardship concerns, the family was carefully evaluated as to their readiness for cross-cultural ministry.
5. In working with the missionary agency, they were able to discern the right time for leaving home and family.
6. Following careful examination and prayerful dialogue, the family was selected and matched to the assignment they felt called to do.

If a sending body will follow this model, they will be able to wisely send out those people who are called, prepared, and ready to impact a dark corner of the world with the gospel of Christ.

Works Cited

Creswell, Mike, "The bittersweet call to foreign missions," *Commission* magazine, December 1982.

Guthrie, Donald, ed. "Tyndale New Testament Commentary, 1 Timothy" Eerdmans, Grand Rapids, 1971.

Lea, Thomas E. and Griffin, Hayne P. "1 Timothy, New American Commentary," Broadman Press, Nashville, 1992.

Roberts, Bob, Jr. "Glocalization," Zondervan Publishing, Grand Rapids, Michigan.

About the Author

Jim Riddell grew up in Colombia and Chile where his parents served as missionaries for thirty-six years. He attended college and seminary in Texas, receiving the Master of Divinity and Doctor of Ministry degrees from Southwestern Baptist Theological Seminary. He has served as a Pastor and Campus Minister. In addition, he worked for over twenty-eight years in various roles related to interviewing, evaluating and selecting prospective missionaries for overseas service with the International Mission Board.

3

The Five Components of an Applicant's Life
by Joel Sutton

All people are complicated. That's not a complaint or a negative statement. I've simply found that we all have multiple layers. Getting to know people well—understanding their deepest thoughts and motives—can often require years of gradual revelation. Husbands and wives discover after decades of marriage that they are just beginning to figure out their spouse.

This complexity of the human heart is by design. God created us in His image, and that automatically produced a multifaceted individual. "Then God said, 'Let Us make man in Our image, according to Our likeness'" (Genesis 1:26a). Just as God is three persons in One, we are also a shadow of God's complexity.

- We have an **inner person** where we think, feel, and make decisions. Our mind, will, and emotions interact, creating attitudes, motives, and priorities.
- Our **outer person** is more than a shell. Our physical body is what enables all our thoughts and feelings to be expressed. When people interact with us, they can know only what our outer person is revealing, whether verbally or through body language.
- If we were simply intelligent animals, we could stop with the first two persons. However, God made us to be more than that. We also possess a **spiritual person**. There's a part of us that is not hindered by space, time, or dimension. Our spirit is able to enter eternity and commune with God Himself. And when we die, our spirit isn't bound to the body. We are able to leave this earth and travel to heaven. We can be "absent from the body" and "present with the Lord" (2 Corinthians 5:8).

- Even though we are three persons, we still only have one identity. We operate under a single name, the one given to us by our parents. But in psychological terms, we use the Latin translation of "I am" to identify ourselves. It's the word "ego." So we are three persons, all wrapped up in a single ego envelope, one identity.

With this understanding of how God designed us, it becomes even clearer how complicated we can be as individuals. Our inner person is composed of several elements—mind, will, and emotions—and all of that is enmeshed with our spiritual person. If those puzzle pieces were visible to the naked eye, people would be less difficult to understand. Instead, we have a thick curtain covering all of our inner secrets. Our outer person is capable of hiding the details about what we're thinking and why. Our words and body language can convey messages that are the opposite of what we're genuinely thinking or feeling.

In addition, we have another layer to penetrate. Our ego or personal identity can cloud the picture. If we're pretending to be something that we're not, we can mislead others as they try to get to know us.

Because we are all complex, it can be difficult to know missionary applicants and whether or not they are ready for the mission field. When I first met Jim* and Sandy* in a Dallas restaurant, they were the picture-perfect couple. She was highly energetic, physically fit, active in church, and had a business of her own. He already had missions experience and continued to feel a burden to share the good news of Jesus with those who had no access to the gospel. He was a successful businessman working for a huge international corporation.

As we moved into the application process, the image this couple had portrayed started to unravel. Jim had significant anger issues, especially in his marital relationship. On top of that, he spent his private moments gazing at pornography. And it turned out that his anger and pornography use were deeply rooted in his past. The things that happened to him as a child were still affecting his habits.

Sandy had equally dramatic issues. She was functioning with Jim in a codependent mindset. She was suffering from low self-esteem and was attempting to manipulate Jim by withholding sex. But the roots of her dysfunction extended much further into the past than just her relationship with Jim. She had gone through a difficult upbringing as a child, and she was traumatized as a teen when she was raped. As a result, she was bound up with multiple fears—without even realizing it.

We cannot depend on what we observe with our five senses when assessing missionary applicants. It's necessary that we penetrate all the layers in order to get a good picture of the total person. If there are issues that will cause a problem on the mission field, they are usually well-hidden. Cross-cultural stress will cause those issues to emerge and worsen, but by then it is too late. That person, even their family, may be permanently damaged. And the advancing work of the mission cause may be stymied or set back considerably. Consequently, it is supremely important that those responsible for recommending missionary applicants conduct a comprehensive assessment.

In order to not miss any elements as we examine our multifaceted missionary candidates, it's helpful to take all the pieces of the puzzle and categorize them. That helps the assessor keep track of whether or not the full picture has been assembled. As we have examined the totality of a person's character and life experiences, we've come up with the following five components that seem to summarize a missionary applicant's full identity:

1. Christian and Church Identity
2. The Missionary Call
3. Missionary Competencies and Qualifications
4. Health and Wellness
5. Missionary Preparation Pragmatics

In the coming paragraphs, we'll examine briefly what is included in each component and why it is important to assess that area of a person's life.

Component One: Christian and Church Identity

This category covers an individual's spiritual life, from beginning to the present. It includes beliefs and how they've been verified through action and attitude.

- **A genuine profession of faith**—In this area, we need to make sure the applicant is genuinely born again and not just religious.
- **Local church identity or membership**—An applicant demonstrates consistent affiliation with the sending body or denomination and is faithfully engaged in ministry through the church.
- **Spiritual disciplines**—The vitality of a candidate's relationship with God is often exemplified through the disciplines used to cultivate that person's connection with the Lord. This includes habits such as focused prayer, intentional Bible reading, fasting, witnessing, and so on.
- **Christian beliefs**—In today's world of diverse influences, we can never assume what a person holds as true in regard to foundational doctrines. And those beliefs are the bedrock of a missionary's priorities and call to ministry.'
- **Other requirements**—Depending on the sending group, whether a church or an agency, there may be specific views or practices that are considered important as part of that group's identity. This would include non-core doctrines such as mode of baptism, view of tithing, glossolalia, and many others.

Here's an example of a couple who needed to find a missions agency that would fit their spiritual background. Charlie* and Roberta* had several different influences as the Lord sought them out and matured their faith. Roberta gave her heart to Jesus in an international church in which believers from all around the world gathered. She absorbed many of their ideas regarding spirituality. Charlie was saved in a church that believed you could lose your salvation. In addition, his aunt came from a charismatic church. When you combine all that together, you can end up with a rather confused spiritual identity.

In time, this couple determined for themselves that they were very conservative in their beliefs. As a result, Charlie actually left a ministry position in his church. He realized he no longer fit that denomination. After serving several years as independent missionaries, they finally solidified their allegiance with a specific group of churches. With such a multi-colored patchwork of experiences in their background, it was necessary for their new sending agency to carefully evaluate their Christian and church identity.

Component Two: The Missionary Call

There are different views as to whether or not a specific call to serve overseas is necessary. However, there are some things that are mandatory in making sure that a person who is preparing to leave family and home is not doing so out of improper motives.

- **Call to obedience**—Is the applicant seeking overseas service because of scriptural commands and a sense of God's personal leading, or is missions simply a noble aspiration?
- **Call to cross-cultural missions**—Everybody has been tasked with sharing the gospel within their own home culture. But not everyone is gifted or called to leave all that is familiar and step over cultural boundaries in order to incarnate the gospel message among another people.
- **Confirming the call of both husband and wife**—With a couple, it is entirely possible that one of them is prodding the other to consider overseas service, yet that spouse has not yet discerned God's direction or timing. If both are not equally called to serve cross-culturally, it can ruin the couple's relationship and ministry.

Tom* and Shelley* experienced God's call to serve overseas in such different ways, it was obvious the Lord was using this to show them the right timing for the move to another country. Tom had sensed a tug toward missions when he was a teenager, and he took a trip to Zimbabwe. That experience ignited a passion in his heart and he was certain that God had equipped him for overseas ministry. Shelley was open to being a missionary, but God had not indicated that such was His will for her.

Tom and Shelley fell in love, got married, had children, and gained ministry skills. Through all these experiences, they grew in maturity and perspective. When they were finally ready for cross-cultural missions service, God touched Shelley's heart. He placed a burning passion in her heart for the nations and assured her that this was His desire for them as a couple. In retrospect, they were glad they waited until both of them sensed that call to missions. Had they gone earlier, they would not have been ready emotionally or spiritually.

Component Three: Missionary Competencies and Qualifications

Just as you would not hire a trained plumber to fix your computer, or employ a landscaper to lay tile in your kitchen, you don't want to accept someone for missionary service just because they have an interest in other cultures. You want to make sure they've prepared themselves for this specific niche of ministry.

- **Ministry experience**—This would include involvement in evangelism efforts and discipleship either in groups or one-on-one.
- **Evangelism training and experience**—Does the applicant take the initiative to share the gospel on a regular basis? And can he or she share the full gospel clearly, to the point of inviting a person to become a follower of Jesus Christ?
- **Cross-cultural ministry experience**—When God has been working in someone's life, preparing the person for full-time, cross-cultural ministry, He will often have led the individual to gain experience dealing with other cultures and languages. This can happen through ministry to internationals or frequent involvement in mission trips.
- **Spiritual gifting**—Part of assessing potential missionaries' readiness for service involves examining their motivational gifts and how they've been expressing those spiritual abilities in ministry. If they have a passion flowing out of God's grace, it will be noticeable.

- **College or other education requirements**—A cross-cultural worker cannot have a narrow view of life, the result of limited experience and education. In order to be open to a new culture, new value systems, and new experiences, an applicant needs to have a well-rounded view of life. There must be an ability to connect with others on multiple levels, and college education is often the means to achieve that flexibility.
- **Theological training**—If your applicants are going to be involved in cross-cultural evangelism, discipleship, church planting, and development, they will need the appropriate tools gained through seminary education.
- **Specific job match qualifications**—If the situation on the mission field calls for someone who can work in a different type of job, just so they can have a valid presence among the people, then your applicants may need specialized preparation. Some assignments may call for English-as-a-Second-Language (ESL) certification, medical training, or a background in communications.
- **Age limitations**—The ages of children may be important to the sending body in determining if the family can make a successful adjustment to the new culture. Also, it may be necessary to consider the impact of an adult's age on learning a new language.

A country in South America was making progress in developing its own missionaries. However, they needed help with giving good theological training and ministry tools to their new personnel. Who could possibly help them? Enter Bob and Patty Williams.* They had already served for eight years as missionaries in a Spanish-speaking country. Most recently, Bob had been working on his doctorate. Interestingly enough, his thesis was on theological education in South America. Patty also was an educator with a degree in childhood education and years of experience in the classroom.

It appeared at first that the ages of their children would be a problem; they were 15 and 13. But actually this was a plus. They were mature emotionally and spiritually. In addition, they already had skills in speaking Spanish. It seemed that God had prepared this couple specifically to meet this need on the mission field. Their qualifications and competencies were evident.

Component Four: Health and Wellness

This category may be the most far-reaching and impactful of all the categories. If a person or family does not have a foundation of good health, it can negatively impact every aspect of their ministry.

- **Physical health of each family member**—Physical wellness often determines a person's ability to function on the mission field. And if the sending body is unable to provide appropriate medical care, it could short-circuit the ministry. Some health conditions don't preclude missionary service, but they could determine where a person should be located. I've heard sending bodies say that if a person can breathe, they can serve as a missionary. That may be true for a limited time, but when it comes to being a good steward of available funds, it is important that the assessing team consider carefully if a person is physically fit to withstand the rigors of cross-cultural living.

- **Emotional health**—As mentioned earlier, it's much easier to see and diagnose the health of the outer person. But illnesses and wounds of the inner person are no less important. If individuals have not experienced healing in their soul, they don't need to go into a stressful situation in another culture and language. That would only exacerbate the problem. Areas to be examined include depression, anxiety, traumatic experiences, abuse (sexual, physical, emotional, verbal), vulnerability to pornography, inappropriate sexual behavior, eating disorders and the use of alcohol, tobacco, or drugs as coping tools.

- **Marital wellness**—In order for a couple to survive and thrive in another cultural setting, they need to have a healthy level of communication. They must understand each other's needs and be committed to loving each other wholeheartedly, regardless of the sacrifice. Also, there needs to be a unity of heart, direction, and values. As the couple goes, so goes the ministry.

- **Children's educational needs**—If a child has special educational needs, it is possible that they won't be met outside of the home culture and language. It is prudent to assess a child's level of development. If there are needs that must be addressed, it is best to do so before trying to have the child learn a new language and navigate a new culture.

Hal* and Charlotte* were impressive candidates for missionary service. He had accomplished more by the age of 40 than anyone I had ever met. He worked extremely hard and was committed to the highest quality of work. I later learned that his father was a workaholic, and Hal was simply following in his parent's footsteps. Just recently, Hal had been forced to accept a job that was more obscure and moved at a slower pace. The challenge was almost too much for him.

Also, we discovered that with Hal's workaholic tendency, he usually did not dedicate enough time to his wife and children. They were suffering in the areas of emotional, physical, and spiritual intimacy. As for Charlotte, she had one absolute on which she would not budge. No one would have permission to care for or educate their children, even while in language school (which was a requirement with their mission agency). Obviously, this family was not ready to commit to cross-cultural ministry.

Component Five: Missionary Preparation Pragmatics

This is a category that gathers several miscellaneous issues. Most of these are circumstantial, but a few deal with an applicant's character. They all pertain to a person's readiness for uprooting, learning a new language, adapting to a new culture, and carrying out a successful spiritual ministry.

- **Support package**—Can the applicants live on the proposed salary and benefits? Are they able to adjust their priorities accordingly?

- **Personal finance and debt**—Many people enter the application process with some level of debt. Part of the assessment is making sure they can pay their debts in a reasonable time frame while on a missionary level of support. You also want to make sure they are good stewards of their resources.

- **Citizenship/visa issues**—The assessing team needs to be aware of any legal implications for non-citizens traveling abroad.

- **Background check**—Sometimes there are hidden, legal complications from past financial mishandling. Also, you want to make sure there are no potential problems of criminal charges. Visa applications often ask if there have been any past charges or convictions.

- **Reputation/references**—Even with a thorough examination of all five components, it's possible that you won't see the whole picture. That's why it's good to request the opinions and perspectives of those who see the candidates on a daily or weekly basis.

Gary* had a felony conviction many years ago. When he was a troubled teen, he had robbed a convenience store at gunpoint. But he had changed and become pastor of a small country church. And somehow that felony conviction had been expunged from the public record. It appeared that he could move ahead as a missionary applicant.

Later we heard from one of his church members. Gary still had quite a temper. He didn't handle criticism well, and he expressed his anger in inappropriate ways. We learned that Gary was yelling at his wife and was throwing things in the home (even though she had told us that all was well in their marriage.) This couple had painted for us the picture of a pastor and his wife, passionate for God and ready to serve overseas. What they really hoped was that they could start anew on the other side of the world where no one knew them. It didn't work.

From these five examples of the various components, it's obvious that examining missionary candidates thoroughly before approving them for service is of utmost importance. A sending body doesn't want to commission new personnel and place them on the mission field if they're not truly prepared. It would be a waste of precious, limited financial resources, as well as unfair to the potential missionaries.

Covering all five components is necessary in order to get a full picture of an applicant's readiness. However, you usually don't want to ask individuals about their deepest secrets, fears, and sins during an initial interview. It takes time to develop a relationship with the applicant and establish a bond of trust. Therefore, it's helpful to start with surface information that is non-invasive and then gradually go deeper.

Once the assessment team feels they know the candidate well, they can move on to considering a potential match to a field assignment. Until that time, no promises should be made. As much as we may want to send workers into the fields, we must exercise caution until we are certain that they are ready.

About the Author

Joel Sutton earned a BA in Music Education from Southern Ark. Univ., an M.Div. from Southwestern Baptist Seminary, and a doctoral research degree from Evangel Christian University of America. He has served the Lord as a music minister, bivocational pastor, missionary to France, missions supervisor for Western Europe, and consultant for missionary applicants (16 years). He is now the Lead Consultant for the Personnel Selection Team, IMB. He and his wife, Rhonda, are blessed by their three adult children and their families.

4

Evaluating Spiritual Maturity
by Randy Rains

Evaluating spiritual maturity in potential missionary candidates is not an easy task. In reality, the assessment of people's relationships with God and their spiritual depth is included in every aspect of the total selection process. Candidates do not have a silo labeled "Spiritual Life," a distinct part of their existence, which can be evaluated in isolation. They are spiritual beings.

From this perspective, every aspect of the selection process—whether it is the evaluation of the physical health, mental/emotional health, marital/relational health, or competency/gifting—may be seen as a part of the assessment of a person's walk with God. Part of the task of evaluating spiritual maturity is learning how each element of the application process reflects spiritual growth or a lack thereof.

When evaluating a candidate's spiritual development and maturity, it is best to look at a candidate's life "in Christ" from the motif of a journey. Often we lean toward evaluating spiritual development as if it can be measured by a series of events, commitments, and achievements in candidates' lives. Normally we want to hear about their salvation experience, how they were discipled, if they are able to articulate a clear call to cross-cultural service, whether or not they have a solid understanding of the basic doctrines of the Bible, and their demonstrated competency in ministry/service.

As important as this information is, and it certainly must be looked at carefully, it alone will not give a clear indication of the spiritual development and maturity level of a candidate. Length of church attendance and the amount of "Christian" activity in a person's life are not the only measures of spiritual growth.

If we evaluate the spiritual maturity of candidates based solely on the outward aspects of their faith walk—knowledge, commitments, and activity—then even the best of the Pharisees would have been accepted. The evaluation process must go much deeper than mere knowledge and outward commitments. We must go beyond collecting and evaluating information about the candidate. It is necessary to look at how much life transformation has occurred. This is why it is vital for those involved in assessing applicants to have a solid understanding of the Christian life as a journey and what that journey looks like.

Many have written about the spiritual journey, developing a variety of wonderful models of what the spiritual journey may look like. The early church fathers wrote of the various stages of the journey, speaking often of a four-phase journey from *awakening* to *purgation* to *illumination* to *union*. Augustine's *Confessions* and John Bunyan's *Pilgrim's Progress* are two well-known works that speak of the Christian journey, one based on an actual life and the other an allegory. Theresa of Avila's *Interior Castle* and St. John of the Cross' *Dark Night of the Soul* are classic works on the spiritual journey.

I would like to offer a brief summary of a modern day model of the spiritual journey offered by Janet O. Hagberg and Robert Guelich from their book, *The Critical Journey*. Based on this model, I will give a few comments and several practical steps that may be utilized in exploring the spiritual maturity of a potential candidate for service.

Of course, a map is not reality, so we acknowledge the limitations of using such an approach right from the beginning. Each person's spiritual journey is a unique, never to be repeated, experience. However, to have a general model or map of the stages of the journey will be helpful and instructive in determining how far along a candidate may be in his or her spiritual development.

Yet, we must keep in mind that any candidate, no matter how maturely developed he or she may be at the point of departure, can always through stress or temptation fall back to earlier stages of the journey or even end in failure. Unfortunately, there are too many examples of this to be listed in this short chapter.

The following is a contemporary journey model that incorporates key insights from scripture and the wisdom of the church. This is an integrated model that brings together patterns of knowing, being, and doing in the quest for deeper relationship with Christ. What follows is an adaptation of Janet Hagberg and Robert Guelich's six-stage journey model.

Season One: The Converted Life

The pilgrim journey begins with joyful discovery of God through conversion and the new birth. Although excited about the new life they have found, converts initially are unsure and unsteady in their faith, much as a newborn fawn falters in its first attempts to stand.

Season Two: The Disciple's Life

Young Christians seek growing understanding of the faith by reading scripture and developing a theology or worldview; they also seek to practice the basics of Christian living. With their limited understanding, new Christians may become rigid in their convictions and may even absolutize some bright idea (for example, speaking in tongues, or soul-winning, or scriptural knowledge) as the exclusive key to growth. They may see themselves as the sole purveyors of "the" truth, with others mistaken in their beliefs.

Season Three: The Productive Life

This is the doing, or the "roll-up-your-sleeves-and-get-busy," stage. Some disciples receive the false message that busyness and accomplishments endear them to God. Here Christians may fall into the trap of serving "in the flesh" or seeking the applause of others to boost the ego. They may find themselves pressured into assuming responsibilities before being spiritually prepared. Viewing ministry as performance, servants may lose personal contact with God. A disturbing distance between the soul and God develops, ironically, at the same time disciples appear to be so productive in the "Lord's service." Overextended, they may become embittered and angry with colleagues or with God Himself.

Often in this third stage believers may experience a major crisis—a wrenching, face-to-face encounter with their own inadequacy. The crisis may be precipitated by a natural development (such as a midlife transition), an external event (loss of a job), or a personal condition (a serious illness). Some who once were riding high now feel disillusioned, betrayed, and angry. But those who genuinely re-examine their relationships with God use the crisis to catch the vision of a new beginning.

Season Four: The Inward Journey

"Hitting the wall" in stage three serves as the catalyst for pursuing a transforming inner journey. Persuaded that the old pattern does not work, believers enter deeply with the soul to engage God. They may practice spiritual disciplines that foster reflection and prayer; they may take retreats, work with spiritual directors, and experience fresh integration of faith to life. Surprisingly, these people discover that God has been waiting for them all along. The healing of Peter's brokenness (see John 21:15-23) illustrates the transformational nature of this inward journey.

Season Five: The Outward Journey

God directs those who have made the renewing inward journey back outward into the active world with clear vision and purpose. The call may be to the same ministry, but the motivation is radically different. Filled with deep love for God, disciples now serve not themselves, but the interests of others. Christians who navigate this passage marvel that earlier they were blind to what following Jesus is all about. But in the "productive" stage, "We were just too busy, too noisy, or too successful to see it." Paul's service as Christ's bond slave to the Gentile world illustrates the outward journey stage.

Season Six: The Journey of Love

Here, the Christian senses God's call to lay down his life in Christ's name for others. Filled with the Father's love, like Jesus, he washes others' feet, either figuratively or literally. The focus is not on success, notoriety, or achievement. Rather the emphasis is on being a vessel through which God can pour His spirit. In this stage servants live simply and sacrificially because their focus is God and His priorities. Disregarding success and reputation, they appear to others to have wasted their lives. The elderly apostle John illustrates well the life of selfless love (see 1 John).

This model serves well as a general framework in which we can assess the overall development and growth of a potential candidate. For the most part, the majority of the evangelical Christian world is well trained in and fairly knowledgeable about the first three seasons of this journey, while lacking in a deep understanding of the latter three seasons. It is of vital importance to select people to conduct interviews and make decisions about selection who are themselves mature followers of Christ who have moved beyond season three in their own journey.

Here are a few practical suggestions based on this model that may be helpful as interviews are conducted and decisions are made regarding the spiritual maturity of potential candidates. First of all, information needed to make decisions about spiritual maturity must be gathered in a personal, face to face, relaxed, unhurried interview time.

Although much helpful information can be collected via forms, questionnaires, references, etc., the kind of information needed to make a decision about someone's spiritual development is best done in person. Body language, relational skills and many other non-verbal clues play a vital role in assessing a person's spiritual health. In some rare cases, an interview via Skype or some similar means may suffice but is best used in follow-up situations after a face-to-face interview has taken place.

The information gathered during an interview must go beyond collecting basic facts about decisions, commitments and activities of the candidate's pilgrimage as a Christian. Penetrating and personal questions must be asked that lead far beneath the surface to find out what has shaped the candidate's life and where he or she is currently being transformed.

Using the six-season model presented above as a general framework, it would only make sense that candidates who have not reached some level of season three are not in a place spiritually to be approved for service. There have been many candidates through the years who have been fairly established in season two, but who have not had much experience in leadership or any proven competency in ministry.

I remember a young man some years ago who applied for a two-year service opportunity. His pedigree was without question, the son of a prominent pastor. He had a genuine conversion experience and was well versed in many areas of the scriptures as well as being doctrinally sound. However, he had absolutely no experience in leadership of any type and very minimal ministry competency.

Needless to say, following the interview and discernment process, this young man was not approved for service but was encouraged to gain further experience and competency in season three and then re-apply. I am happy to report that he did just that and a few years later served a successful two-year term.

In most cases, unless you are dealing with candidates in their early 20s who have had limited life experience, you want to find candidates who have moved beyond the experience of season three, the productive stage of the journey. It is vitally important to access the ways candidates have hit "the wall" at various points in their faith journey and discover how they have handled those experiences. Often those who have faced tough life experience or life choice situations and have worked through them are in a stronger place than those who have not.

A young woman, raised in a strong Christian family and sheltered from the hardships of life, was sent to the field to work among immigrants from the Middle East who were now living in Western Europe. Her lack of experience in relating to the opposite sex, along with her sheltered life, left her in a vulnerable place. Not knowing how to effectively handle the advances of the young men she was working among, she fell into an immoral relationship that led to pregnancy.

This scenario is not only true for younger candidates but can also be true for older applicants who have not successfully navigated the "walls" they have faced in their own lives. It is important to investigate what kind of "walls" candidates have faced in their lives and evaluate how they have navigated their way through those walls to become stronger and deeper in their faith.

Many candidates will have faced walls of various kinds only to become more rigid and less flexible in their faith. This can be a red flag for someone who is facing the challenges of cross-cultural life and ministry. When evaluating how candidates have responded to the walls of their life, you will want to make sure they are not stuck at the wall, but have been able to work through the challenges to become more open, grace-filled people. This area of discovering what walls candidates have faced and how they have navigated their way successfully beyond the wall is key to evaluating spiritual maturity.

Ideally, you would hope to find a candidate who has matured to living a fairly stable life vacillating somewhere between seasons four and five. It is doubtful that you will discover many, if any, candidates who live consistently at the maturity level of season six. Those who have stabilized and live consistently between seasons four and five will usually have the inner, reflective maturity to navigate the walls they will certainly face in living cross-culturally while also being able to remain productive as they do so.

These candidates are not often the high achievers and may not appear to be the most successful. However, over the long haul, they are the candidates who are often able to stay the course over time and participate well with what God is doing instead of burning themselves out trying to perform for God—which is often what happens with a candidate who is stuck in season three.

There is much more that could be written about using a journey paradigm as a tool for evaluating the spiritual maturity of potential candidates. However, I think this introduction to such an approach should serve to provide basic information for developing a model. The key is to spend quality, face-to-face time, in listening to and looking carefully at the faith journey of each candidate in a prayerful, discerning spirit.

As mentioned earlier, there is no guarantee that candidates who are spiritually mature when they are sent will remain that way for the course of their assignment. Spiritual maturity is not a place you reach or something you accomplish. It is a lifelong process of walking faithfully with Christ, learning as the apostle Paul says in Philippians 2:12-13, to "… work out your own salvation with fear and trembling," knowing that it is "God who works in you both to will and to do for *His* good pleasure."

Works Cited

The Critical Journey by Robert Guelich and Janet Hagberg

"Reflections on Developmental Spirituality: Journey Paradigms and Stages" by Bruce Demarest, Journal of Spiritual Formation & Soul Care—2008, Vol. 1, No. 2, 149-167

About the Author

Randy received a B.S. degree from Union University and an M.Div. degree from Southern Baptist Theological Seminary. He also attended Baylor University, plus completed a two-year Certification Training in Renovare's Institute of Christian Spiritual Formation. Randy is married to Betty and they have 3 adult children and 5 grandchildren. Randy and Betty have served in Rwanda, Kenya, Bangladesh, Australia, and the Philippines, and as Associate Area Director in Singapore. Randy has served in various roles on the IMB staff in Richmond since 1995. In his current ministry assignment, Randy seeks to raise the awareness and understanding of spiritual formation and the practice of the spiritual disciplines.

5

Facets of a Call to Missions
by Andy Tuttle

The term "call," more precisely "God's call," may refer to all of the areas of service given to man by God. When we speak of the call of God, we most often think of the Lord choosing specific individuals for some type of special service. They are set apart for missions, ministry, or other assignments.

Unfortunately, a call from God is invisible to others. It cannot be seen or proven by an outside observer. It is a personal experience, and only that individual can absolutely verify that he or she has received a call from God. The call is unique in every situation and doesn't follow a specific formula. However, there are some common denominators in understanding God's call. Through these elements of a call, we can better visualize God's will and purpose for someone's life.

The Call of God in the Bible

One of the most significant biblical teachings is the concept of calling. This theological doctrine has its roots in the Old Testament with Abraham being the first person with an explicit call (Genesis 12), though it can easily be argued, and rightly so, that individuals preceding him also were "called" for various purposes.

Other Old Testament stories also include the element of a divine call. God appeared to Moses in the burning bush (Exodus 3). He called Samuel as a boy in the night (1 Samuel 3). God revealed to Jonah that he was to go to the despised city of Nineveh to represent God and call the people to repentance (Jonah 1). Joshua (Joshua 1), Gideon (Judges 6), Isaiah (Isaiah 6), Amos (Amos 7:14), and Jeremiah had a call to a distinct ministry and task. Jeremiah even testified that God had planned that call before he was born (Jeremiah 1:5). And then we have many others who were called by God for a special task, such as Noah who built the ark.

In the New Testament, there are many references to God's calling, in different contexts. The Greek verb *kaleo*, which means "to call" appears 148 times. There are three broad categories of the use of *kaleo* in the New Testament that are theological in nature. The first is to summon or invite. The invitation that Christ issued was to sinners. It was a call to repentance, faith, salvation, and service (Brown, p. 274). Jesus was calling people to come and be His disciples and to follow Him (John 6:44, John 6:65, Eph. 1:18).

God's people are referred to in the New Testament as the Greek word "*ekklésia*," which is often understood as "church" or "an assembly," but literally means "the called-out ones." "But you are a chosen generation, a royal priesthood, a holy nation, His own special people, that you may proclaim the praises of Him who called you out of darkness into His marvelous light" (1 Peter 2:9). This refers to a general calling and not specifically a call to missions, but it is the first call we experience. We are first and foremost called to God Himself through salvation in Christ.

In the writings of the apostle Paul, the "call" also describes God's work of grace as the disciple seeks to carry out God's purpose and will (Romans 8:28-30). An example of this can be seen when Jesus selected and sent out 70 disciples to be kingdom witnesses (Luke 10:1). We also can point to the special call to the Twelve who were to leave home and family and vocation to follow Jesus and give themselves fully to His kingdom purpose (Luke 6:12-16).

There is a third usage of the term "called" in the New Testament. Only three instances of this kind stand out in scripture (Friesen, pp. 312-313):

1. God's call to Paul to be an apostle (Romans 1:1; 1 Corinthians 1:1)
2. God's call of Barnabas and Saul to be the church's first missionaries (Acts 13:2)

3. God's call to Paul to take the gospel to Macedonia (Acts 16: 9-10). This third use of *kaleo* seems to be the exception rather than the rule. However, there still exists the possibility that not all instances of persons who received such a vocational call are recorded in the New Testament.

Different Levels of Call

Starting with the **initial call,** we can see in the Bible a progression in the "calling" that God gives to His servants. It is helpful to look at this calling in terms of five concentric steps, with the progression from the center (most common) outward (diminishing frequency). (Tuttle)

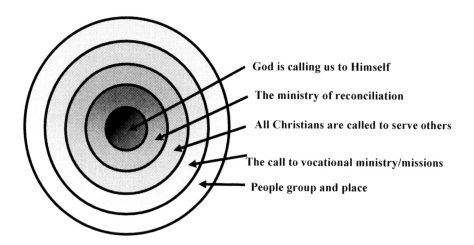

God is calling us to Himself

The ministry of reconciliation

All Christians are called to serve others

The call to vocational ministry/missions

People group and place

As we've seen, at the heart of the call, God is calling us to Himself through Jesus Christ. It's a call to salvation that is universal to all men. "For God so loved the world that He gave His only begotten Son, that whoever believes in Him should not perish but have everlasting life" (John 3:16).

Once we have accepted that call to salvation, we then move to the **next level**. All Christians have been called to a **ministry of reconciliation**, of helping bring others back to a right relationship with God.

Therefore, if anyone is in Christ, he is a new creation; old things have passed away; behold, all things have become new. Now all things are of God, who has reconciled us to Himself through Jesus Christ, and has given us the ministry of reconciliation, that is, that God was in Christ reconciling the world to Himself, not imputing their trespasses to them, and has committed to us the word of reconciliation. Now then, we are ambassadors for Christ, as though God were pleading through us: we implore you on Christ's behalf, be reconciled to God. For He made Him who knew no sin to be sin for us, that we might become the righteousness of God in Him. (2 Corinthians 5:17-21).

The ministry of reconciliation is seen in the symbol of the cross (Tuttle). The relationship between God and man is represented by the vertical bar and the relationship between men is the horizontal bar. Unless we have both the vertical and horizontal, we do not have the full significance of the cross; it's an incomplete picture of the gospel.

Through this ministry of reconciliation, God builds our spiritual and moral character, making us holy and fit for the Master's use. The more we grow in the grace and knowledge of our Lord, the more He will use us to carry out His work, and the more He uses us, the more growth experiences we will have. Thus we enter a never-ending cycle of glorifying God by doing His will, the ministry of reconciliation. John 15:16a says, "You did not choose Me, but I chose you and appointed you that you should go and bear fruit."

When some Christians begin to sense a call from God to share the gospel, they refer to the Great Commission and assume that God wants them to be missionaries in another country. However, the Great Commission is not a personal call to residential overseas missions. It is critical that we read and apply biblical passages in context. Look carefully at the Great Commission. To whom was it given? It was given to the disciples (followers) in particular and the church (followers) in general. Why was it given? To spread the gospel and teach others to obey the ways of the Lord.

> Jesus came and spoke to them, saying, "All authority has been given to Me in heaven and on earth. Go therefore and make disciples of all the nations, baptizing them in the name of the Father and of the Son and of the Holy Spirit, teaching them to observe all things that I have commanded you; and lo, I am with you always, even to the end of the age" (Matthew 28:18-20).

Jesus has stated, with authority, that we cannot keep the gospel to ourselves. But how and when do we share that good news? Consider the word "Go." This is not a command in the Greek text. The disciples had *been* going, doing ministry with Jesus for three years. So this is not a command to go and do what they had not done previously, but an admonishment that they should continue going. Here is the sense of that phrase: "as you are going about your normal daily activities, share the gospel and make disciples." This Great Commission is for the local church and not simply unique to the missionary or preacher.

Jerry Rankin, retired president of IMB, wrote of this in his book, *A Challenge to Great Commission Obedience.*

> "There seems to be three steps that are prerequisite in discerning a specific, personal call to missionary service. The first is obviously an awareness of God's kingdom purpose and desire for His people to proclaim the gospel literally to the ends of the earth. Second, is a recognition of the needs of a lost world and the consequences of those who do not know of the salvation God has provided through Jesus Christ. And third, is a relationship with God that is expressed in an availability to go—a willingness to offer oneself and follow God's leadership in that direction.

> "Our confusion regarding God's call is often created by an egotistical and self-centered perspective on God's will. I once heard Henry Blackaby speaking to a group of students who were in a critical time of preparation for what they would do

with their life. They wanted to know, as so many young people do, 'How can I know God's will for my life?' Blackaby readily pointed out that they were asking the wrong question. He said that the appropriate question was, 'What is God's will?' When we understand and discern God's will, then we can begin to discern how His purpose for us fits into it.

"There can be no question about God's kingdom purpose and desire to bring a lost world to saving faith in Jesus Christ. This was inherent in the call to Abraham through which 'all the families of the nations would be blessed' (Genesis 12:3). It was expressed through the Psalmist, 'All the ends of the earth will remember and turn to the Lord, and all the families of the nations will worship before Thee. For the kingdom is the Lord's and He rules over the nations' (Psalm 22:27-28). It was expressed in the call to Israel to be his chosen people. They were to 'proclaim good news of His salvation ... tell of His glory among the nations, His wonderful deeds among all peoples' (1 Chronicles 16:23-24). In Psalm 67:1-3 we read that God chose to bless them, to be gracious to them and favor them, but it was for the purpose, 'That Thy way may be known on the earth, Thy salvation among all nations.'" (Rankin, pp. 5-6)

Consequently, Great Commission ministry can include all the work of the church. Anything in which the primary goal is to share the gospel and make strong disciples can be an expression of the Great Commission: children's programs, worship, maintenance, organization, administration, nurture, teaching, discipleship, social ministry, and many others. Ministry and missions are two sides to the same coin; you cannot have one without the other. At the core is the gospel, and so a church without missions at its core does not understand the desire of God. It is the responsibility of the local church to evangelize, make disciples, and ultimately send out missionaries.

The **third level** of call upon believers is that **they serve others in the body of Christ**, using their spiritual gifts and natural talents. Those spiritual gifts, and some of the functions in which they're used, are listed in Romans 12:1-8 and 1 Corinthians 12. A careful examination of the New Testament churches reveals a shared ministry philosophy.

Under the leadership of the Holy Spirit, each member was expected to function in a role or ministry. Each member was called to touch lives in the name of Christ in his or her own unique way.

> [We] may grow up in all things into Him who is the head—Christ—from whom the whole body, joined and knit together by what every joint supplies, according to the effective working by which every part does its share, causes growth of the body for the edifying of itself in love (Ephesians 4:15b-16).

Within this call to serve, there may be a more precise call to a specific station in life. Some are called to be faithful husbands and wives, or respectful sons and daughters, within the context of a family. Others experience like Paul a call to singleness so they can be focused entirely on God's kingdom (see Matthew 19:12; 1 Corinthians 7:17-35) (Platt, Chapel message, IMB, Richmond, VA). Regardless of their station in life, all Christians have received a call to some degree of involvement within the Body of Christ. This is their spiritual avocation, a call that is above and beyond their regular occupation or responsibilities.

> "Calls to service are fluid, operating at varying levels and open to varying assignments from God. Calls to service are continually discerned and affirmed through Spirit-led examination of a disciple's desires, gifts, abilities, and opportunities as a member of the church on mission in the world" (Platt, Chapel message, IMB, Richmond, VA).

At the **fourth level** of call, that avocation becomes a more specific **call to full-time, vocational ministry, which can include missions**. This level involves a greater commitment of time and resources, and it will often require more extensive preparation in both education and experience.

> And He Himself gave some to be apostles, some prophets, some evangelists, and some pastors and teachers, for the equipping of the saints for the work of ministry, for the edifying of the body of Christ, till we all come to the unity of

the faith and of the knowledge of the Son of God, to a perfect man, to the measure of the stature of the fullness of Christ (Ephesians 4:11-13).

Only a small percentage of people will get paid vocationally for their avocation, but that does not make individuals any more or less called or less of a missionary just because they must be a "tentmaker" (Acts 18:3).

Many of those who experience a call to missions also will sense a **fifth level** of call. The Lord will burden their hearts for a **specific people or place**. This is what happened with the apostle Paul: "To me, who am less than the least of all the saints, this grace was given, that I should preach among the Gentiles the unsearchable riches of Christ" (Ephesians 3:8).

However, this specific call can change at any time as it pleases the Father, and He may cause or allow anything that He wishes to accomplish His purpose. When a missionary experiences a change of location due to illness, political unrest, war, or anything else, nothing has caught God by surprise and nothing is beyond His control. At this level of call, one needs to be fluid and undaunted by change.

As we consider God's call to His people, we find it is the intimate connection with the Father that is at the heart of the call. Our primary calling is not to do the work of the missionary, evangelist, or preacher but rather to walk in a personal relationship with the Lord. It is only through the overflow of our experience with God that we can actually do the work of the ministry.

The Call to Missions

Is it true that "everyone is a missionary and we are all called to be missionaries?" Yes and no. We all have a calling from God, including the ministry of reconciliation. However, not everyone is called to be a residential missionary in another country or even another region of his or her own country. A missionary is "a person who, in response to God's call and gifting, leaves his/her comfort zone and crosses cultural, geographic, or other barriers to proclaim the gospel and live out a Christian witness in obedience to the Great Commission" (NAMB/IMB).

In a certain sense, Abraham was the first model of a missionary call (Genesis 12:1-3). He clearly experienced that distinct command from God to leave his home and kindred, even though he did not know where God would lead him. That call was the foundation for missions because in responding, he and his descendants would become a blessing to the nations.
The call to missions is a unique experience, and it is not good to compare one person's call to that of another. We especially should not compare a typical call to serve overseas to that of Paul. He saw a bright light and was affirmed by God's message to Ananias: "Go, for he is a chosen vessel of Mine to bear My name before Gentiles, kings, and the children of Israel" (Acts 9:15).

For some people, it would be easier if God provided them with a dramatic call experience so they could be sure that it was indeed God speaking. But for most it does not happen this way. In fact, God often speaks in a whisper. "Your ears shall hear a word behind you, saying, 'This is the way, walk in it,' whenever you turn to the right hand or whenever you turn to the left" (Isaiah 30:21b).

When I interview potential missionaries, I want to hear their call story. It always is unique and special. There are no standard words that I expect to hear, but I do want the applicants to express their understanding of call in their own words. Often there is confidence as people share their story, along with interesting details that provide clarity.

But other times I hear of wrestling with God, searching for direction and a desire for God to affirm the call through some sort of proof. Regardless of the person's experiences, we find that "God is able to call in ways that man can understand and man is able to respond in a way that will bring glory to God and blessings to mankind" (Pearce, p. 2).

Being certain of this call to missions is critical to success on the field. Take, for example, this missionary couple that we sent overseas a couple of years ago. They presented very well in the application process and the interviews showed no concerns. They appeared to have good potential for long-term service. The assessment process took over a year and included two months of residential orientation and training before leaving the U.S. They quit their jobs, sold their home, and left their family. They told us they were sure of their calling and they had counted the cost of missionary service. Several weeks after their arrival in their new country, we received their letter:

"We have made one of the hardest decisions we will ever make. We are coming home. No one is sick (not even homesick). It has not been an easy process by any means. The stress of wondering if you are doing God's will or your own, plus the culture shock is not a good combination. It causes spiritual, emotional and physical exhaustion that is overwhelming.

"It is not a matter of having been given the responsibility of reaching the world with the gospel, as are all Christians, but a matter of having a call to a specific place or people because God has burdened your heart with them.

"While being here we were told by many missionaries, 'On the hard days, the only thing that will keep you on the field is your call, when you get out amongst your people.' We do not have such a call. We do not feel a specific call holding us here. This has not been easy.

"God has shown us even through our application process, missions conference, and orientation that we did not share with one another our true feelings and real reasoning for coming. Ultimately it was pride, discontentment in our daily lives, fear of failure in life, and the unfed desire for adventure. Not until the past few days did these hidden agendas and unshared truths surface. These were things they told us to share and discuss in orientation, but we kept them hidden out of fear of what others might think. God has been working to bring these things out during our time here. He has shown us that we do not belong here and has given us a peace in this extremely hard, life-changing decision.

"As we talked this over with the leadership here, they listened to us pour out our hearts and cry, and they cried with us. They talked with us, touching on every area we needed to consider, and they prayed with us. We told them that our only fear was returning home and disappointing our family and friends. They assured us that you would wrap your loving arms around us and continue to pray for us and support us as we seek God. We know you will."

The difficulty with a call to overseas ministry is, as mentioned earlier, the fact that it is invisible. It occurs within the human heart. God initiates that call, external to the human mind, will, and emotions. He may propose a new sense of purpose or a change of direction. Often this includes an inner conviction concerning a change of vocation. But then comes the internal response of the believer. That inward call requires self-examination. And it is at this level that the difficulties in accepting the call, or even verifying the call, begin. Today's society is "feeling oriented." Often Christians elevate their personal feelings to the point that they confuse "feelings" with the working of the indwelling Holy Spirit.

Jerry Rankin provides us with some insights into the struggles that occur in the heart and mind when God issues a call to missions:

"But most likely we never hear and respond to God's call because of a reluctant will that is unwilling to trust God to lead us and use us. It is tragic that we have to term a response to God's call as a decision of 'surrender' to His will. It does mean giving up our own selfish plans and ambitions, but the natural inclination of every Christian should be to willingly and joyfully place their lives in the Father's hands and count it a privilege of following wherever He leads.

"When we accept Jesus as our Savior there should be no other desire except to serve Him and be obedient to His lordship. It is at the point of a surrendered will that most Christians struggle with God's call, rationalizing how to be obedient without sacrifice or denial of material comforts. Negotiating with God, expressing a willingness to serve Him where we are without having to go to the other side of the world. We seek to justify disobedience by questioning whether or not God is really calling us. But I assure you it is not Satan that is breaking your heart over a lost world and stirring your emotions with an inclination to walk the aisle and lay your life on the altar to go wherever God leads. That's your Lord speaking to your heart in the still small voice of His Spirit, and if He is Lord, your response is not optional." (Rankin, pp. 8-9)

Affirmations of the Call

The call to missions has many facets, like a cut gemstone, and each one must be considered when validating that call. The three major facets are: 1) direction, 2) preparation, and 3) timing (Tuttle). Within each facet are multiple questions that need to be asked by both the missionary candidate and the assessing team.

Direction—Following God's direction is a journey. He will open and close doors, but one must be careful and not take everything at face value. An open door is not an automatic sign that the believer should go through it. There must be discernment of which direction to take. Also, a closed door may be simply God's means of testing. The door could open at a later time.

The following are some questions that a missionary applicant should consider when evaluating God's direction toward missions.

- Through what means does God want to send me?
- Am I to serve as a volunteer, as a short-term worker, or as a career missionary?
- Does God want me to simply support missions through praying or giving financially?
- Has God burdened my heart with a specific people group or country?

- How do my gifts and talents fit the needs on the mission field?
- Am I able to learn another language? Do I have any hearing difficulties?

The body of Christ, the local church, also needs to be a primary part of the affirmation process. The church cannot confer the call to missions on an individual, but those within the body of Christ who know the missionary candidate well enough can speak into that person's life by giving affirmation and wise counsel (see Acts 13:1-3).

As much as the inward call is critical to have, there must also be an outward calling, a sense of affirmation. "The purpose of the outward or external call to ministry is to examine and confirm the preliminary intuition of an inward call by deliberately testing and assessing the candidate's potential for service to the body of Christ" (Oden, p. 20). In this quote, Thomas Oden is referring primarily to those candidates for ordination to gospel ministry positions, but I feel this would also include missionaries.

It's tempting, when considering someone's talents and experience, to rule out missionary service as a possible option for them. However, they may have a skill set that could be used on the mission field in an unconventional way. We have sent a professional surfer, a bass player for a Christian band, a couple of rodeo cowboys, a man with no arms, blind people, deaf people, a horse trainer, a woman crippled by polio, a man who built roller coasters, mountain bikers to Africa, baseball coaches, football coaches, graphic artists, dancers, professional fishermen, kayakers to do a travel service, water well drillers, photographers, writers, coffee drinker/storytellers, agriculturalists, medical doctors, computer programmers, wedding coordinators, and countless others who thought they were just plain vanilla people. Those who assess new personnel must be cautious to not discount someone and what they have to offer.

Preparation—The call to missions also is a call to preparation. Missionary candidates are generally not ready to depart immediately for the mission field. There are many areas where more time is required before deploying to a missions assignment. It's the responsibility of the assessing team to review all areas of an applicant's life to see if the needed preparations have been completed.

- Education (college, graduate school or seminary)
- Experience as a volunteer
- Mentoring and discipleship experience
- Growth in emotional/spiritual/social maturity
- Victory over sin and lifestyle issues
- Experience in effective evangelism
- Counseling to deal with strongholds or issues rooted in the past
- Financial preparations, including selling a house or business, and eliminating debt
- Specialized training, such as English as a Second Language ESL
- Resolution of relationship difficulties
- Care for aging parents

Timing—How can an applicant, as well as the assessing team, know that all needed preparations have been completed and that it's time for the prospective missionary to go overseas? There are several indicators God often uses to affirm the timing for leaving home, family, and country.

- *Circumstances* in their life have been coordinated by God, indicating that this is the best time to leave. There are no pending, unresolved issues.
- *Other believers* are able to see and affirm their calling and the rightness of their departure.
- After praying consistently and fervently, they sense a *peace* about moving overseas (John 20:21).
- God has used *specific scriptures* to signal that the time is right for them to leave.

There is no standard formula for discerning the call of God to personal, full-time involvement in missions. Sometimes He provides details such as a specific people group to whom He is sending them, or the exact country He wants them to reach with the gospel. But that is not always the case. Each situation is unique. However, God will always provide affirmations. Even though we walk by faith and not by sight, the Lord knows we need confirmations of His direction in our lives. "'For My thoughts are not your thoughts, nor are your ways My ways,' says the Lord" (Isaiah 55:8).

Affirmations can come from different people and in different ways. However, not every Christian gives good advice or has the identical opinion as others. Even our most trusted advisors and mentors have to deal with their own human perspective. For example, mature godly parents may not give the best advice to their children who are sensing a call to missions because they don't want to see their only grandkids move to another country.

Summary

A call to missions is a call to walk with God as He leads someone to move overseas and share the gospel. That call could potentially change since the average career missionary serves for about nine years. God's call to missions in a specific assignment is most likely temporal, while the call to be on mission with God is for a lifetime. Only God can say when the task is done. Therefore, it is critical that those who are assessing a candidate's potential for the mission field not focus uniquely on a possible call to a specific people, country, or type of work. Those things can change. It is wise to look at the five levels of God's call, see how the applicant has responded at each step, and look for the affirmations He has provided.

Works Cited

Brown, Colin, ed. *New International Dictionary of New Testament Theology*. Milton Keynes: Paternoster Press, 1986.

Friesen, Garry, and Maxson, J. Robin. *Decision Making and the Will of God*. Portland: Multnomah Press, 1983.

Harrison, Everett F., ed. *Bakers Evangelical Dictionary of Theology*, "Call, Called, Calling." Grand Rapids: Baker Book House, 1960.

(NAMB/IMB) Definition of a missionary—as approved by the North American Mission Board, in partnership with the International Mission Board.

Oden, Thomas C. *Pastoral Theology: Essentials of Ministry.* San Francisco: Harper, 1983.

Pearce, J. Winston. *God Calls Me.* Nashville: Convention Press, 1958.

Platt, David. *"Calling"* (Unpublished study).

Rankin, Jerry. *A Challenge to Great Commission Obedience.* Nashville: B&H Publishing Group, 2006.

Tuttle, Andrew W. *Ministry Skills and Preparation for Missions.* Copyright © 2001

Tuttle, Andrew W. *Understanding the Call to Missions* (adapted from "God's Call to Ministry," dissertation, 1987, California Graduate School of Theology)

Tuttle, Andrew W. *How Do I Know if I Am Called to Missions?* Copyright © 2002

Tuttle, Andrew W. Cross Illustration, copyright © 1988

Tuttle, Andrew W. "God's call to Missions = Direction + Preparation +Timing," Copyright © 2001

About the Author

Andrew W. Tuttle received a B.S.D. from the College of Architecture of Arizona State University, M.R.E. from Golden Gate Baptist Theological Seminary, D.Min. from California Graduate School of Theology with additional studies at Fuller Theological Seminary. He served as youth pastor, associate pastor, a hospital chaplain part-time and a university professor. Tuttle served as an IMB missionary in Costa Rica, Peru and Chile, and since 2001 as an IMB Personnel Consultant. He and his wife, Sherry, have two grown children and three grandchildren.

6

Missionary Competencies and Qualifications
by Alan Garnett

Although many people feel called to serve overseas and share the gospel with the unreached, not everyone is prepared. Sometimes God will direct someone toward mission service, but He knows they'll need some time to grow and mature. Therefore, it is helpful for a selection team to set a standard for the competencies, qualifications, and giftings they view as necessary in order to determine if the applicants are ready to be deployed.

In the coming paragraphs, I'll examine a wide spectrum of qualifications including spiritual maturity, ministry experience, cross-cultural experience (both domestic and international), evangelism training and experience, spiritual gifts, education, theological education, interpersonal/social skills, and possible age limitations.

Spiritual Maturity

Spiritual maturity is the first priority in preparation for any kind of ministry involvement. People's spiritual lives can be viewed as the base upon which a life of ministry is built, and this foundation is what they are going to stand on the rest of their lives. If the foundation is not solid, it will crumble over time and under stress—in their home culture certainly, but even more so in a new culture.

This foundation development starts with missionary candidates' personal relationship with God and how that manifests itself on a daily basis. What does their devotional life look like? Are they having a "quiet time" or devotional time on a consistent basis? A regular devotional life is crucial for spiritual survival in our own culture, and it is a critical element in the ability to survive and thrive on the mission field. Their ability to feed themselves spiritually will often make or break their missionary experience.

Another consideration is church involvement. Are the applicants actively involved or just passively attending on Sunday for worship? There's a whole spectrum of what church involvement could look like. The potential missionary should be actively engaged, usually with some leadership responsibility. Someone who is just attending worship and not involved beyond this experience is missing the dynamic of being a part of a church body.

Examples of further involvement include teaching Sunday School, working with youth or children, leading a small group, teaching a Bible study, discipling others, involvement in evangelism and outreach ministries, being a part of or leading a serve team. This will be addressed further in the following section on ministry experience.

Spiritual disciplines are an often overlooked area of expectation today. We all practice personal disciplines at some level, though the practice of spiritual disciplines is often neglected because of a lack of understanding or expectation. Richard Foster's book, *Celebration of Discipline,* contains a very insightful range of spiritual habits and how to practice them. Without getting too involved in the breadth of these practices, there are basic disciplines that should be expected of applicants who hope to serve successfully as missionaries—a consistent devotional life (as referenced above), prayer, and tithing to name a few.

A final aspect of spiritual maturity that we will consider is one's reputation. Strong believers will be respected by family, friends, and co-workers. They will be recognized by their church family as spiritual leaders. One way to gather information in this area is through references. Both primary and secondary references will generally give a well-rounded perspective of who the applicants are and can serve as a reflection of how/if they can serve successfully on the mission field.

Ministry Experience

As indicated in the previous section, ministry experience should be a basic expectation. Someone going overseas to do ministry should have first gained experience at home in the safe context of his or her church/community. Often that experience will grow into leadership roles as well. Missionaries on the field have to be leaders—leaders of their family, people group team, house church, discipleship group, evangelism team, etc. Let's look at a couple of missionary applicants and see whom you would choose to serve with your organization.

Jared* and Angie* have been married a little over two years and are both taking seminary classes. They are confident in a call to cross-cultural missions and hope to leave for the mission field soon after they graduate. They both participated in one overseas volunteer trip while in college. They are now working part-time jobs trying to make ends meet. However, they dislike their jobs and feel threatened if they try to share their faith in the work context. They are members of a local church, though they travel back home as often as possible to stay in touch with their family and church where they grew up.

Unfortunately, between school and work they have little time to be involved in ministry. They attend worship regularly on Sunday morning but often don't make it in time for Bible study. The small group they "joined" meets on Tuesday night, which is usually a work night for both of them. They have been at seminary for two years but have not successfully gotten involved in any ministries or outreaches of the church.

Tom* and Julie* also have been married two years and are pregnant with their first child. He has one more semester to complete his seminary degree. She has a bachelor's degree and has taken some women's study classes through the seminary where he attends. They were both active in a college ministry, and both held leadership roles for a couple of years. After graduating, they missed the ministry outlet they had through the campus ministry, so they became actively involved in a local church when they moved to seminary.

They serve now in the children's ministry, teaching on Sunday mornings, and co-lead a small group Bible study on Wednesday nights. On Saturdays, they are often found relating to international students at a local university. He works full time at a retail job and goes to school part time. Julie works part time but plans to quit when the baby is born. They are intentional about inviting co-workers and neighbors into their home for meals and social activities. The church has just asked Tom to consider serving as a deacon.

As we compare and contrast these two couples, even with the limited information available, we can quickly see the differences in perspective of ministry experience, intentionality, and even spiritual maturity. Taking the initiative to be involved in others' lives does not automatically equal a successful ministry. Experience does, however, lend itself to growth and hopefully evaluation and training as part of the preparation to lead.

Cross-Cultural Experience

What is cross-cultural experience? If you're reading this book, you probably have a pretty good grasp of "crossing cultures" and relating to people unlike yourself. Cross-cultural experience used to mean going overseas, or at least to a neighboring country where one would experience different cultures, language, foods, etc. Given the eclectic nature of the U.S. today, one doesn't have to go overseas to experience another culture.

In fact, someone who has grown up in the rural Midwest, moves to the Northwest to do college ministry, and then takes a team of students to New York City on a mission trip has a lot of cross-cultural experiences to process and debrief! Such was my experience as I started out in ministry many years ago.

As we consider candidates' readiness for missionary service, we must consider their cross-cultural experience, not simply overseas but also their involvement right where they live. What are some ways someone can be involved cross-culturally in their home culture? This may include ministering to international students (language partners or "adopting" a student), serving in a refugee ministry, doing low-income housing or inner-city outreach, sharing with ethnic co-workers or clients, frequenting an ethnic restaurant in order to build relationships with staff or owners, or participating in an ethnic church.

It is amazing how often God will provide opportunities to cross paths and build relationships within a people group before we ever leave our country. It is easy to think about cross-cultural experience as being exclusively overseas, but we mustn't overlook the many opportunities right here in our backyard—or front yard or side yard or across the street!

International experience also is a significant preparation for long-term service in another culture. It is a rare thing in today's world of easy travel to have a missionary applicant for long-term service who has never before been outside of the U.S. Most often, they have multiple overseas experiences. Travel has become easier, and churches and campus ministries provide frequent opportunities for volunteer trips around the world. Many colleges provide study abroad opportunities as well. Why not be a missionary while traveling to another country as a student?

Any cross-cultural experience helps to broaden one's world view, and the more this happens before immersion into another culture long-term, the better prepared the individual will be to adapt and adjust and accept his or her new context. The deeper a person's cross-cultural experiences, the more "shallow" the pit of culture stress/shock will be when he or she goes to the mission field long-term.

Evangelism Training and Experience

Evangelism is the intentional verbal witness of sharing the gospel with the purpose of giving the opportunity for someone to make a faith commitment in Jesus Christ. Evangelism is not just random acts of kindness, or a godly lifestyle, or service projects. The past few years we have so watered down the concept of evangelism that we have not only lost effectiveness, but we have also lost a solid understanding of what evangelism really means. We often are afraid to offend others because we don't want to scare them off. But actually the gospel is naturally going to be offensive to many people.

Missionary applicants are saying they want to go overseas and share the gospel message with those who have not heard. Yet how can they share that gospel message if they don't understand what they are sharing? Solid evangelism training that includes a practicum is essential preparation for missions. There are various trainings available, and one can usually be found through a local church or campus ministry.

If people are feeling led to travel to another country to share their faith, are they sharing their faith here at home? To be certain of this, you may want them to keep a witnessing journal to record where and when they are being intentional in sharing the gospel. The act of keeping a journal is a way to establish and demonstrate a focused lifestyle of sharing one's faith. A journal also is a good source of self-accountability.

We also can expect that if applicants have a lifestyle of sharing their faith they are going to see results. We should see the fruitfulness of their evangelistic ministry at home before we send them abroad as a missionary. Sometimes we see faithfulness in sharing and a consistent evidence of witness in their journal, though they are not seeing results. This may indicate a need for further training; maybe they just need help in knowing how to "draw the net" and ask for a decision in such a way that leaves the person understanding the urgency of making a faith decision. Before we commit to sending people overseas long-term, we would want to see that they've been instrumental in seeing others make first-time faith decisions.

Think back to our two couples introduced above. Which one do you think is more prepared for cross-cultural evangelism?

Spiritual Gifting

What are spiritual gifts? And why is it important to know one's spiritual gifts? Carrie* responded to a question on her missionary application asking about her spiritual gifts.

"I enjoy working with children and serve in the nursery almost every Sunday. I also am talented at music and play in the church orchestra on Sundays and for special events. I think I have a gift of talking to people, too. I enjoy hearing people's stories and helping them solve their problems by sharing a different perspective."

Does Carrie understand spiritual gifts? I think not, though this type of response is not uncommon when someone is asked about their spiritual gifts. Scripture indicates every believer is given spiritual gifts (1 Peter 4:10), yet many in our churches today have no idea what their particular gifts are. There are many spiritual gifts assessments available—a simple online search will yield multiple options. Missionary applicants should have a basic understanding of their unique giftedness and how to use those gifts in ministry. Scripture tells us spiritual gifts are given to each believer and are for the edification or benefit of the congregation as a whole. We each have a role to fill in the body of Christ. How can we fulfill that responsibility if we don't know where we fit?

Once we know an applicant's giftedness, we will have a better idea of what type of job he or she might best fill on the mission field. In the current environment where many field personnel around the world are in restricted-access locations, knowing one's gifting should be a significant consideration in choosing the type of assignment he or she is offered. For example, someone who is looking at a logistics or administrative role would serve well in this area if he or she has a gift of administration.

Education/Theological Training/Certifications/Experience

There is great debate about how much training a missionary needs to be effective, and we're not going to try to attempt to answer this question in a definitive way. The reality is there is more to consider in the area of education than just whether a person completed a degree. Knowledge is certainly a part of the equation, though there is something to be said for other aspects of completing an education: learning time management, refining interpersonal skills, and gaining perseverance.

We recommend a minimum education of a bachelor's degree, though we have some two-year assignments where this is not the case. Those two-year assignments are designated for a select segment of applicants and are a finite commitment on the field. These assignments primarily are support roles to other personnel, such as information technology, bookkeeping, media functions, and so on.

Students who are pursuing an undergraduate degree and are feeling called to missions should not automatically aim for a Bible or missions degree. They should pursue a degree in something that interests them and with which they could get a job, if five to 10 years later they were to find themselves back in their home country and in need of a means to support themselves and their family. Most applicants who are headed toward missions or ministry as a vocation are probably going to pursue a seminary education anyway.

We also recommend a minimum of 12 credit hours of theological education for long-term personnel before they go to the field. If the applicants are married, we ask this of both husband and wife. Eventually, we will require 20 to 30 hours of seminary education for the head of household. And if someone will have the responsibility of theological education or training national pastors, we may then require a full seminary degree.

Transcripts are readily available, usually at no cost for an unofficial copy, and they are an easy way to verify the required education/ courses have been completed. But reviewing a transcript can also reveal a bit about missionary applicants: What kind of students were they? Did they take a foreign language, and if so, how did they do in learning another language? If they "scraped by" with grades of C and D, and barely passed their German class, we need to consider how they might do in learning a new language on the field.

Additional training or experience may be required for certain assignments. If someone is serving on a creative access platform, which is a doorway of ministry in places where typical missionaries are not allowed, he or she should have the experience and/or credentials to be legitimate. Platforms vary greatly around the world so there is no "right" certification or degree specified. It is exciting to see God's creativity around the world as He uses the passions, gifting, and education of those He has called out to serve cross-culturally. In order to enter and stay in restricted-access locations, a legitimate business presence is needed.

Below are some examples of degrees or certifications that would be expected to fulfill a particular role on the field.

- ESL or TESL certification for English teachers
- Business degree and/or experience for a business platform
- Finance/accounting degree and experience for a finance support job
- Media background and experience for media roles
- IT education and experience for a tech support assignment
- Medical background for a medical coordinator role.

Age Limitations

There is a practicality in considering age limits, both for children and adults. A couple with an infant baby is already in a time of major adjustments: a growing family, sleepless nights, new responsibilities, older children adjusting to not having as much of mom and dad's attention, etc. It is wise to not rush into the additional transition of moving cross-culturally too soon. It's perhaps best to delay the move overseas until the baby is at least 6 months old to give everyone in the family time to adjust and get to know each other before entering the stresses of transitioning overseas. This also gives time for the baby's health to be evaluated and initial immunizations to be completed.

The other end of the age spectrum for children is a family with pre-teens or teenagers. Experience has shown there are many challenges for a teenager in adjusting to a new culture. They are already going through a tremendous amount of developmental issues, and compounding this with learning a new language and making cultural adjustments has often resulted in a family having to return to the States. There also are significant educational concerns during the teenage years, notably whether or not they'll be able to stay on track educationally in the midst of transitioning to a new culture and language.

For example, Dan* and Jaylin* went to Southeast Asia with their four children ages 14, 9, 8, and 5. The job assignment meant they would spend 12-18 months in one location for language acquisition before they moved to their assigned destination and people group. During language school, the children all attended a private school and did well. They made friends and adjusted appropriately to their new environment. Dan and Jaylin completed their language studies and were excited to move on to their job assignment.

About a month before the planned move, their oldest began having issues at school and respect issues at home. The closer the move came, the worse things became. He became sullen and withdrawn from both family and friends. He didn't know how to communicate what he was experiencing, and he erupted in anger. He didn't want to move again, and he didn't want to learn another language and go to yet another school. Things became so stressful and such a distraction for Dan and Jaylin that, in consultation with member care personnel, a third-culture kid (TCK) specialist, and their field leadership, decided they should return to the States so their son could have a stable environment where he could get the help he needed.

The preceding scenario is vague at best, and certainly does not convey all of the details, emotions, stress, or expense involved in such a case. Although not every young person is going to respond negatively, we have found it best to be cautious. We do not want to jeopardize a teenager's development or education by sending him or her to a cross-cultural context during these already challenging years. This is an area where applicants tend to think, "This wouldn't happen with our kids." Unfortunately, many of those who've gone in the past have had those same thoughts but ended up leaving the field prematurely.

Age limitations for adults also are a consideration. A minimum age of 21 is appropriate for long-term missionaries since most 21 year olds will not have the experience or education to be ready to make a long-term commitment. Could there also be an upper age limitation? Language learning and the number of years of potential service before retirement age are valid considerations. The older an individual is, the more difficult it will be for him or her to learn a new language.

Depending on the organization and the support provided, there is a stewardship consideration for the overall cost of putting an individual or family on the field, learning the language, and developing a legitimate platform to stay there long term. The assessing team must decide if the investment of resources is worth just a few years of service.

Summary

There are many dynamics when considering the readiness of someone to serve cross-culturally. We have touched on several of these elements, and it is important to remember God's sovereignty in the midst of the whole process. Sometimes we can have tunnel vision to the point that we miss what God is doing in and around us.

Many times I have had applicants tell me at the end of their selection process that they grew significantly as a result of examining themselves and their readiness for the field. They would say, "Whether I ever go overseas or not, this process has been worth it because of what I've learned about myself and what I've learned about my relationship with God."

About the Author

Alan Garnett has a BS in Business Administration/General Management, University of Central Missouri, and a Masters of Divinity, Golden Gate Baptist Theological Seminary. Alan served as campus minister in Oregon for 13 years prior to moving to Richmond, VA as staff at the IMB where he has served the past 13 years. Alan has now been to over 50 countries as a volunteer, team leader, strategist, and trainer. Alan and Summer have been married 25 years and have two grown children, Christopher and Becca.

7

Qualifications that Match the Assignment
by Ken Eells

There are many key qualification areas that are vital to making a good job match. The person guiding the matching process must have knowledge of how and why the assignment was written. Understanding the assignment's underlying rationale is imperative. The person writing the job description had a clear purpose in mind with regard to what he or she wants the assignment to accomplish as well as the type of person that needs to fill the role.

Understanding the Assignment

The first consideration is to determine if the job is primarily a support role or church-planting assignment. At a time when reaching this world for Christ is the paramount goal of evangelical churches and sending groups, all assignments should be strategic and have the purpose of sharing Christ as their ultimate objective. However, the support job, while also having evangelism and discipleship as its ultimate goal, will have a specific area of responsibility that makes it possible for others to remain on the mission field.

Missionary families have support needs such as children's education, medical treatment, member care, financial bookkeeping, IT support, and logistical requirements. It's of great benefit to know this information as you look for a person who has training and experience in a field that matches the job requirements. It is important to stress that support assignments are strategic.

In most cases, the church-planting strategist assignment will not have responsibilities for any of the support roles mentioned. While it shares the primary role of evangelism and discipleship with the support type job, it will have added responsibilities for overseeing the big picture for unreached people and places. It will focus on locating, mentoring, and training nationals to assist in reaching their own people. The strategy job will focus on developing strategies for engagement as well as a plan for assessing the health of the work as it progresses.

Within the two categories of strategy and support, there are other factors that are important for the job-matching process. The person involved in matching applicants to the right assignment should be asking several pertinent questions. Will the job be that of a team leader? Is the assignment for a new team or one that is established? On which unreached people and places will it focus? Understanding the type of assignment will help in finding the right person for the right assignment.

Another area that is significant to job matching is the specific expectations of the assignment. In most cases, cross-cultural ministry will be done within the national and cultural context of the country and/or people group of focus. Being familiar with the language(s) required and the cultural adaptation plan for new personnel is essential.

In some instances, there will be a mentoring program for those in their first term of overseas service. An excellent example is the International Mission Board's apprentice mentoring program, referred to as AMP, where the new missionaries are assigned a coordinator/trainer who guides them through their first term. If there were not a formal mentoring program, the individual missionary would be wise to develop his or her own plan of orientation appropriate for the assignment. A good start will pay rich dividends in the months and years to come. Being able to identify with the people God has called one to minister among is vitally important.

The person responsible for determining if a missionary candidate's qualifications match the assignment should be knowledgeable of any specialized training, skills, security training, or certifications required to be matched to the job. For example, does the assignment require the person being matched to enter the assigned country on a legitimate visa platform? If so, this is information that must be known to make a good job match. Specific credentials may be required for obtaining a visa such as a college or seminary degree, certifications, and work experience, just to name a few.

Other information to be aware of includes knowledge of the assignment's people group focus. The demographics of population, birth, marriage, disease, and death are helpful to know. Is the assignment location urban or rural? What is the primary religion of the people group: Muslim, Orthodox, Jewish, animistic, post-modern, other—or none? What are the ultimate goals and objectives of the assignment? Church-planting movements? Sowing, watering, cultivating, and harvesting? Mobilizing partners locally and globally?

As a consultant with responsibilities for strategic deployment in the Middle East and Northern Africa, I have many opportunities to cast vision to interested candidates for missionary service. After one such opportunity of sharing a strategic assignment in a difficult part of the world, there were several people who indicated their interest in the assignment. Using my knowledge of the job's background, including most of the items shared above, I was able to determine the best match among the people who had expressed interest in the assignment.

Was this a guarantee that they would adjust well to the new culture and language of their assignment? That they would not experience any difficulties in their work? No. But experience over time has taught that attrition is lower when the particular needs of the assignment are known, understood, and then carefully followed.

Understanding the Applicant

Another necessary qualification area to consider is having a good understanding of the candidates you are working with. While we acknowledge each person is unique in the way God made and gifted him or her, not every person is qualified for just any assignment. Having a good understanding of each person you are working with will make it possible to correctly assess and match people to the right assignment.

There are other demographics that also need to be considered. Education is always important, but it carries greater weight with some sending groups than others. For those that have no or limited educational requirements, the job-matching process is fairly simple and straightforward. There is a nuance, however, that needs to be considered when it comes to educational requirements. Some assignments may require a minimum educational level due to the country being considered having work-related entry requirements. For example, one country may require a degree to teach ESL while another only minimal certification.

In addition to having the right education in place, ministry and work experience are important considerations for overseas service. It is a given that many new missionaries are going to be formally and experientially trained for their work overseas once on the field. At the same time, many sending groups will require a certain level of experience before deploying their personnel.

Assessing both ministry and work experience of the potential missionary prior to deploying to the field is critical to a good job match. Depending on the assignment, both secular and religious work experience are important considerations. One assignment may ask for a person who has a business background or particular secular work skill. Creative access is an important means for gaining entrance in limited-access countries and making contact with the focus people group. Another assignment may focus more on someone with strong ministerial experience.

In either case, evaluating a candidate for job match while taking both his or her secular and ministry skill sets into consideration is imperative. It does not matter if the person is on a creative access platform or missionary visa, evangelism and discipleship are the primary goals. For those of us charged with the responsibility of deploying missionaries, assessing someone's experience and training, ministry or secular, will pay rich dividends in making a good job match. It will go a long way toward helping individuals do well in their assignments.

While it may not be possible to match applicants to assignments where they meet *every* requirement, the more they meet the better. The more qualified and equipped the potential missionary is, the greater likelihood of a good match. It is important to keep in mind that while written job descriptions are not set in concrete, they are important guides to follow. As one begins to assess a person's background, it is important to decide if he or she meets most of the assignment's requirements.

For example, life and work experiences give each person a unique skill set. By considering the whole picture of background and experience, we can begin the process of seeing if and how people match the assignment. A good example of this is previous overseas mission service. Even though such experience may not be a requirement to match a particular assignment, any previous overseas mission experience is always good to assess. Was it long or short term? How did they like it? What do those who observed them say about their experience?

Also, if the job being considered has education requirements, you will need to assess applicants' college and seminary hours or degrees. Some assignments may call for specific certifications such as ESL while others may suggest specialized training such as the CrossFit strength and conditioning program. It is best to review one's educational credentials early in the job-matching process. This will make it possible to filter the assignments the candidate might match. The same process is recommended for life experiences as well as secular and ministry passions the person may have. These will be a window into the person's real interests and the things he or she enjoy doing the most.

A good example of how a review of a person's education and experience can lead to a good job match can be seen in the following couple. Glenn* has his Master of Arts degree in intercultural studies. Jill* has her bachelor of science in health promotion. In addition, she also earned 18 hours toward her master of arts in intercultural studies.

Both served overseas as short-term missionaries before marrying. Glenn served two-and-one-half years in North Africa. Jill served two years in the Arabian Peninsula. Both received affirming evaluations from their supervisors and missionary colleagues. Glenn and Jill personally spoke in very positive terms concerning their time overseas. When they applied for long-term service, they were well prepared and equipped, educationally and experientially. They verbalized a strong confirmation of their call to return overseas. It was easy to determine that this couple met all of the educational and experiential requirements for the team strategy leader job they now fill in a Middle Eastern country.

In the world of missionary sending organizations, many are affiliated with a particular denomination. When this is the case, there will likely be requirements related to the doctrinal and ecclesiastical practices of their group. In many situations, a person at the point of job matching will likely have already been assessed regarding his or her doctrinal beliefs. However, there are sending groups that are either non-denominational or inter-denominational that do not require adherence to any one particular denomination or doctrinal statement.

In such a case, knowing what the individual's doctrinal beliefs are is central to making a good job match. For example, if evangelism and discipleship that leads to church planting is a core goal/value for a sending group's assignments and the candidate being considered for matching does not share this belief, you would want to know this.

Depending on the guidelines of the organization deploying personnel overseas, sending a person back to his or her country of origin may or may not be permitted. While it is not the purpose of this discussion to debate the positives and negatives of such a guideline, it is important to note it is a major consideration for job matching. It needs to be on the radar of the person working with the candidate seeking to serve.

My personal experience has been that each case is unique and must stand on its own merits. A word of caution is needed here. Don't stop the job-matching process until all information has been gathered. It is quite possible in some cases that an exception to the policy or guideline could be made.

Similar to the discussion in the previous paragraph, one's ethnic background could be a factor when it comes to filling an assignment. Racial prejudice, ethnic hatred, cultural bias, or tribal barriers are just a few examples of how one's ethnic background needs to be considered when looking at a particular assignment's location. The goal is to place people in an ethnic and cultural setting where they can assimilate without having to overcome substantial hurdles related to their ethnic background.

It should be noted there is likely to be some ethnic prejudice in most countries where missionaries serve. The goal of job matching while taking one's ethnic background into account is not to automatically eliminate the person because there will likely be prejudice, but to determine if it is possible for someone to serve effectively in the face of that prejudice.

Gender is another distinctive that must be considered when seeking to have the right person in the right assignment. In some cases, specific job descriptions must be written in a way that takes into consideration the cultural and religious mores of the country and/or people group of focus. The classic example is ministry in Muslim countries or cultures. Since approximately one-half of all people in a Muslim country are female, the assignment must make provisions for ministry among women by female missionaries. Conversely, this is true for male candidates in the job-matching process. As a result, there will likely be jobs available for men and women, in both single and married categories.

For the non-Muslim world, there still may be a need to take gender into consideration when matching someone to an assignment. An example of this would be in male-dominated societies and cultures. There may not be any overt discrimination, religious or otherwise, toward women but simply the reality that a man will not listen to a female missionary in the same way he would another man.

The marital status of those being considered for a specific assignment must be considered when making the best match possible. It has already been mentioned there will be needs that only singles can fill. The same is true when it comes to married couples. In the organization where I work, we have jobs that specify a single male or a single female as well as those that are limited to married couples.

This in no way has anything to do with gender or marital status prejudice by the sending group, but rather the cultural mores where the assignment is located. Even though there may not be any religious beliefs at stake for the people group as there is with Muslims, there can be strong divisions of culturally acceptable gender roles. We must be sensitive to these if we hope to have the opportunity to share the message of God's love. Of course, some assignments will be open to any gender or marital status.

It is helpful to understand how the principle of having a good understanding of the people you are seeking to match to an assignment plays out in an actual job match. One of our field strategy leaders for a country in North Africa had a burden for reaching a particular unreached people for which he is responsible. These people live in one of the most dangerous locations in the world.

After doing the necessary mapping of the people and spending time in prayer, he wrote an assignment that requires missionary personnel to live in a very challenging and dangerous location. The extremely difficult climate, isolation, lack of infrastructure, unstable government, and terrorist activity in the area, called for a person who could come to grips with the extreme negative circumstances of living among these people in order to share the gospel.

After reviewing the files of a number of people I was seeking to match to an assignment, it became clear to me that Tom's* profile was a good match. He was a single male doctor in his early 40s. He was able to count the costs mentioned above and prayerfully consider filling this job. As a result, God led him to take the assignment. Many of the characteristics discussed earlier in this chapter were considered in Tom's profile and this led to a very good job match.

Spiritual Qualifications

Up to this point we have looked at how and why the assignment was written and the importance of having a good understanding of the candidates. Another vital part of good job matching is being aware of the candidate's spiritual qualifications. The call to missions is discussed elsewhere in this book. It is, however, impossible to discuss one's spiritual preparedness without considering a person's sense of call to a specific cross-cultural ministry assignment overseas.

There have been situations, in the case of a married couple, when one feels called to a particular job and the other does not. It is crucial that both husband and wife are in agreement. Be it a single person or a married couple, having a sense of God's call and confirmation to the assignment is tremendously important. In reality, I much prefer to focus on the person's call to the people group rather than the country or written description. No doubt these are important considerations, but one's burden and passion for a particular people is far more strategic. We are not called to fill job descriptions but to love people. God calls us to love Him and to love those who do not know Him.

Knowing the spiritual gifting and spiritual practices of a missionary candidate also are fundamental to making a job match. The person's application can be impressive on paper but if the spiritual life is not healthy, no piece of paper can make him or her a spirit-filled missionary! When you discuss spiritual gifts with a candidate you are seeking to match to a job, you will be given foundation stones for that job match. I would much rather know that the person I'm working with has the gift of mercy than to know he graduated magna cum laude. Do not misunderstand. One's educational training is important, but it cannot take the place of being gifted by the Father.

There are spiritual disciplines that are basic and fundamental to followers of Christ being spiritually prepared for service in their homeland or in a foreign land. Prayer is so important to all we do. If people don't practice a life of prayer, how can they expect God to bless their life's ministry? I know it is a well-worn cliché, but it is true: prayer is the lifeline for living the Christian life. When potential missionaries pray, they need to hear from the Father. And reading and studying God's Word is the way we are fed and nourished.

On the mission field, it is the Bread of life we share with those God has called and sent us to. If applicants are not reading and studying God's Word, how can they expect to have the spiritual nourishment and strength to faithfully live for Him? Someone once described evangelism as "One beggar telling another where he can find bread." That is so true! I am a beggar. You are a beggar. Someone showed us where to find the Bread of life, and that is what missions is all about.

It is difficult to imagine making a job match if this is not a part of the person's spiritual DNA.

Then there is this thing called "spiritual passion." When I'm talking with others about finding the right place and assignment overseas, I want to know what they are passionate about. There are many things in life we can have a passion for: sports, education, family, work, religious activity, and friends, to name a few. For the Christian, and more specifically the missionary candidate, is there a passion for those without Christ? "Going to the mission field" is so much more than a love for international travel or exotic places. It is joining God in what He is doing in His world. It is thanking the Father for allowing us the opportunity to join Him in what He is doing in His world. If this passion is missing in a person's sense of calling to a lost people group, it should raise concerns.

It was my privilege to work with a married couple, Sam* and Veronica,* who demonstrated the spiritual disciplines we have been discussing. Sam was called to missions around age 18. His spiritual gifts included shepherding, encouragement, and service. Veronica's call developed over the years and was settled during a two-year assignment overseas. Her spiritual giftedness included encouragement and teaching.

Both were self-starters and had a number of skills that were well-suited for the mission field. Sam and Veronica had been trained in personal evangelism and shared their faith on a regular basis. As a result, both had led numerous people to receive Christ as their personal Savior. I remember well the time we discussed God's call to a specific assignment overseas. They discussed their deep passion for the people group to whom God had called them to serve. Individually, and as a couple, they demonstrated outwardly through their words and facial expressions the inward spiritual reality of God's Spirit at work in them.

Counting the Cost

Finding the right place overseas should not be finalized without considering an applicant's family status. Singles and married couples alike have family needs that must be met wherever they are in the world. Moving across the ocean to a foreign land does not change this need. It may make them more intense. Those of us who help to deploy people to the far corners of this world have a responsibility to shine a bright light on this area of people's lives.

For singles, a part of this process must include a discussion of gender. As noted earlier in this chapter, one's gender potentially could be a factor in some locations such as the Muslim world. This is not to say single females cannot serve in a Muslim culture. Many are serving effectively. Being part of a dynamic team is critical for both single males and females wherever they serve in the world. The assessment process leading up to the job match must include a thorough look at the single's contentment with his or her singleness. Are they OK going to the mission field not married?

Similarly, married couples must have strong marriages in order to serve effectively in their assignment. If there is dysfunction in the home, or if one in the marriage is not called to missions or to the specific people group as his or her spouse, it is impossible to make a solid and healthy job match.

Whether the applicant is single or married, a good job match depends on much introspection by each individual. It also depends on good exploration by the one guiding the job-match process. I realize a discussion of single and married identity may seem out of place in a chapter on qualifying for a job match. But having such information aids those working to deploy new personnel. Decisions must be made about how the individuals will fit into the team they will be joining. The way people feel about their singleness or marriage will be critical to their healthy adjustment on their new team.

This becomes even more significant for married couples when there are children in the home, whether currently or in the future. Can the assignment location provide for education needs, health care, and security? What about social needs for each family member? Has each of them counted the cost?

There are two family units I remember well who demonstrated having counted the cost for moving overseas. Their job-matching process exemplified what we have been discussing concerning one's family status. Myra* is a single lady who served short term for two years prior to being deployed as a long-term missionary. In both instances, she demonstrated her ability to serve effectively in a Muslim context as well as her ability to maintain a healthy view of her singleness. Myra wisely counted the cost of serving in a high-security location where war had taken its toll for many years.

The same held true for Ron* and Tammy,* who had a large family. They, too, are now serving in a very dangerous part of the world. The job-matching process was lengthy for this family due to many factors that had to be considered related to the size of their family as well as their assignment location. In both of the examples given, a single female and a married couple with a number of children, the process was similar to determine the right assignment. There were a number of options for each family unit. But in the end there was only one good match for them.

Personality and Character

Up to this point, we have looked at a number of important qualifications for a person to be a good match for a strategic assignment overseas. We now consider a qualification that can be a deal breaker for almost any assignment. Even if all other qualifications are in place and this one is not, it has the potential for creating many problems.

What could be so pivotal to be a game changer in this process? I refer to the personality and character of the person being considered. The job-match process is not complete until all issues have been explored and resolved. Education and experience can be in place. Family dynamics may even appear to be healthy. Spiritual background seems to be appropriate.

As the job-matching process has moved along, what impressions have been formed about the individual's personality and character? Each of us has core values that guide us throughout life in our decisions and choices. There are a multitude of lists out there, some with as many as 300-plus core values noted. Most of us would agree on a much shorter list as the basic, essential core values for life.

A few values my parents taught me are integrity, discipline, accountability, perseverance, and diligence. Because we are followers of Christ, our core values grow out of our Christian faith. For those who live according to the teaching of God's Word, these and other basic core values take on greater meaning. While we may not think of the Beatitudes of Jesus as a list of core values, the blessings He mentions are certainly powerful demonstrations of attitudes, actions, and values that are a part of Christian character:

> Blessed are the poor in spirit,
> For theirs is the kingdom of heaven.
> Blessed are those who mourn,
> For they shall be comforted.
> Blessed are the meek,
> For they shall inherit the earth.
> Blessed are those who hunger and thirst for righteousness,
> For they shall be filled.
> Blessed are the merciful,
> For they shall obtain mercy.
> Blessed are the pure in heart,
> For they shall see God.
> Blessed are the peacemakers,
> For they shall be called sons of God.
> Blessed are those who are persecuted for righteousness' sake,
> For theirs is the kingdom of heaven. (Matthew 5:3-10)

A good job match can be made when God's Word is actively evident in the person's life. Core values, especially spiritual core values, will greatly impact and influence a person's character in positive ways. As the job-match process unfolds, candidates' strength of character should be noted. What are their core values related to ministry overseas? Are they teachable? Can they be trained? What about their personal attitude? Is it mostly positive or negative? How do they feel about being a part of a team? Do they require certain team dynamics to be satisfied and effective? How does their singleness or marital relationship impact their core values?

I realize that some of the things we are considering as essential to finding the right person for the right assignment can seem idealistic. The idea is not to find someone who is perfect. We know that person does not exist. Rather, we are looking for candidates who are committed to God and willing to be led by His Spirit. If they are willing to learn and grow, they will grow into the overseas servant God desires them to be.

If we are not careful, we can go to the extreme when looking at one's qualifications and completely miss the person who is moldable and teachable. The goal in job matching is not to find the person who has everything in place and has "arrived." I am what I am today because different people I encountered on life's pathway saw potential in a young follower of Christ. They saw the core values were in place and set out to educate, train, and equip me to be the best I can be in Christ.

So don't overlook the brass vessel that is tarnished. With the right polish and labor it can shine brightly. Experience has taught me to see through the outward façade of the people I work with who are following God's call to cross-cultural missions.

Over the past 20-plus years, I have been blessed to encounter some of the most committed, dedicated people God has called to missions. With regard to some of those the Lord brought into my life, I could not have made that statement when I first met them. Over time, as I got to know them and learn of their heart's desire to do whatever was necessary to prepare and go wherever God led them, I began to see the potential for cross-cultural service. I have been with a number of these people in their places of field service through the years. I am thankful to say they are still faithfully serving our Lord in some very difficult places.

For example, Cindy* served extremely well overseas in a short-term assignment for five years with a very positive attitude. She did this while serving in a difficult place on the African continent. Her spiritual life was strong and vibrant as she completely relied on God to meet her needs as a single female and make it possible for her to impact the people she worked among. She demonstrated a team spirit throughout her time on the field. Her supervisor stated that Cindy was the "real deal."

It was noted in her field evaluations that she was coachable and teachable yet competent. Cindy was culturally appropriate and completed difficult projects on time. She demonstrated maturity and was a self-starter. Her being a single female was not a factor on her team. Cindy was a good example of someone who had the right core values in place and was living her life by them. Because they were a part of who she was, we could be certain that her Christian values and character would permeate her life. Therefore, her long-term job match was made with confidence, based on the life she lived.

Summary

The right people in the right assignment, on the right team among the right people group, is our goal. While a good job match is not the only factor in being an effective missionary, it is certainly a very important one. For a number of years, I have had the blessed privilege to practice what I have written about in this chapter. This is not just theory; it is a proven model.

As I mentioned earlier, I work with a part of the world where it can be difficult at best to live and share one's faith. Security is an ever-present reality that personnel must deal with. In the face of tight security, our personnel have many opportunities to share and some are seeing God's Spirit move. I mention this now as an encouragement to all who are significantly involved in deciding on the right assignment for the right person at the right time. Even if the location is fraught with many barriers, God prepares the way for those who go.

In the part of the world where I work, we have an ethos of families reaching families. This includes all persons on all teams. It has been my blessing to see that singles, married couples, and children all have significant opportunities for sharing the good news of Christ. My prayer is that many people will have the opportunity to hear about the Savior and be able to respond in faith to His invitation to come to Him.

About the Author

Ken Eells is married to Carolyn and they have two daughters and a son as well as eight grandchildren. Ken has his B.A. from Lamar University and MA from Southwestern Baptist Theological Seminary. Ken pastored several churches in Texas for 22 years. In 1992, he and Carolyn were appointed by the International Mission Board, SBC to serve in Malawi, Africa as church planters. Before retirement, Ken served as the Strategic Deployment Consultant for Northern African and Middle Eastern Peoples.

8

Assessing Physical Health
by Van Williams

In previous chapters we have been looking at aspects of an individual's calling and preparation that are considered before going overseas. This chapter will look at another important facet in the decision process: the applicant's health and how it might impact his or her ministry. We will look at this answering some of the well-known "W" questions: who, what, when, and why. We will begin answering the "why" question by giving some of the rationale and thinking about health assessment initially and throughout the time of ministry.

Why is Assessment of Health Important?

We believe that personnel are our most valuable resource in the missions effort, so it is important that a health assessment be done to assure individuals will be able to serve their full time and be successful in ministry. Unexpected health consequences may still develop, but evaluating beforehand enables decisions to be made that can limit the impact of existing health issues. Both the individual and the sending agency make a financial investment in the process of preparation for ministry.

For the individual this could include resignation from a job, selling housing and transportation, or obtaining education in the skill set needed for the new ministry. An assessment is especially important for those desiring long-term ministry where the complications from a current health condition could take several years to develop. For the sending agency there is the cost of the assessment process, training and orientation to a new community, as well as expenses to establish the new ministry. An inability to be productive or to remain in the new locale for ministry because of health issues results in a poor use of financial resources. Here are some questions that need to be asked when assessing a health risk:

- Will applicants' health cause limitations in their ability to perform the ministry duties expected of them?
- Will they be able to complete the assignment before their health conditions limit what they can do?
- Do their health conditions require routine follow up, and if so, will this be available in the location where they minister?
- Will their pre-existing health issue be a problem when they return and try to integrate back into the health system of their country?
- Perhaps the most important question is the following: Will their living in the new environment be life-threatening or place them at risk for deterioration of their health?

Paramount in the assessment of health is the importance of the applicant being aware of and understanding his or her health. An awareness of one's health issues, the limitations they might cause, the need for follow up, and how this might impact life in another country are all important factors that help determine one's fitness for ministry in a new country. Will their lifestyle and daily activities be impacted by their health? If so, what can they do to minimize that impact? What cautions and changes need to be considered? As these questions are answered by applicants, they gain insight on how to limit the impact of their health on their ministry.

Health awareness includes an acceptance of the limitations that a health issue may cause. Some disease processes such as fibromyalgia require an individual to slow down or rest some each day. If the missionary and their colleagues understand this, work schedules might be altered, allowing the individual to accomplish his or her work assignments. One of the most difficult conditions to overcome is denial of one's health status and the limitations that it could impose. This denial is often seen more at a younger age when individuals think they are indestructible or immortal. Before one can move ahead in learning to live with a health condition, it is important to accept it.

Understanding how the new environment may affect one's health also is important. Individuals may have adapted to their environment and work conditions to the extent that they rarely experience problems with their health. This is particularly noteworthy in individuals who have an allergy history. Things to which they are allergic may be more pronounced in a different environment and lead to new or increasingly severe medical problems.

A person with a known allergy to mold and mildew may find that living in a hot, moist, tropical climate will cause their allergies to be more severe. The severity of many allergies and their progression is affected by the environment. It may be impossible to know how these will affect the individual until he or she has lived within the environment for a period of time. However, assessing these before transition to the mission field may prevent the need for an assignment change in the future.

Who Should Have a Health Evaluation?

The most obvious answer to the "who" question is the adults who will be responsible for the ministry. Their health certainly impacts their work. However, when the work/ministry requires a move to another location, other family members are involved and such decisions can affect the ministry. Thus, the health of these family members should also be considered.

Experience has shown us that the physical or emotional health issues of children often are the things that cause limitations to the ministry of the parents and may be the reason for which the family needs to change locations or return to their home country. It is important for not just the adults, but also all the family to have some type of health evaluation before going to an overseas assignment.

How long the individual plans to be in the ministry overseas is another factor that should be considered when evaluating the health of applicants. When missionaries remain overseas for longer periods of time, there are more chances that health issues will develop or cause problems in ministry. Most organizations send individuals for varying lengths of ministry in an overseas setting: long term, short term, volunteers, students, etc. All of these groups should have some evaluation and awareness of their health and health-related issues they may face while overseas.

Long-term applicants should be the most extensively evaluated due to the length of time they'll be involved in ministry and the responsibilities of the sending group. When health problems are progressive or have a high risk for developing future complications, these applicants may be excluded from long-term service. In such cases, these missionary candidates might be allowed to consider a short-term program. Following that term, we could then re-evaluate their health and any issues that developed during that first term before approving them for further short-term assignments.

Short-term personnel also should complete initial health evaluations similar to those completed by long-term personnel. However, they may be evaluated at different levels, with consideration given to those whose disease processes are well controlled, can be monitored while overseas, and when the risk of development of complications during their anticipated time of ministry is low.

While we may not have responsibility in inviting or medically clearing volunteers and students for their time of service with overseas teams, it is important that their host or contact person discuss their health and any limitations that might be found. Once missionaries are on the field, the development of health issues has been shown to impact the teams and ministries with whom they work. These volunteers will likely have less understanding of the culture and language. Therefore, they will need the assistance of those with whom they work to direct them toward appropriate medical care, provide transportation to and from care, and provide language/interpretation assistance during these times.

Should a medical issue arise with a volunteer or student, it is less likely that they will elect to remain overseas in their ministry, especially if more complicated medical care is required. They will not have developed the support system and trust for national medical care that has been developed by personnel who have spent more time in the new country.

When personnel leave their known environment to minister in a new area, there are risks involved for both the missionary as well as the sending agency/church. Many illnesses or medical conditions have specified risks for developing further complications. How important is it to understand and weigh these risks as part of the assessment of health? The risks for the worker are certainly as important as those for the sending source and often may be overlooked due to a lack of information about the consequences of living in an environment with a health condition.

One of the best examples of this is the fact that individuals who have had their spleen removed for any reason have increased risks for experiencing much more severe problems with malaria. In countries where malaria is not present and physicians may not be accustomed to treating it, this fact is not one of the first pieces of information shared after one's spleen has been removed. In addition, an applicant's desire to minister in a specific location or among a specific people may overshadow and limit his or her personal concern about the seriousness of malaria.

As our medical team grappled with the question of risk, we developed a risk assessment grid to identify health conditions that presented a risk of such significance that it may be wise not to send individuals with these health histories for a long-term ministry. We chose to evaluate five basic areas—productivity, need of travel for health care, the risk of future complications, length of expected service, and associated costs.

We then rated some of the more troublesome chronic diseases for each of these five categories, with four being the most severe and one being the least severe. These ratings were developed using information about the natural history of the disease, need for ongoing regular follow up, and treatment costs. Refer to the grid below.

	4	3	2	1
PRODUCTIVITY	-Requires intensive assistance in daily living -4 weeks' work loss annually with illness -Less than full workload on regular basis	-Physical impairment requiring occasional assistance -3 weeks' work loss annually with illness -Less than full workload on regular basis	-Physical impairment requiring infrequent assistance -2 weeks' work loss annually with illness -Less than full workload on infrequent basis	-No significant assistance needed -Infrequent work loss -High energy level and stamina
INTENSITY OF TRAVEL FOR CARE NEEDS	-Tertiary medical care needed -High travel intensity and cost involved	-Mid level medical care needed -Moderate travel and cost involved	-Basic medical care needed -Minimal travel and cost involved	-Limited medical care needed Infrequent care needed, locally available
RISK OF FUTURE COMPLICATIONS	-High	-Medium	-Low	-Minimal
FIELD SERVICE CAPABILITY	-Less than or equal to eight years -Risk of attrition Before age 55	-Eight to 15 years -Risk of attrition by age 55-60	-15 to 25 years -Risk of attrition by age 60-65	-25 years plus -No attrition risks
COSTS	-Anticipated medical expenses greater than $25,000 annually	-Anticipated medical expenses $5,000-$25,000 annually	-Anticipated medical expenses less than $5,000 annually	-Limited expenses for disease, only routine medical care

This assessment grid is to be used primarily for those seeking long-term ministries. There might be times when one would not be considered for a long-term ministry but could be considered for a short-term assignment or two. The risk of future complications and the productivity of the individual are obvious concerns, as they would prevent the worker from accomplishing his or her job or being able to complete a long-term ministry.

Over the years, we have noted that the completion of two four-year terms is a time when we see a high frequency of attrition, even without medical causes. So we set the most severe rate of attrition because of health issues to be less than or equal to eight years. We also established a tenure of 25 or more years of service to be the least severe. Applicants given the more severe rating in this area might be considered for short-term assignments, provided other factors did not show them to be at the high-risk level.

Travel for medical care outside of one's ministry locale is considered since it contributes to decreased productivity due to days away from ministry. The frequency of travel is rated from "infrequent need to travel" as less severe to "high travel intensity needed" as the most severe. As more remote areas of the world become the target for ministry opportunities, these locations are less likely to have acceptable medical care. Thus, personnel may need to travel to larger cities within the country, or even to a nearby country for acceptable medical care.

Associated with the need to travel are the logistical costs involved. Can travel be done by ground, or are expensive flights necessary? Is lodging necessary and available, and is the cost reasonable? Our experience has shown that other care providers, either family or team members, may need to travel with the missionary who has the health concern. At times, full families may need to travel and remain in a distant location for an extended period of time to accommodate the medical needs of one member of the family.

An example is the situation where an entire family must accompany a wife who has a high-risk pregnancy. They must relocate for an extended period of time during the pregnancy so that adequate follow up, monitoring, delivery, and newborn care can be provided. When there is a prior history of such high-risk pregnancies, physicians may expect the missionary to be near better medical care early in the pregnancy for monitoring and remain there through delivery.

As medical care progresses and new diagnostic and treatment options are developed, the cost of medical care continues to increase. Some newer medications or special treatments now cost as much as $60,000 a year. In order to be good stewards of the resources provided to the sending body, these costs should also be part of the assessment of risk. This is particularly important for any organization that provides the funding for a significant portion of the health-care costs for their personnel. After looking at average medical costs, we determined that expenses in excess of $25,000 annually for a single disease process to be at the higher end of the scale.

We began using the risk assessment grid to evaluate some of the more common chronic illnesses that individuals were reporting and determined the degree of anticipated risk associated with them. Medical conditions receiving a rating greater than 15 were felt to present a high enough risk for the agency and individual over the years that these were generally not approved for long-term ministries. The most common ones we saw on applicants' health histories and also experienced with field personnel were type 1diabetes, multiple sclerosis, current therapy for cancers, and type 1 bipolar disorder. Therefore, we felt they should not be considered for a long-term assignment.

As indicated, we look at whether or not it is possible for these individuals to participate in one or more short-term assignments and re-evaluate at a later date. For those conditions with ratings in the 12-15 range, we felt that they warranted consideration for a long-term assignment. This group of illnesses is significantly longer and some of the more common ones include type 2 diabetes, type 2 bipolar disorder, fibromyalgia, lupus, ulcerative colitis, Crohn's disease, rheumatoid arthritis, and childhood ADHD. In some of these cases, we recommend an assignment where medical care is more easily accessible, cutting the need for travel and days away from ministry.

Is decision-making all about calculating the risk, and not looking at other factors? Are there some times when an individual might be such an ideal person for a ministry that the health risks and concerns for the individual or other family members could or should be overlooked? There may be times when applicants' job skill sets, their prior experience, their association with other team members, or their ethnicity might make them ideal candidates for a new ministry.

In these situations, both the individual and the sending agency/organization may decide to overlook some of the health risks. This could be done as long as it does not require placing individuals or family members in an environment that would be life threatening or detrimental to their health. When doing this, both the applicant and the organization should agree to the risks taken. In these cases, it also may be easier to consider these workers for short-term experiences and see how their health is maintained during that time.

How Can the Physical Assessment Best Be Done?

The amount of time and resources involved in physical assessment should be appropriate to the length of time the worker will be overseas and the level of relationship or responsibility between the missionary and the sending agency/organization. Those who are going as volunteers should undergo the least formal assessment, but they would do well to be aware of how their health might impact their time overseas.

In today's Internet world, it is easier for individuals to obtain information about their health and medical conditions from a simple search. But one must be aware of the source of the information on the Internet. Larger medical institutions and medical associations have websites that offer public access and information about many disease processes. Gathering information from such sites as Mayo Clinic, the American Cancer Society, the American Heart Association, the American Academy of Pediatrics, and the American Diabetes Association enables volunteers to learn more about health issues that they already have.

Primary care physicians also will know what testing should be performed on healthy individuals to be sure that new medical conditions are detected early. Several groups have developed guidelines on what testing should be done and at what age these should start. The American Cancer Society has these, with special attention given to those that aid in the detection of cancer. The American College of Physicians also produces a series of guidelines, and the U.S. Preventive Services Task Force (USPSTF) provides information that weighs the benefits and disadvantages of various forms of testing, making recommendations along these lines.

The American Academy of Pediatrics makes similar recommendations regarding evaluations and testing to be done on children. These various groups do not exactly agree in their recommendations, but tend to provide more testing of children at a young age and adults during their fourth or fifth decade of life. Our medical team evaluated these recommendations and decided what was appropriate for our personnel to undergo before leaving the USA for a term overseas.

A better understanding of an applicant's health also can be obtained by completing a comprehensive medical history. This should be considered for workers who are planning to be on the field on more than a volunteer basis. Such a review will often lead them to think of a disease process that is common in their family. They may be at an increased risk for developing such a disease. This review also may trigger the memory of conditions experienced in the past but that still could cause problems in the future.

Traditionally the "annual physical" has been a means for an ongoing evaluation of one's health. These may provide new information at times, but usually a good medical history and the age-appropriate screening mentioned above will provide the most needed information about a healthy adult. Thus we began relying more on information from our health questionnaire and less from the physical exam.

However, we have continued to require physical exams on children and older adults who are at stages where a direct interaction with a physician may be more beneficial. A primary care physician can provide information and should be consulted when plans are made to spend time in another country. The physician will have good advice about the natural history of a disease and needed follow up for a medical condition but may have limited knowledge about what is available in other settings.

When Should the Physical Assessment Be Done?

Health issues should be surfaced early in the decision-making processes between applicants and the sending agency/church. This prevents the building up of hopes and expectations that may later be shattered if health issues are a reason for the person not to be involved in overseas ministry. Looking at these issues early also is good stewardship, both of time and resources. When a sending agency or church determines that specific health conditions prevent an applicant from participating in a long-term ministry assignment, these conditions should be made known to the applicant at the outset.

It is helpful for applicants to complete a few health questions that assist in determining if they have those conditions that might exclude them from serving long term overseas. If their health is stable enough or their condition is one that is not expected to develop significant changes in the short term, they could be considered for a shorter assignment.

In addition to those medical conditions with greater risks, there also are conditions that would not impact someone's ministry as long as the environment and work circumstances are right. For example, there will be locations where medical care is acceptable for monitoring and managing any anticipated emergencies that might arise. These personnel could be allowed to serve in one of these locations but not other areas. If an applicant were not focused only on a specific ministry or destination, having health information early in the process would allow discussions about other possible ministries.

No matter how early in the process a person's health information is obtained, that health is going to be a dynamic process. Changes can and will occur throughout the application process and time of ministry. Because of the possibility for change, a relationship of trust between the missionary and the sending organization must be encouraged so that information will be shared openly as new problems arise, and changes can be made that contribute to the success of the ministry.

Does Health Assessment Contribute to the Success of a Ministry?

This is not one of the "W" questions that we learned to use in evaluating events or situations. Yet when the health of applicants is one of the factors assessed during the application process, the information obtained can be used to make wise decisions about the location and length of ministry. Both the missionary and the sending agency/church will be aware of the risks involved and they can work together to limit the impact of those risks.

As a result, the likelihood for a full and successful ministry is enhanced. Those personnel will be able to accomplish their ministry goals and feel good about completing their work. Also they will not have created new health risks caused by living in an area that would be detrimental to their health. Both the missionary and the sending body will reap the benefits of being good stewards of their resources.

About the Author

Dr. Van Williams earned his medical degree from the University of Mississippi. He served as a Medical Missionary for 11 years at the Bangalore Baptist Hospital before joining the staff of the International Mission Board in 1987 as Medical Consultant. He then became Director of the Medical Department in 1989. Retired now, he and his wife Sarah have three adult children.

9

Emotional and Psychological Health
by Duane Hammack

Considering an applicant's emotional and psychological health may be the single most important factor in missionary retention and overall success. While churches and mission agencies lose missionaries to wellness problems and/or moral failure, a relative few are lost due to a weakness in theology or missiological practice. For this reason, it is imperative that the methods used to select emotionally and psychologically healthy missionaries are an important consideration in any application process.

It should be noted that for the sake of this discussion, we are distinguishing emotional wellness elements from medical wellness issues. However, this separation of terms in no way suggests that there will not be simultaneously experienced physiological or medical components to a given emotional wellness scenario.

The phrase "emotional wellness" is an umbrella term that includes several key elements. Emotional wellness is the composite of a person's non-medical health, which includes emotions, thoughts, and spirit.

1. **Emotion**—the God-imaged part of our inner person that involves the full continuum of feelings that missionaries experience in day-to-day life.
2. **Thought**—the God-imaged part of our inner person that describes specific words and phrases that missionaries "say" to themselves as they evaluate real life experiences.
3. **Spirit**—the foundational part of our creation that proportionately (righteously or unrighteously) informs our thoughts and feelings, as well as our behavior.

We recognize that not all missionary applicants will have significant emotional wellness issues. In a 2010 internal study at the International Mission Board, we found that about only 10 percent of the overall applicant pool required some level of focus on their emotional wellness issues. This is important to know because while it can be labor intensive to assess these issues, it is usually not a large percentage that requires this type of attention.

The Emotional Wellness Evaluator

Before we go any further, it is important to pause and identify some of the needed qualities for those who might be tasked with evaluating the emotional wellness of missionary applicants. If possible, it is good to have someone with an academic training in the social sciences as well as personal cross-cultural experience. If that type of person is not available to the assessing team, then a combined approach using former missionaries alongside a mental health professional might be more realistic.

In addition to the cross-cultural perspective, the evaluators need to have a good level of emotional wellness plus a healthy sense of personal boundaries. Those involved in this level of assessment should possess the same (or greater) level of maturity and emotional fitness as those who are applying. They must be able to identify their own feelings and thoughts about the applicants and then separate those feelings from the assessment process. They must remain unbiased and objective.

Spiritual maturity is perhaps the most important quality for the evaluator. These people should sense a confidence that God has called them to help make these important decisions about a missionary applicant. That means they know how to listen to the Holy Spirit and follow His lead. Spiritual discernment, following prayerful evaluation, should be the bedrock for recommendations of "going," "waiting," or "not going."

Working with missionary applicants is fundamentally about people, not a process of gathering information. This is not to imply that using technical skills when gathering information is not critical to the overall emotional wellness review process. In fact, gathering the best specific and detailed information can sometimes make the difference between a good decision and a bad decision that is later regretted. However, there must be a balance between skills, spiritual discernment, and personal rapport.

Jerry* is a good example of someone who did not have all these qualities in proper balance. He was a former long-term missionary who had to return home unexpectedly due to the educational and developmental needs of one of his children. Jerry was asked by the pastor of his home church to be the organizer of a new missions ministry at the church, which would include the selection of missionaries sent directly to the field from the church. Unbeknownst to Jerry and his pastor, he had not yet examined his own feelings about having to leave the mission field.

When Jerry eventually worked with an applicant family with small children, he was unaware that his unprocessed feelings of disappointment and grief were still affecting his perspective. Because of those deep feelings, he gave his opinion that the developmental needs of this family's child could be met on the mission field. While Jerry consciously and verbally committed to be objective in his thinking, his personal feelings obscured both his perspective of this family's overall application as well as his ability to discern God's direction for the eventual needs of the child. Quite simply, Jerry could not say "no, not now" due to his own strong feelings about no longer being on the mission field himself.

Foundations for Emotional Wellness

In our previously stated definition of emotional wellness, we saw three key components: emotion, thought, and spirit. Because the spiritual state of applicants feeds their thoughts and feelings, it is truly foundational. Although there are many ways that a person's spiritual life impacts thoughts and feelings, there are two pillars that provide the basis for emotional wellness: the person's **identity in Christ** and his or her **concept of God as Father**. Knowing the truth about "who we are" and "who God is" shapes the ways we experience stress, how we see our past/present/future, set expectations, and perceive traumatic life events. It is not uncommon for missionary applicants to have a strong head knowledge of these concepts, but what really matters is what their actions and behavior say about what they believe. The importance for a missionary to live out of a true biblical identity in Christ cannot be over-emphasized. Satan is scheming every day to compromise or destroy what God has done in the life of a missionary (Ephesians 6:10-12). He will use second-culture stress and adversity to tempt a missionary to doubt and be distracted. As sinful people, we all seek to define our worth and value based on some variable that is temporal and built on the sand (as the parable goes in Matthew 7:24-27). Spiritually mature applicants know exactly what the Bible says about who they are through the eyes of Jesus as their supreme advocate to the heavenly Father. What we really believe about ourselves will impact the thoughts and feelings we have as we experience adversity.

Of equal importance is missionaries' ability to demonstrate what they really believe about God, their benevolent spiritual Father. Satan routinely challenges missionaries around the world to question the love and care of God when facing challenging circumstances, slow prayer response, rampant evil, and the reality of hell for those without Christ.

A missionary applicant with a strong spiritual foundation should possess the following insights:

- Knowledge of and life-tested belief in a personal, biblical identity in Christ
- Knowledge of and life-tested belief in God's biblically-revealed character
- A healthy, biblical worldview of suffering
- Ability to do battle with Satan over falsehoods that are intended to hurt or destroy
- Skills in knowing how to spiritually care for his or her own soul

Built upon that spiritual foundation are the other two elements of emotional wellness: thoughts and feelings. This includes but is not limited to the following skills:

- Have the capacity to be "self-aware" of his or her internal world of thoughts and feelings
- Possess a good, working knowledge of the full continuum of life emotions
- Have good skills in labeling and verbally processing feelings
- Does not deny or minimize those feelings that bring discomfort
- Resolution of past hurts, emotional wounds, and the grief that accompanies them

These emotional and cognitive elements of personal wellness are important but not readily understood by many. All behaviors are preceded by a chain of internal events of which most people are unaware. All of us have deeply held core beliefs about nearly every aspect of our lives. These powerful but typically non-verbalized beliefs are the foundation for our thoughts. These thoughts are then the seedbed for our feelings. Many times the end of this chain of events is a behavior that reflects the core belief that birthed it. Here is a diagram of this chain of events:

Core Belief $\longrightarrow$ Thought $\longrightarrow$ Feeling $\longrightarrow$ Behavior

Joy* was a vivid example of hidden beliefs bearing visible fruit through her behavior. She had never studied a second language before going to college where it was required for graduation. Unfortunately, she soon discovered that she was not a natural linguist. While she successfully completed the course requirements, doing so was a struggle and she was never able to attain conversational skill. Along the way, Joy developed a core belief about her ability to learn languages that was primarily the result of her difficult time in college. Her core belief about language learning was "It's impossible for me to learn another language."

117

Years later, when she heard God call her to international missions, she was struck almost immediately with panic as her mind raced forward to the inevitable expectation that she would need to learn another language. Within seconds of hearing God's voice saying "Go," Joy heard another voice in her head say "You can't learn languages; you'll never be a missionary."

As Joy pondered the reality that she would never be able to be obedient to God's call to go overseas, she was overwhelmed with fear and sadness. Her sad feelings were nearly instantaneous and the direct result of the thought she had just seconds before. The longer Joy sat with her sadness, the more resolved she became that she would never be a missionary overseas.

Joy never applied to be a missionary, so an assessing team did not counsel her appropriately. But Harry and Jill did apply for service, and the following example is a great illustration of why it is necessary to go beyond the surface expressions of wellness and dig down to the depths of a person's true character.

Harry* and Jill* were a young, highly productive ministry couple who had been extremely successful leaders in their local church. In fact, all who knew him as their senior pastor loved Harry dearly. Jill was a stay-at-home mom, raising their two small children, and also had a part-time women's discipleship ministry. Harry was a prolific preacher and was asked regularly by other churches in his area to fill the pulpit. Harry's church had grown by leaps and bounds in the three years that he had been senior pastor, seeing significant increases in church membership and baptisms.

When Harry came home one night from a state missions conference, he shared with Jill that he was sensing God's call to international mission service. Being called to full-time ministry along with Harry, and having her own childhood experience of admiration for missions, Jill was certain that this was the next logical step in God's plan for their family.

When Harry and Jill officially announced their sense of calling to be cross-cultural missionaries, everyone who knew them was ecstatic that God had now equipped this fine young ministry couple and was sending them to the "real" ministry field overseas. They had all of the necessary qualifications for their proposed work: seminary training, church experience, and effectiveness in their local ministry. Harry had the moral support and strong references from many key ministry leaders in his city and state.

As Harry and Jill began language learning overseas, Harry had difficulty staying focused on the task since it required him to study again, and in an area of linguistics that was conversational and not academic. In a short time, he began to loathe the daily grind of studying language. It felt like he was getting nowhere fast, and he resented the way the teachers seemed to talk down to him when he did not perform well. Harry began to show his stress through brief outbursts of anger toward Jill and the children. Jill was concerned about Harry and his stress but knew that in time he would adjust and settle into his new role as a missionary. She prayed often and did her best to support him.

Unfortunately, Jill's support was not enough. One year into their term, Harry was discovered to have pornographic movies on his computer. He admitted that an old habit of viewing pornography had re-emerged and that he had been compulsively viewing pornography every week for the past six months. He had been driven by his feelings of incompetence, anger, and helplessness to escape into an imaginary world of power, sexual conquest, and feelings of being desired or needed. Harry quietly feared inside that he would never feel competent and empowered in his new ministry setting overseas.

Harry had not shared the complete truth in the application process about his history of pornography use or the extent of his childhood physical abuse at the hands of his alcoholic father. While Harry had everything he needed to qualify as a skilled worker in the missionary task, he lacked the necessary spiritual maturity and personal wellness to qualify him to stay on the field.

Elements of a Wellness Profile

As the assessment team begins gathering information on a missionary applicant, there are at least five important elements that need to be examined.

1. **Temperament**—Temperament is the God-given "bent" of a person when he or she is dealing with problem solving and stress. It does not typically change over time because it is part of our nature, much like our hair texture, height, and body type. Temperament can be viewed like the blank canvas of an oil painting. The basic texture, color, and shape of the canvas will always be the same whether covered with paint or not. We may grow through teaching, study, and life experiences, thus adding paint to our canvas.

    As we add this learning and shaping to our temperament, they combine to create a more colorful and full creation that I consider to be the personality. Over time, our personality may grow such that our temperament may not be as easy to detect by observation alone. However, we will always tend to manage stress from the same temperamental leaning. Most people deal with stress either through a "feeling" response or a "thinking" response.

    Either approach is fine for processing stress, but both have unique needs in order to bring balance to their coping response. I believe that Jesus was ambidextrous when it came to temperament. He knew the exact balance of paying attention to His feelings and thoughts when dealing with life's stress. The mature believer in Christ will imitate Him, avoiding the extremes and finding balance through the use of adaptive skills.

    Another example of temperament includes the tendencies toward introversion and extraversion. Personally, I am a shy, introverted, quiet person. I tend to need time alone in order to recharge and be ready to engage the world. I am naturally reflective and can spend hours evaluating my internal thoughts and feelings. I am not a naturally social person.

In the course of my maturation and learning from life experiences, I have found that if I will push myself beyond what is temperamentally "natural," my life will be enriched. By reaching for this balance, I'll spend more time in meaningful social relationships with friends, feel less vulnerable to sin by focusing outwardly, and find enjoyment in standing and speaking publicly to a group of people. All of these abilities have been learned and are appreciated, but at the end of the day I still need my downtime for recharging.

There are several objective ways to measure temperament, but perhaps the most common instrument used in mission circles is the Myers-Briggs Type Indicator (MBTI).

2. **Healing of Life's Wounds**—Some missionary applicants have experienced emotional or psychological wounding in their lives. They have had hurtful experiences in their original families, at school, at church, in their social peer group, etc. These wounds can range from small offenses to what might be considered traumatic. These wounds can be significant because they shape people's souls and personalities: how they view themselves, others, authority, God, and society. They may be the root cause behind an applicant's response to stress, even though the original wound happened years ago.

   Roy,* a missionary applicant, was 10 years old when his live-in grandfather began to sexually abuse him in his own bedroom. Because his grandfather was a trusted authority in his life, Roy's understanding of trust in relationships, trust in authority, personal boundaries, view of his own "goodness," and his belief in God's sovereign power were decimated as he entered his own adult years. We'll see later how those experiences, which remained unhealed, affected his experiences overseas.

3. **Family History**—Important events that impacted the family as a whole also are important, such as birth order, the effects of debilitating physical challenges of a parent, a trauma that occurred within the family, etc. A familiar adage among our

assessment team goes like this: *Whatever "bugs" you in America will "hippopotamus" you overseas!* This saying wisely alerts us to the fact that past experiences, if unresolved, can potentially mushroom and become even larger issues in the cross-cultural environment.

The power of family history can be illustrated using the previous example of Roy. Everyone in his family dearly loved Roy's grandfather, especially Roy's sisters who adored him as a cherished model of stability and manhood in their lives. When Roy was 12, he decided to share with his parents about the abuse he had been enduring. When he did, the authorities were called, his grandfather was arrested, and he was later convicted and sent to prison.

Along with the personal pain of having been violated by a trusted adult family member, Roy also had to cope with the impact on his family. His father was angry that the abuse had been exposed, and two of his sisters would no longer speak to him due to their grief over "losing" a treasured family member. In the end, the abuse perpetrated upon Roy became the whole family's shared story of loss and damaged relationships. For Roy, he would later find that on the mission field, it was difficult to build trust with his supervisor and to develop the needed support relationships with his team.

4. **Identification of Clinical Symptoms**—Emotional and psychological woundings, if not properly addressed, can result in clinical symptoms such as depression, mental illness, and personality disorders.

There also is a theory of symptom development called the "stress-diathesis" model that suggests that we all inherit from our families certain degrees of potential to develop physical, emotional, and/or psychological problems. This model suggests that stress is the factor that can push some people over their personal, genetic threshold of stress tolerance, thus triggering problems that are common to their particular family.

As we know, unprecedented levels of stress are typical for cross-cultural missionaries. Their stress can be expected to come more frequently, more intensely, and in a cumulative fashion.

Whether from wounding, genetics or both, unhealthy coping skills in a person's life can sometimes be so severe they create clinical symptoms, which need to be addressed medically and by trained professionals. Examples of clinical symptoms are panic attacks, cutting behavior, suicidal thoughts, obsessive thoughts/compulsive behaviors, and restricting or binging with food. When clinical symptoms increase in severity or are allowed to remain for a length of time, they may develop into identifiable, diagnosable mental problems.

There are some clinical problems of this severity that may prevent an applicant from being considered for overseas missionary service. Some of these diagnoses are schizophrenia, bi-polar 1 disorder, any diagnosis that involves psychosis, and personality disorders. These types of problems are usually identified with the help of a clinical psychologist and/or psychiatrist.

There are other less severe diagnoses that deserve great caution but may not indicate that overseas ministry is prohibited. These emotional wellness problems are worthy to be considered but only when balanced with many other factors in a strong missionary application. Some of these cautionary problems include obsessive-compulsive disorder, panic disorder, and eating disorders. When a history or presence of these problems is discovered, good information gathering is imperative so that a healthy decision about the overall application can be made.

Let's return to the story of Roy. He eventually married Julie* and together they felt that God had called them to be missionaries. Roy had not explored his sexual abuse history with many people. In fact, he had made a concerted effort to put the abuse behind him, which meant not thinking about it and minimizing its impact on his life. As he and Julie made their way to the mission field several years later, Roy struggled to adjust to the culture of his new country and was not finding success in learning language. He felt depressed and in the quietness of his own thoughts, he told himself that he was a "slacker" and asked himself repeatedly why "he was such a loser."

In addition, in Roy's sexual relationship with his wife, he began finding it impossible to sustain an erection during intercourse. As Roy was faced with the challenges of learning a new culture and language, his past feelings of self-blame and helplessness with his grandfather were stirred and became overwhelming. Because Roy continued to unknowingly believe that he was responsible for the abuse, and therefore a reprehensible person, his struggles with cross-cultural adjustment only confirmed in his mind what he already knew: "losers can't be missionaries." This feeling of being out of control and helpless, just as he had been in the past, resurrected those old emotional wounds from his prior abuse. His sexual shame as a 10-year-old completely killed his desire and ability to feel competent sexually with his wife in the present.

4. **Current Use of Healthy Coping Skills**—Coping can be defined as "a person's ability to face and deal with responsibilities, problems, or difficulties, especially successfully or in a calm or adequate manner." All people have coping skills, but not all those ways of dealing with stress are appropriate. A few examples of unhealthy coping are addiction, binge eating, blaming, using pornography, and denial. Using unhealthy coping will usually lead to increased and expanded negative coping over time if not changed.

In Roy's situation, although it would appear that he had few coping skills, the truth is that he used healthy coping every day. Those skills prevented him from giving in to his feelings and buying his airline ticket to return home. He persevered through the strength available to him through his relationship with God. He stayed focused on the mutual calling he and Julie felt they had together. From time to time, Roy refused to remain stuck in his negative thinking. He got active and did something constructive such as studying language or taking his wife on a date.

While these are all legitimate coping skills, they are not particularly hearty skills that will continue to perform effectively over time. Therefore, the cumulative stress for Roy would eventually lead him to conclude that the risk to his own long-term health and that of his marriage was too great. The couple returned to the States, and though Roy felt confused about his handling of the situation, he also felt relieved to be out from under the stress. Had Roy turned to a skilled counselor for help, he could have possibly gained the needed insights and coping skills that would have allowed him to stay on the field.

Gathering Emotional Wellness Information

For any missionary assessment team, whether in a church or with a sending agency, it is wise to develop a solid process of gathering current and historical emotional wellness information from an applicant and then using that information in the decision-making phase. Here is a helpful list of seven specific sources when gathering important information.

1. **Health Questionnaire**—A thorough, written questionnaire that asks comprehensively about physical and emotional health is essential. Emotional wellness issues, and especially diagnosable mental health problems, must be understood first as having not been caused by another diagnosable medical condition. Sometimes it is possible to discover that a problem classified as "emotional" is really the result of a physiological, medical issue. A questionnaire needs to also ask the broad questions about emotional wellness issues such as depression, pornography use, anxiety, eating disorders, etc. These initial questions will surface the major emotional wellness vulnerabilities for the applicant, either historical or current.

2. **Assessment Inventories**—There are many assessment inventories that are scientific in design and proven to be reliable in objectively assessing emotional wellness readiness. While these tools all rely on self-report information, they provide a rich context that surpasses that of simply asking questions in an interview format. Some assessment inventories measure the presence of major forms of severe mental illness, such as the Minnesota Multi-Phasic Personality Inventory 2 (MMPI-2). Others measure marital health, such as the Prepare/Enrich Marital Assessment. Still other useful measures, such as the Myers-Briggs Type Indicator (MBTI), provide great information about temperament. These are just a few of the many objective and scientific inventories that can provide important applicant information.

3. **Reports of Previous Counseling**—If applicants have used the services of a mental health professional in the past, it is always wise to have a report of the benefits of that counseling submitted by the counselor who delivered the services. This report will identify the number of sessions/dates of the counseling, credentials of the provider, goals, motivation of the applicant, and progress realized in the course of counseling. Most mental health professionals also are willing to elaborate or even answer additional questions by telephone if asked. One of the purposes of these reports is to evaluate the issues identified by the counselor against those that have been self-reported by the applicant.

4. **Self-Reports of Previous Counseling**—How an applicant is able to report the benefits of past counseling is critical in understanding the real quality of change in his or her life. It is safe to expect an applicant to be able to share in a written report what specifically made the counseling helpful. If the counseling transformed an applicant's perspective and quality of life, he or she should be able to tell you how things are different now.

This report should include number of sessions and/or dates, what identified issues were discussed, and how counseling changed the individual's understanding of himself, God, and other people. If an applicant is unable to share well in either written or verbal form how the counseling was helpful, it is wise to conclude that there was essentially no real benefit.

5. **Issue-Focused Clarification Questions**—Once the major emotional wellness issues have been identified, it may be necessary to go deeper with the applicant by using a written set of clarification questions about an issue. These more specific questions and self-report responses by the applicant will shed even more light on the experience of symptoms and the periods of time experienced. These sets of questions also can assess the absence or presence of an applicant's spiritual, emotional, cognitive (thought), or social coping skills.

6. **Personal References**—Personal references can provide a unique form of applicant information in that it is not self-reported but provided by others who know the applicant. Many times a reference will mention personal knowledge of important historical events in a person's life that may be associated with an identified emotional wellness issue. Another trusted person's perspective of an applicant's emotional wellness in the real context of life is of high value. If secondary references also are gathered, these references may provide even more valuable help in that this information comes from someone recommended, not by the applicant, but by a primary reference. References that waive the applicant's right of full disclosure are particularly useful in that it is possible to also call or inquire further if the reference information provided suggests a need for further clarification.

7. **Applicant Interviews**—The most reliable and valuable sources of information are the applicants themselves. Personally interacting with and dialoguing face-to-face with an applicant has no rival. Though other sources of information are helpful, it is uncanny to see how often hypotheses related to a person's emotional wellness state are rendered invalid after quality time is spent with the applicant. Not only is it possible to understand better the life context of reported events,

but interviews are free-flowing and can be directed on-the-spot as additional pieces of information are learned. Beyond this, though, is the opportunity to sit with a fellow believer who shares the indwelling presence of the Holy Spirit and to watch the Spirit rightly interpret application information.

Risk as a Reality

From a position of logic, one might assume that God's perspective of risk-taking in kingdom work might be ultra-conservative. After all, we are called to sound stewardship with all things given by God, and He, being sovereign and omnipotent, could find it unnecessary to take risk. When we look to the Bible, however, we see a very clear command to take risks that are Spirit-driven and ultimately a venture of faith building for us as His children.

In the parable of the talents (Matthew 25), the master entrusted his goods to his servants, knowing there was a risk that they might not use those funds wisely. Similarly, there is a risk of sending any sin-natured person into a world still manipulated by Satan. Because of this, whether it appears to us that there is a small or large risk with a given missionary applicant, we will never be able to eliminate risk entirely from the missions equation. Such is the spiritual dynamic of assessing and sending missionaries.

Grace* is a good example of a risk worth taking. She was a young, 26-year-old missionary applicant who was applying with her husband of four years. She had struggled in significant ways with depression. In fact, she had a major depressive episode when she was 21 years old. Grace appeared to be "sensitive" in temperament as well. There was documentation that told the assessing team that since Grace's episode five years ago, she had worked with her physician to find the right dosage of the right medication and also had worked with a counselor to educate herself and implement the spiritual and emotional coping skills that might help her stave off another episode.

In interviews, Grace was transparent, genuine, and relaxed about her emotional wellness history. She acknowledged her vulnerability. The interviewer sensed great spiritual depth in Grace, partly because of her struggle with depression. During the interview, the Holy Spirit seemed powerfully present as Grace was both appropriately sober regarding her chance of future depression but also willing and able to wield spiritual weapons in combatting errant thoughts and feelings. Despite the risk of future symptoms, it was recommended that Grace be affirmed for service, based mostly on the sense of spiritual discernment in the interview.

It can be very helpful to use an outline of factors of importance when evaluating an applicant's level of risk. I tend to look at these factors in the order that they are presented here. The overall strength of an application can be broadly gauged by considering the following factors:

- **Age**—The older the applicant, the more life-coping skills gained through the maturing process. The opposite also is true; the younger the applicant, the fewer life experiences and opportunities to develop healthy coping skills. As a rule, fewer years of life equal fewer healthy coping skills.
- **Family History**—If there is a history of the same emotional wellness problem in the applicant's family, there will be an increased possibility of occurrence for the applicant overseas.
- **Personal Symptoms**—The greater the number of symptoms for a particular emotional wellness problem, the greater the chance of experiencing the same symptoms overseas. This includes a consideration of both past and current symptoms.
- **Severity of Personal Symptoms**—The intensity of the symptoms experienced is important when thinking about the challenge that the problem will bring to the available coping skills. This includes the greatest severity of any symptom that has ever been experienced.
- **Number of Life Occurrences**—Some symptoms are experienced more continually than episodically. If usually experienced episodically, the number of lifetime episodes where symptoms were present and active is a significant factor.
- **Time Distance since Last Occurrence**—Generally speaking, the longer it has been since symptoms have been experienced, the more positive it is for potential reoccurrence of the

problem. This factor must be weighed carefully in consideration of the other factors.

- **Relative Strength of Overall Application**—It is important to evaluate the "30,000 foot view" of the larger application against the strength or weakness of the emotional wellness view. There are times when an application is extremely strong in other areas. In contrast, the overall application may be weak with a high risk of a reoccurrence of emotional wellness problems.
- **Strength of Healthy Coping Skills**—The emotional wellness assessor needs to examine the presence of an applicant's spiritual, emotional, cognitive, and behavior coping skills, their frequency of use and the strength of their impact.
- **Proposed Assignment and Location**—The anticipated assignment and the degree that it matches an applicant's previous experience and skill set will help estimate future stress and the potential need for increased coping with change or vocational transition. Also, cultural and economic development factors in the new location may suggest increased levels of stress.
- **Anticipated Support System**—The missionary's support system can be a significant factor to consider. This may include geographic proximity to supervision, presence of ministry teammates, support from other like-minded believers in the community, availability of social technology such as Internet and telephone, and access to support persons such as pastoral caregivers and/or member care providers.

Conclusion

Missionaries are no less human than anyone else. The proof is in the reality that mission field caregivers provide hours of pastoral and clinical counseling for exactly the same problems: marital conflict, depression, pornography use, eating disorders, sexual deviancy, anxiety disorders, sexual abuse, inappropriate anger, addictions, sex outside of marriage, panic disorders, etc. Cross-cultural stress, both momentary and cumulative, is enough to weaken even the best coping skills.

This is why it is mandatory for an assessing team to gather all the necessary information about an applicant's emotional wellness, view the whole picture of the person's readiness for the mission field, and then reach a consensus decision. It is only by doing this work as a team that such a large task can be shouldered and carried out effectively, and with spiritual discernment.

Recommended Resources

The following study resources are excellent for establishing a strong identity in Christ and knowing God's character.

The Search for Significance, Robert McGhee (2003). Nashville: Thomas Nelson.

God: Discover His Character, Bill Bright (2002). Wayne: New Life Publishers.

About the Author

Duane Hammack has a Masters in Clinical Psychology plus three years of seminary training. In the 90s, he served two terms in East Asia as a Member Care Consultant to missionaries using pastoral care, training, and counseling. In the 2000s, he returned stateside to his mission organization's home office. For 12 years, Duane served alongside a team of missionary selection consultants as an emotional wellness consultant with missionary applicants. Duane is married to Sandy, has three daughters, and is most assuredly "Papa" to two grandsons.

10

The Necessity of Marital Wellness
by Mark Whitworth

In the spring of 1986, my wife, Linda, and I were appointed as missionaries to Japan. Linda and I were soon transitioning to Tokyo, sent out by a deeply loving church body, supportive families, and having greatly benefited from the experiences in our respective careers. Prior to overseas deployment, Linda was employed as an accountant in a fulfilling work environment while I was employed as a psychotherapist in a private setting.

Married for about 10 years prior to deployment and having been blessed with the affirmation of the consultants who screened us at IMB, we were not overly confident but did share the belief that we had a fairly high degree of resilience in our marriage.

We proceeded to Tokyo, firm in the belief our solid and satisfying marital existence would serve us well as we navigated the deep waters of cross-cultural adaptation. One month after arriving, swimming around in the deep end of language and cultural acquisition, we were both seeing and hearing from one another things we had never seen or heard before.

I was withdrawn and extremely lonely on an emotional level. Linda, while not in a full, clinical depression, was moving through many days with a glazed and empty expression on her face, frequently moved to tears. Normal activities and functions we previously did without thinking took incredibly more effort and left us completely drained many days.

Our residence in Tokyo was a 600-square-foot apartment deep in the heart of the city. We commuted daily on jam-packed subways to attend Japanese class 20 hours a week and studying another 20 hours outside of class. None of our neighbors spoke English, and daily life— getting food into the house, commuting to school, attending Japanese church, managing the daily logistics of life— were so much more draining than we ever imagined.

We have one child, Brooke, who was attending international school in Tokyo during this phase of our career. The Lord and His servants surely provided for her during this time as we simply did not have much reserve for her in those initial months on the field. I was just an uninformed (read clueless if you will) young missionary, but it did occur to me as a trained family therapist that, had we not been pretty solid as a couple upon field arrival, we would never be holding up under all this transitional stress.

It was a level of isolation, grief, stress, and adaptation that we had never experienced before and it was impacting our marriage in significant ways. The Lord used that initial term on the field and subsequent terms to teach Linda and me about Himself, our areas of need, and how to be more fully aware of His provision for our marriage.

In the following pages of this chapter we will examine why a healthy marriage is so foundational for effective overseas life and ministry. We will delineate what constitutes a Christ-centered marriage. Then in a fairly detailed fashion, we will look at the various facets of a healthy and/or robust marriage that are capable of impacting a lost world for Christ. In other words, will those witnessing this couple see, hear, and feel Christ's presence at the center of the couple's life?

Christ at the Center of Marriage

In the midst of this suffering, our dependence on God and the truth of His Word sustained us in ways we had never experienced before. Our marriage was far from perfect, but it was a Christ-centered marriage. In my role here at the IMB I have interviewed, visited overseas with, taught, and counseled hundreds of missionary couples. The married couples we send out have Christ-centered, Bible-based marriages. The individuals in these marriages most frequently take an Ephesians 5 approach to relating to one another in marriage.

We are looking for men who love their wives as Christ loved the church—in a sacrificial manner and constantly giving of themselves—and women who respect and respond to their husband's God-ordained leadership of the home. A husband who appreciates his wife as one of God's most precious gifts to him and then makes sure his wife knows that, is fostering a marriage full of warmth and gratitude to God. A wife who trusts and affirms her husband at every turn is a woman who testifies about a God who is perfectly trustworthy and to be constantly praised.

Any couple that has a dynamic and effective overseas ministry life will have mature individual walks with the Lord. Those walks are characterized by quality times alone with the Father and daily feeding on His Word, which they use to fuel and focus their lives. Effective public ministry flows out of those private times in devoted dependence on a loving heavenly Father.

They have been discipled well over their years together and are instruments in God's hands as they minister first to one another before ministering to a lost world. Worship would be seen as foundational to the health and wholeness of their married life, and they would see it as absolutely essential in their lives. Service would flow out of all the above, and the best case would have them serving together in some significant ministry opportunities.

In terms of their history as a couple, there is a notable lack of separation patterns when it comes to conflict or stress. Of course there would be an absence of physical or emotional abuse, and the acting out of issues outside the marriage. The marriage would be remarkable in terms of harmony and health. The marriage should appear to be robust and that appearance supported by references reflecting the same. No marriage is without periods of challenge and in a later section we will discuss the reality and assessment of conflict management in a couple's relationship, but you would expect couples to be able to resolve conflicts in a biblical manner.

A significant aspect of overseas ministry for married couples has to do with call, which has been more thoroughly addressed in another section of this book. For the purposes of this chapter, suffice it to say that both husband and wife need to be similarly called and committed to overseas service. I frequently counsel with couples where one of the spouse's call to overseas service has somehow lessened, or in some cases completely dissipated. Naturally this is a very delicate area of discussion and one that is fraught with major ramifications. Our organization strongly affirms both husband and wife expressing a strong call to missions or otherwise they are not sent—but what if that original call begins to wane over the years?

As stated above, the ability to communicate these thoughts and feelings to one another is incredibly helpful in those times, as is having the maturity to not judge the one suffering in the midst of reaffirming God's call. There are a myriad number of unique situations that arise in married life overseas and it is critical that one hallmark of a missionary couple's life be the strong level of commitment they have to deep sharing of thoughts and feelings. Any healthy marriage has at its core quality communication.

It is vitally important that any couple considering, or being considered, for overseas service be able to communicate effectively. They must have the ability to discuss the full range of issues that impact all marriages, from the mundane matters of daily life management to critical, pressure-filled decisions they also confront. We seek couples that are able to share freely and listen, both with equal skill. There should be a free flow of give and take in the communication with healthy couples. Even when discussing weighty matters, there is clear evidence of love, mutual trust, and respect of opinion.

Several years ago I met a young couple in a great deal of distress; they wondered if they should return to the States to seek weekly marriage counseling. During their first term on the field, this childless couple had withdrawn from one another on several levels. Living under the stress and isolation of field life, they had become emotionally withdrawn, going days with minimal words exchanged and frequent hours-long periods of silence.

More notable to me was how they had withdrawn from one another in matters of the heart and Spirit. They reported no longer being drawn to pray together or read the Word together, and it was breaking both their hearts. Of course, one can imagine how it impacted their public witness in a very lost overseas setting where a missionary couple's marriage is on constant display. They recognized their need and committed their situation to the Lord.

These precious folks sought counsel and accountability and over time God spurred significant insight and produced change in their lives. A healthy married life is truly foundational for effective overseas service, but there are some factors that can make it very challenging to maintain that health.

Unique Factors Impacting Marriages in Cross-Cultural Ministry Settings

The high stress/low support environment in which most of our personnel serve is not always conducive to enhancing the quality of a marriage. By high stress/low support I am referencing the reality that most personnel will live and serve in settings where the availability of support is lower than they have ever experienced, and the stress higher. Personnel will be living in conditions very dissimilar to the ones they were called out of, living with a dramatic downturn in the availability of goods and services, isolation from family and friends who know and love them most, outright danger in some settings, feeling frustrations with work and colleagues, and worshipping in their second language.

Couples who have taken short-term trips to their eventual field of service sometime mistakenly believe long-term life will be as it was during the short-term trip. Seldom is long-term service as simple, well-planned, and provisioned as the volunteer trip.

Another factor impacting personnel early in their overseas life will be the grief that accompanies the loss of physical contact with family and friends on a regular basis. Eventually the Lord brings meaningful relationships into missionaries' lives, but it can take a significant period of time as cultural and language acquisitions do not typically occur at a rapid pace.

Most folks can handle high stress for short periods of time as long as the stress eventually subsides. Personnel also tend to do much better in high stress when they have high levels of support. The case, however, with many personnel is they are deployed in settings where high stress is the norm and support is not significantly high enough. Of course, lower stress environments such as a Westernized capital city do not typically require such high levels of support, but paradoxically sometimes the lower stress environments do offer higher levels of support.

For instance, there are overseas settings where quality public worship in English is available, which can be incredibly uplifting to missionaries. The availability or lack of healthy food, nearby colleagues, travel safety, clean water, consistent electricity, electronic connectivity, and safe medical services deeply impact overseas personnel on the physical and emotional levels.

Married personnel who are deployed on teams often report one significant, positive aspect of team life is the emotional and spiritual benefits of being sent out together. There is much support in the New Testament for the sending out of individuals in teams, and it would never be wise to consider a married couple as a team unto itself.

Linda and I served on a church-planting team with two other couples during our time on the field. We functioned as a team for almost seven years together, and it would be difficult to highlight all the ways those precious friends encouraged us, challenged us, and pointed us to the Lord with their lives. It was absolutely His will that we serve alongside them as God, time and again, enabled us to be more than we ever could have been had it been Linda and me serving alone. Linda watched and questioned how those wives served, and it impacted her on deeply significant levels as did my observations of the two husbands. We were intentional about pouring into, praying for, and just loving one another.

Cross-cultural stressors often impact couples in different ways and at different rates. It is very rare to hear reports of couples acquiring language or comfort in the culture at the same rate. Typically one spouse will acquire facility in the language sooner, and one may report the second culture feeling much more like home than the other. Many factors play into the reality of this difference in comfort levels, but healthy couples recognize it and do not let it become a hindrance in their lives and service.

Family of Origin Issues

Genesis 2:20-25 reveals to us God's plan of man and woman coming together to form the most intimate of all human relationships. The husband-wife relationship is more intimate than the parent-child or child-parent relationship. Yet as we move away from our families of origin to unite with our spouse, those families continue to impact how we live in profound ways. One significant influence of our families of origin is the model of marriage we witnessed in our families.

If you were raised in a family where your parents were believers, loved one another, modeled healthy marital patterns in front of you, and stayed married throughout their lives together, then God no doubt has used that in a powerful way in your life. You do not have to guess what a healthy marriage looks like; you saw it lived out in front of you. I was raised in such a home and to this day, when I do not know what to do in my marriage, I tend to default to what I saw my Dad do.

My Dad dearly loves my Mom and has loved her sacrificially for almost 60 years. We saw him love her with his actions and his words. He insisted his children respect her, publicly praised her, expressed his love out loud, and blessed her by never forgetting special occasions. For sure my parents did not have a perfect marriage, but I did see two people loving one another for decades and working their way through the ebb and flow of a life knit together by God.

You may contrast this model of marriage I witnessed with someone coming out of a single parent family, or a family where divorce was a reality. We have numerous individuals on the field who come from broken homes and yet have established very healthy, Christ-centered families.

Individuals coming out of families where the birth parents were not present in the home, or whose parents were unable to maintain their marriage, really do wonder at times about what constitutes a healthy married life. Not having seen one lived out in front of you on an intimate level can make your own married life somewhat more challenging.

That is not to say that other models such as extended family's marriages, or your grandparent's marriage, pastor's marriage, or older siblings' marriages cannot provide very healthy models for you. The presence of loving step-parents and their relationship to your birth parent also can be an excellent model at times. It is essential for individuals heading into overseas life to be fully cognizant of how their family of origin's model of marriage impacts their own marriage.

During my first few years on the field, I was deployed on a church-starting team. However, in my second year on the field my leadership, in consideration of my background, asked me to go meet with a young couple serving in a nearby Asian country. Over the course of their first term of service, this couple had grown increasingly alienated from one another to the point where they were ready to resign and return to the States.

In the first hour of our meeting, they both indicated they were miserable as a couple but somehow were doing fine in public ministry and life. They did not believe others could yet see the tears in the fabric of their marriage. In taking their history, it became abundantly clear that their families of origin, specifically the models of marriage they witnessed, were definitely impacting their current situation. The wife's father was emotionally distant and lacking in his ability to affirm her mother. He traveled frequently for work and simply did not model a loving and present husband. Interestingly enough, she fell in love with and married a man who was in many ways much like her father.

This young missionary husband was very driven in his ministry life, often away from the house in the evening on weekends. Under stress, he tended to withdraw from his wife and expected her to give him space to recharge his physical and emotional reserves. The wife constantly compared him to her father and in times of frustration was prone to stating in a very negative fashion, "I married a man just like Dad!"

Interestingly enough, the husband was affirmed for his ministry success but they were miserable as a couple. The wife valued the praise he received for his ministry but in their home had begun to deeply resent the impact it was having on them as a couple. As we worked together over a period of several days, they both began expressing insights into how they had incorporated various aspects of their own parents' marriages into their relationship, and of course some of these aspects were not healthy.

Not all overseas-based counseling cases, even with timely intervention, resolve well on the field. In this case, the couple returned to the States to receive counseling and as a result of the insights gained from the counseling, they sensed God calling them back to the States to resume ministry in a setting that was less demanding and more supportive. Would this couple have been able to serve longer overseas had they fully understood their families of origin? Only the Lord knows, but it would not have hurt for this couple to be fully cognizant of how their models of marriage impacted their own expectations, attitudes, and behavior toward marriage.

The Significant Impact of Stateside Family Support

Another substantial way in which families of origin impact overseas personnel is whether they are supportive of their children and grandchildren moving overseas for years at a time as they serve in strange and faraway places. Highly supportive families are a tremendous source of strength and encouragement as personnel deploy and spend years immersed in other cultures. Less supportive or strongly opposed-to-service families can be an immense drain or distraction to personnel serving in already difficult circumstances.

I have witnessed numerous cases where parents with deep faith-walks somehow have strong objections and fail to support their adult children as they receive God's call to serve Him overseas. On the other hand, I have seen parents who do not express faith in Christ be very supportive of their adult children's call. I know in our own families,

Linda and I had the full range of responses in terms of support and understanding.

Personnel must do all they can to bring their families along, recognizing the impact it will have on the entire family, as they work through God's call to overseas service. I simply do not know many parents/ grandparents who would choose to be separated from their children/grandchildren for years at a time, only having access if they spend significant amounts of money, time, and energy to have contact. You factor into the emotional equation the stateside family's fear and anxiety for those children and grandchildren moving into a lonely, unknown, and hostile-to-the-gospel setting overseas and you have a family finding it difficult to be enthusiastically supportive. Missionaries who keep their families informed as much as possible, get them to the field regularly, maintain healthy relationship boundaries, and bathe all family-related matters in prayer tend to have the most positive kinds of relationships with stateside family.

The Reality of Grief in Overseas Service

Finally, it is essential to be aware of the reality of grief and joy that permeate a family as they send out members to share the gospel with a lost world. It will be a source of great joy at times for families as their loved ones serve cross-culturally, but there also will be the accompanying sadness and grief that come with any long-term separation from those you dearly love.

Linda and I thought our goodbyes would get easier and longing for contact would abate over the years of our overseas service—but we were wrong. We missed holidays, births, weddings, graduations, funerals, and other significant events in the lives of our families over the years. We felt secure in our call, but there were times of longing to be at the table, or in the pew beside our folks as they celebrated or grieved. Families who recognize this reality and are able to talk and pray it through tend to do best over the long periods of separation required in serving cross-culturally.

It is of paramount importance that individuals and couples take into account how their families will respond to their being deployed for years at a time with little or no physical contact. Of course with the increased electronic connectivity around the world, there are many creative options for maintaining meaningful contact, but the reality is that for most overseas personnel, physical contact is very limited. God does supply the comfort and peace that only He can, but there will be tears of joy and sadness over the years of service.

Managing Marital Conflict Well

Unless you are just headed out on your honeymoon, you will be quick to agree that conflicts are going to be a clear and present danger in any marriage. In the routine and in the unusual events of life, most couples will find themselves occasionally in conflict.

On our honeymoon Linda and I were driving home, headed north from New Orleans toward Kansas City. The first afternoon of that drive, I got drowsy and Linda took the wheel as I crawled into the back seat for a nap. I slept way too deeply and woke up to find us *way* off course and deep into Texas. Linda had failed to take a significant right turn *north* and ended up extending our trip significantly.

I wish I could say I laughingly took the wheel, gave her a quick kiss, and corrected course with nary a negative word, but that was not the case. I will spare you the details, but we took about a hundred miles to work through the situation. Of course I was gentle, kind, and patient throughout the discussion—at least that is my memory (I believe Linda has a slightly different version of my reaction, but she is unavailable for input at this time). As best I can recall, this was the first conflict we experienced in our married life. Over time we learned better ways of resolving the regular small matters of conflict and the occasional large issues.

Married folks heading overseas must be able to resolve conflicts in a manner that reflects lives given over to Christ. They bring glory to Him as they subject themselves to His authority and allow the Holy Spirit to fuel the necessary resolution. Couples being sent overseas need some healthy history of conflict resolution so when tensions arise on the field, and they absolutely will, they have some tools and experience on which to draw.

They need solid, proven, conflict-resolution skill sets. It takes maturity, insight, humility, and patience to work through most marital conflicts, and individuals who have a strong dependence on God's Word and strong personal devotional lives evidence those qualities more quickly and in fuller measure. It is not a question of whether marital conflicts might occur overseas, but when.

Satan loves to distract couples from their focus on the Father and His call in their lives, and nothing can more readily and completely put you off of that focus than to have a huge fight with the person you love most. Linda is the world's leading expert on me, and the Holy Spirit impresses her to pray for me in ways no one else possibly could. God uses Linda to draw me to Himself as I watch her in the midst of resolving conflicts.

She loves me completely, and yet there are times when I can be incredibly frustrating for her. There were times in Tokyo, in the midst of really high stress, where neither one of us was at his nor her best in terms of resolving conflicts. The higher baseline of stress present in most overseas settings can create an atmosphere where marriages fail to resolve small irritating matters because missionary couples simply do not have the energy to address the conflict.

I once sat with a missionary couple in a hotel lobby overseas who had requested to meet with me. This couple was in their mid-40s and had been on the field more than 10 years. They knew I was in town, and the husband indicated they had a small issue they wished to discuss with me. According to the wife, the basic issue was that the husband "drove like a maniac" and over their years of service it had reached a point where she was afraid to get in the car with him.

The husband did admit he drove very aggressively and at high rates of speed, but rationalized it as necessary to get anywhere on the streets of the major metropolitan area where they lived. They used their car daily in ministry and lately she had taken taxis rather than ride along with him to points of ministry service.

Despite weekly efforts to resolve the conflict, they had not been successful. They had no team in the city and therefore no local support or accountability to assist them in working through this. While not a terribly complicated matter in terms of dynamics and resolution, this would be an example of how a small matter can mushroom into a substantial distraction from Spirit-led, effective service overseas.

Couples serving overseas need healthy self-esteem, solid conflict-resolution skills, some history of successful utilization of those skills, and above all else rock solid dependence on the Lord and His revealed Word in the midst of conflict. Couples considering overseas service should apply only when they have a healthy history of conflict resolution.

Maintaining Intimacy in a Marriage

Any couple who has been able to maintain solid intimacy in their marriage prior to overseas deployment stands a much greater chance of replicating that overseas as opposed to a couple who has struggled in that area prior to deployment. The intimacy to which I am referring is the physical, emotional, intellectual, and spiritual intimacy you hope to see in any healthy marriage with Christ at its center. This is a broad topic and one which can be the source of such great joy for couples or, when not present, can be the source of great suffering and longing for more.

When I sit with couples, and I meet with hundreds every year, I often quickly sense whether this couple really likes one another or not. I like to assume they are contentedly married, and in many cases have been so for decades. Sadly however, I occasionally sit with couples who do not seem to really like one another. There is an accommodation and acceptance, but there does not seem to be any discernable attraction to one another.

I love to see couples whose eyes light up when I ask, "What do you admire most in your husband?" or "When did you first find yourself falling in love with your wife?" Intimacy is essential for using marriage as a format of witness for the Lord. Couples who nurture and develop intimacy in their marriages benefit not only themselves but impact all those around them.

As others in the host culture notice the quality of a missionary couple's marriage relationship, they may be drawn to Christ. Many host cultures are excellent observers of human interaction and as they watch personnel go about their daily lives, they frequently notice how they interact with their spouse. Linda would regularly get inquiries from her Japanese friends as to why I behaved toward her in the manner I did. It was always a clear opportunity to share about God's provision and plan for her life and how God was using me in her life.

Cross-cultural ministry can be extremely demanding and draining, and it has a serious impact on the energy available to devote to one another as couples serve those in need. God's gift of intimacy, available in all marriages, requires most of us to focus and work on developing and maintaining that intimacy in the above-mentioned areas. Those personnel who serve on solid, loving teams may have colleagues to affirm and model good marital intimacy, but there can be times of minimal contact with like-minded couples.

Marriages that exhibit healthy intimacy typically have some very intentional patterns that foster such intimacy. Rather than present a comprehensive list, I will mention a few that field personnel have shared with me over the years. First of all, couples that keep the Sabbath tend to have a better sense of weekly pace and perspective on life. The setting aside of a day per week to be with the Lord, along with setting aside the busyness and encumbrances of work and ministry life, tend to bear up better under the strain of cross-cultural life. As couples consider moving overseas, do they have a solid history of good Sabbath-keeping and fully comprehend the value of such practice?

Personnel who budget, schedule, and take regular vacations on the field exhibit a greater sense of enjoyment of life and intimacy with one another. It is not just the enjoyable time away that is beneficial, but also the anticipation of the event and the looking back with fondness that make the actual vacation a much more impactful experience. I strongly encourage personnel to take holidays away from work and their immersion in their ministry settings. Couples who regularly take vacations here in the States seem to have little trouble carrying that pattern to the field, but discussing the need for this, prior to deployment, will make a less loaded topic of discussion after their arrival on the field.

Finally, one important aspect of intimacy is the maintaining of romance in a marriage. Those couples who regularly enjoy one another, plan times alone (whether it be dates or days away), and who really are attracted to one another in a physical way seldom report problems feeling like romance is lacking in their lives. Most couples will report this romancing of one another is much more difficult overseas. Therefore, both husband and wife must be very focused and intentional about making their spouse feel valued, loved, and truly God's gift to them.

Staying in good physical condition can really be helpful in continuing to be attracted to one another. In general, most married folks will indicate it is no easier to stay in shape overseas than it was here in the States. If you take the time and energy to exercise with integrity you will see results, and of course no one will see the results more clearly than your spouse. Marriages where exercise and fitness were a regular part of stateside life will eventually put those patterns in place overseas. It may take some creativity and pursuit of new patterns to work out, but if couples value fitness, they make it happen overseas.

Balancing Overseas Ministry Well in a Marriage

One of the more challenging aspects of cross-cultural ministry for married couples is dealing with the unique demands it places on individuals and marriages. Most folks headed overseas have a rich and varied history of stateside ministry and have utilized their gifting and passion for ministry in a successful manner. What overwhelms many couples is the high level of need present in just about any setting where they might be deployed, much higher than they have ever experienced in terms of depth and breadth of dire need.

Married personnel can find themselves gradually evolving into people who neglect the needs of their families as they attempt to meet the vast physical, emotional, and spiritual needs presented to them on a daily basis. In many cases, as personnel develop networks of influence, the needs present at a higher and more varied rate. There are daily invitations to new opportunities for service and ways to invest energy in those starving both physically and spiritually.

Marriages where the couples thoroughly discuss potential ministry goals prior to deployment tend to handle the transition to overseas life more smoothly. Having a realistic idea of what ministry will look like is extremely helpful. Many couples take vision trips or actually do volunteer trips to the area where they hope to serve long term. Those kinds of opportunities will inform them about what field life might feel like should they pursue extended overseas service. Those trips allow couples to experience firsthand what it feels like to walk the streets, eat the food, and experience the value of language and cultural knowledge and how it enhances ministry.

One reality that sometimes surprises married folks is how stressful it can be to spend so much time together on the field. Linda and I both had fairly separate lives before we moved to Japan. Forty hours a week at work, separate roles at church, and different sets of outside relationships for both of us resulted in us spending dozens of hours a week apart. But from our first day of the eight-week missionary orientation program, it became very clear to us we would be spending a great deal of time together in the coming years. Linda is an extroverted verbal processor, and I am much more introverted and comfortable with silence.

Professionally Linda worked off of schedules, utilizing protocols and proven approaches to task completion and quickly resolving problems. I, on the other hand, spent most of my life listening to clients in a quiet office setting, occasionally consulting with other clinicians about best practices and difficult situations. Suffice it to say it took us a few years to fully comprehend and put into place the best patterns for our lives as we began ministering together.

It is a rare couple here in the States that spends as much time together as missionary couples do, and it is so wise to consider this reality as overseas service is considered. Linda obviously brought many strengths into our ministries in Japan that were simply outside my gifting and passion, and I brought my gifts to bear as well. Over time, I could not believe how much joy we derived from ministering together. The first time we taught a parenting class together utilizing the Japanese language was so intimidating on every level. We based the entire class on God's revealed truth about parent-child relationships, and we saw Him use that teaching as only He could in the lives of those Japanese families. What a fabulous blessing for us to be used in that manner!

The Stress of Constant Decision Making in Missionary Marriages

As we continue to examine the various aspects of healthy missionary marriages overseas, it is important to highlight that couples heading overseas will be under the stress of constantly making major decisions about a variety of involved matters. On the front end of service, there are the obvious issues of where to serve and the timing of entering full-time service. These issues are discussed in other chapters, but it is absolutely essential that couples be on the same page, in the same paragraph, and even in the same sentence on these matters. A couple is called together and must be fully committed to the location/people group as well as to when they deploy.

Once the couple is deployed, the issue of lifestyle takes on much greater weight, and certain questions will need to be answered. Will we be living the moneyed, ex-pat lifestyle of business and diplomatic personnel, or will we be located and living much closer to our people and their style of life? How often will we take vacations away from the field, and how is that perceived by colleagues and the people we serve? When will we return to the States for furloughs and visits, and how long should we stay gone from the field? To what degree do we open our home for ministry—six days a week or very seldom? How much of our personal budget do we utilize to meet the very real needs of those suffering around us? To what degree should we be open to taking on new assignments? These are just a few of the questions overseas marriages must address all the time.

The rate at which these kinds of decisions come into married life overseas is higher than in the States due to the transitory nature of missionary life. The constant moves to and from the field and the fluid nature of overseas ministry require couples to constantly respond to these types of weighty questions. Couples who have highly developed communication styles and spend robust amounts of time in God's Word and in prayer with one another tend to respond to these questions in a much healthier fashion.

Walking with Christ in Marriage while Overseas

I began this chapter sharing how Linda and I were sent out from a very loving and supportive church family. One aspect of our support in that setting was our involvement in small group Bible study and discipleship, but equally important was how we were held accountable in those settings for our individual daily walks with the Lord. We were strongly encouraged to develop a personal style in consuming God's Word and letting its truth permeate every aspect of our lives. The accountability offered in those settings helped us establish patterns of prayer, reflection, and Bible study that were absolutely foundational to healthy and productive overseas service. Prior to deployment, we also put into place our couple and family patterns of devotion and worship.

During our orientation, we were strongly encouraged to take these discipleship patterns to the field and be firm in our conviction to maintain them in Japan. As I said earlier, many things were much more difficult on the field but this pattern was not. Linda and I found ourselves praying and studying the Bible in rich, new, meaningful ways and doing so out of dire need. The demands of field life require married personnel to walk closely with the Lord and that begins with individual time alone with Him and in His Word.

One facet of overseas service that is difficult to comprehend prior to deployment is how challenging it can be to feel comfortable worshipping in your second language. First-term personnel frequently share with me how long it takes and how spiritually dry they can feel as they assimilate to overseas life and gain facility in their people's heart language.

It is not a given fact that personnel will eventually reap as much in second-language worship as they do in their heart-language worship. It can be glorious when it does occur, but again, it is not always the pattern. Many of our overseas personnel do much of the spiritual feeding for others in group settings, and they do find themselves getting depleted.

There seems to be little that couples can do to prepare for this kind of experience while stateside other than willfully attending and participating in a second language body of believers. Having established years-long patterns of personal, marital, and family devotional life is a great predictor of maintaining those patterns once on the field.

Summary

Serving with one's spouse overseas can be one of the most joy-filled blessings one could ever experience on this earth. What more could a couple want than to have their marriage be a place of witness and ministry to a lost and dying world in desperate need of a Savior? That God would call a couple to serve Him in a setting He has chosen for them is almost beyond belief and only indicative of His perfect mercy and grace in their lives.

Couples with a dynamic, vibrant, and Christ-centered marital relationship will find others attracted to Christ as they witness that robust marriage lived out in front of them. Being cognizant of how families of origin impact service, managing marital conflict well, maintaining intimacy, handling ministry in a balanced fashion, making major decisions together well, and walking with Christ in marriage are all vital elements for couples who hope to serve Christ effectively in cross-cultural ministry.

About the Author

Mark Whitworth recently retired as the Member Care Team Leader for the IMB. He and his wife Linda served multiple terms in Japan before transitioning to the Richmond staff. Linda served as the IMB's Director of Stateside Training. Mark received a B.A. in Psychology from the University of Missouri and a M.S. in Clinical Psychology from the University of Central Missouri. Mark and Linda have one daughter Brooke, who is an Assistant Professor of Science Education at Northern Arizona University.

11

Educational and Developmental
Screening of Children
by Areba Houston

Those serving on the mission field face a number of challenges as they adjust to living in a different cultural setting. Any missionary candidate assessment process will attempt to determine the likelihood that the missionaries can successfully live and minister in the new setting. For those mission agencies and churches that send families, the children of the missionary candidates require this assessment as well.

One of the primary areas of adjustment for children in an overseas setting is centered on education and personal growth. Therefore, the educational and developmental needs of the children are of utmost concern. An assessment will be necessary, prior to approval of the family to serve overseas, to see if there are any specific educational or developmental needs that must be addressed for the child to succeed academically.

Many children can learn in a number of educational environments, while others may need a particular educational program to address special learning challenges. It is critical to know if the necessary educational programs are available in the location where the family might serve. Sometimes these development issues could relate indirectly to education, such as speech or hearing concerns, so there must be cooperation and communication between educational and medical professionals as assessments are completed.

First Five Years

The first five years of life for a child are critical because this time sets the stage for success in school as well as the ensuing years. It is important to ensure that each child's development goes well during this period. The sooner a delay or disability is found, the sooner a child can be connected with services and supports that can make a difference. The goal is for children to have a reasonable chance for normal development in the following areas: cognitive, emotional, physical, and spiritual.

Therefore, there must be a confidence that they are in a good place in each of these areas and that proper educational and developmental resources can be made available where they may live overseas. Unaddressed developmental or academic issues can spell disaster for families that move to a cross-cultural environment. Therefore, develop-mental and educational screening is strongly recommended for children from the age of 2 months and up whose parents are in a missionary application process.

Not all pediatricians regularly include formal developmental screening as a part of preschool health care. We have found that a parent-completed developmental screening tool is helpful and even necessary. This instrument can assess children ages 2 months through 60 months for delays in the areas of communication, gross motor skills, fine motor skills, personal-social skills, and problem-solving skills. Parents receive insight into their child's development and can begin to address concerns at an early age.

These screenings are done every two, three, four, or six months according to the age of the child. For each stage of development, appropriate activities are sent to the parents. If the results of the screening show that further evaluation is needed, referrals are made to appropriate professionals for additional assessment. Referrals are sometimes needed for speech articulation, language development, or gross motor skills. Sometimes speech intervention is needed for a period of weeks or months before a child can be cleared for overseas service.

These assessments can seem invasive and unimportant to the parents. However, the earlier an issue can be identified, the more quickly an appropriate method of addressing that issue can be chosen and implemented. For a young child, often this intervention will require only a few months. If an issue is not identified or addressed early, or the child's needs are overlooked, eventual intervention will likely be more costly, take much longer, and require professionals who are less likely to be available in an overseas setting. It is imperative for parents to understand the importance of this screening so they can be full partners with the assessment team in plotting their course.

Not only is the screening process for young children important for their own well-being, it also is beneficial for the adults. This process has helped make our company's families and staff more aware of developmentally appropriate growth and skills. Many parents have said that using the screening tool has helped them know their child better and understand more accurately what is developmentally appropriate for them.

The Haltom* family is a good example of how screening for developmental issues can help parents know their children better. The mother home-schooled the children and felt they were all proceeding normally in their studies and growth. So when their first child went through the assessment process, they anticipated no issues.

However, the mother was so used to reading test questions to her oldest daughter, Cindy,* she didn't realize that her child had a reading deficiency. By not allowing Cindy to read the questions herself in the online tests, the results were skewed and inaccurate. Her son Robert, however, did take the tests by himself, and it appeared that he had some reading issues. Reluctantly, the Haltoms admitted Robert's need for some supplemental help, and he improved somewhat.

When it came time to assess their kindergarten-aged daughter, Sharon,* the Haltoms were fearful of another delay. So when it seemed that she had similar issues with her reading skills, the parents balked and became defensive. They said the assessment process demanded too much of a young child. They didn't want to delay their application process any longer. But they finally yielded to the request for more testing, and it was determined that Sharon truly had a learning disability. As a consequence, the family learned what would be necessary for Sharon to learn and progress normally while living in another cultural setting and language.

As the Haltom family spent time in orientation before deploying overseas, Cindy's hidden deficiencies in reading became apparent, to the surprise of her parents. Immediately they began working with her, trying to rectify the situation created by this learning handicap. Thankfully, they caught these learning issues before it was too late. And the parents learned much more about their three children than they could have imagined.

Since families often deploy to locations overseas where adequate care is not always available, it is important for early intervention to occur in the home country if needed, before leaving for the mission field. It is not uncommon to see a young child's speech and communication assessment results fall into a non-typical area of development. While speech therapists in the home country are easier to find, English-speaking speech therapists/pathologists are extremely difficult to locate overseas.

The same is true for parents and children whose primary language is not English. Many missionary families live in locations away from major cities, and the travel required to visit a speech therapist, if one can be found, is costly and time consuming.

The screening tool is a first step toward preventing a child's developmental problems from becoming more prevalent. If there are no issues to be resolved, the tool will serve to confirm that learning and developmental problems are likely not present in the child.

School-aged Children

For those school-aged children whose parents are in a missionary application process, they are either being home-schooled or attending a public or private school. For this level of assessment, the parents will complete forms in order to provide information about curriculum for the home-schooled children as well as any standardized test score results. For those students attending public and private schools, report cards are requested as well as any standardized test scores results and comments from teachers.

Each school-aged child also is asked to take online tests that are supervised by a certified teacher other than a parent or relative. The tests evaluate multiple sub-skills in reading and math. Each test is about an hour long and is completed over a two-day period or longer. Soon after the testing is completed, detailed and easy-to-understand reports are provided to the assessment specialist.

These reports are sent to the parents along with instructions on how to improve a student's particular reading or math needs. Activities are provided to improve specific areas that are weak. If it is determined that a student is not on grade level for reading or math, the student will be given suggestions on how to improve these skills, and the tests can be retaken a few months later. If a learning disability is suspected, psycho-educational testing by an educational psychologist or an educational diagnostician may be recommended.

The Advantage of Assessments

Many missionary families have a preference for home-schooling, yet the parents are not trained to detect developmental issues. The same is true for those families who assume that national schools will suffice, yet they don't see or understand the developmental needs of their children. In these situations, educational assessments have proven to be quite valuable, with varying results and outcomes.

1. **Adjusted curriculum**—There have been several instances where a student has been struggling in a home-schooling situation, and the online reading or math tests have detected weak skills. After further consultation with the parents, it was determined that the home-schooling curriculum needed to be adjusted in order for the child to have a stronger reading and/or math program.

2. **Testing required**—At other times, it has been evident that psycho-educational testing was necessary. In several instances, a student has been diagnosed with dyslexia after the testing. When this was the case, that student—who was being home-schooled in the states and would be continuing in an overseas

setting—was given an appropriate reading curriculum to help with the dyslexia.

3. **International school**—For some cases, it was determined that the student needed to be in an overseas English school that could provide special reading or math services. Home-schooling, even with adjustments, would not provide sufficient support for the child's normal advancement in education.

4. **School selection**—Yet in other situations, it was concluded that studying in a certain national language school might not be appropriate for a student due to his or her special learning differences. An educational assessment was helpful in planning for the location of a student in school. Once again, early intervention is the key in helping students have a program that is appropriate for their educational needs.

It must be recognized that children are different and have various levels of abilities and talents. Children of all types have successfully grown up in a cross-cultural environment. The goal is not to send only near perfect children. The goal is to help families move to their place of overseas assignment feeling reasonably confident they can successfully raise their children with the resources available.

Case Study

We have seen countless families impacted in a positive way through the influence of developmental screening. While it is impossible to recount all the stories of how children's lives have been changed as they made appropriate preparations for the mission field, let this case study serve as a typical example of why effective developmental screening is so necessary.

As they began the missionary application process, the Greene* family completed the first developmental screening for their child at 9 months of age. Several of the summaries in the skills domain fell in the non-typical range of development and needed to be monitored. The child was examined by a pediatrician and began special activities as prescribed by a local speech/language pathologist. Eventually all levels fell into the typical developmental range except for communication skills.

Both the child's articulation and vocabulary skills needed extra time to develop, with careful therapy and monitoring so that proper adjustments could be implemented as needed. With time, improvement was noted and by the time the child was 24 months of age, the parents felt that no further language therapy was needed. But ending the intervention plan too early led to the child digressing in these two critical areas. Knowing that the child would soon be in a second language in an overseas setting, they agreed for their child to get back into therapy. Two years later, the child had made enough progress to be given developmental clearance for going to the mission field. By 39 months of age, the child showed sustained communication development and it was determined that moving to a different cultural and language environment would not be detrimental to the child's further development.

Two years feels like a long time to be delayed for overseas service, especially for the developmental needs of one child. However, had the couple deployed before these matters had been adequately addressed, the child would have faced significant learning challenges in the second-language environment and would have likely required special educational provisions in elementary school. The time used to address the matter in those early years has led to the family being successfully deployed, and there has been no need for special interventions in the overseas setting.

Parents may be uncomfortable about having their children tested. Their home-schooling methods could potentially be called into question, or they may feel that their family is being labeled as inadequate for the mission field. However, we have found that it is best to assess a child's developmental needs before leaving the home culture. These assessments can help ensure the child's successful adjustment to education in another language or culture and can improve the child's chances of navigating successfully through his or her educational years.

Resources

Brookes Publishing Company—http://www.agesandstages.com - ASQ-3 Questionnaires

Battelle Developmental Inventory— http://www.assess.nelson.com/test-ind/bdi.html

Let's Go Learn—http://www.letsgolearn.com/ — Diagnostic Online Reading and Math Assessments; Differentiated Online Math and Reading Instruction

Phonological Awareness Literacy Screening— http://pals.virginia.edu/tools-prek.html

About the Author

Areba Houston and her husband Larry have a married son and a granddaughter. Kay has a Bachelor of Science degree and a M.Ed. with a focus on Early Childhood Education from East Texas State University. She taught elementary and middle school grades for 10 years in Brazil and in Texas Public Schools before serving for 25 years in East Asia. In Brazil and in East Asia she served as a missionary doing student work, church planting, teaching and training. She is currently the TCK Education Consultant for IMB.

12

Minor Details Are Important
by Carlton Vandagriff

The process of assessing and job matching new missionaries includes five critical components that, if considered carefully, will greatly assist the missionary candidate, the missions organization, and sending church in making good decisions. Christian and church identity, the missionary call, competencies and qualifications, and overall health and wellness are key components that must be researched, assessed, and understood.

There is a fifth component in the missionary selection process that deals with practical details. If the assessment team uses this component appropriately, it can surface significant matters that can contribute greatly to the future fruitfulness of the missionary and the ability of the family to live and adjust to the cross-cultural setting.

Too often in the missionary enterprise, it is the small and seemingly insignificant matters that can cause the most challenge. Even when the missionary call and cross-cultural elements are in place, these little concerns, if not properly addressed, can sap time and energy that would otherwise be focused on more strategic efforts. These issues often come from our blind side and surface when least expected. Looking ahead and preparing for these potential obstacles could help our missionary applicants either avoid rough waters or navigate through them more easily.

Financial and Support Matters

The issue of missionary support will sooner or later impact the life of just about every missionary. Complications arise when there are unexpected adjustments in exchange rates, or expenses for medical care, or fees for children's education, and those costs have not been adequately considered in the support package. For example, international banking or ATM fees, if not adequately included in the planning, can strain a budget that was likely planned on a subsistence level with little allowance for flexibility.

It is important to carefully delineate in advance which expenses are covered from missionary work funds and which expenses are considered the missionary family's personal responsibility. The prospective missionary should have a reasonable knowledge of the funds available each month in order to plan his local budget and consider other needs such as future children's schooling.

Any missionary support package, whether processed via a missions-sending agency or a local church, should have a provision for missionaries to set aside funds for their future retirement. In many cases, plans are developed that include incentives for the setting aside of funds for use in future years. For example, the sending agency might match the missionary contributions to a credible retirement plan up to a certain amount or percent of gross income.

The preparation of taxes for the missionary can be a daunting experience, especially considering the complicated USA and host country tax laws. It is likely that the missionary family will have to submit an income tax report in their country of assignment as well as the United States or their country of citizenship. Assistance and/or advice in the preparation and payment of these taxes could help save the new missionaries time, energy, and anxiety as they are required to meet filing deadlines.

The ease of obtaining credit cards and the availability of student loans for education has left many young candidates shackled with debt. A credit report and score should be obtained as they can reveal not only the candidates' current status but also their history of handling their finances. Any single issue with debt does not necessarily eliminate or disqualify someone, but this information can provide a worthwhile picture into the lives of applicants and give the assessor information regarding their past performance and experience. In any case, missionaries should not have outstanding debt that is more than they can handle, considering the income they'll have available on the mission field.

Candidates who have been working for a period of time may have purchased a house. Generally, missionaries are not able to make house payments while serving overseas. Their salaries are just not enough to sustain those payments. When candidates have a house they cannot maintain while serving overseas, the house must be sold before they deploy to the overseas location. In some cases, a rental contract will be adequate to cover the costs, but even in this case the missionary should have a rental firm or trusted friend take care of these business matters during his or her absence. It is not wise for new missionaries to take care of this sort of obligation. Prospective missionaries should either sell their house or procure a rental contract before they are deployed overseas.

Citizenship, Background, and Other Government Commitments and Obligations

In some countries, there are significant exit requirements before one can be granted a passport or permission to leave the country. This might include a military obligation, a criminal background check, or other governmental requirements that could take both time and money.

Entry requirements into other countries also must be considered. Governments around the world usually view a person's criminal history with a critical perspective. In many cases, those who have a felony on their record will be prevented from obtaining a visa, and they may not even be allowed to travel in that country for a short period of time. Therefore, a criminal background check early in the application process can reveal details of any criminal history that could impact the candidate's ability to live and function overseas.

Military status is usually completed prior to consideration for service as a missionary, but it is possible that someone could have served 20 years in the military, retired, and still has 20 or more years remaining to serve as a missionary. There are some cases where there is still an ongoing obligation to be available for the reserves, which could require a few weeks of service every year plus the possibility of being called into active duty, should the government deem it necessary. The sending church or agency will need to carefully consider whether or not they will send candidates who are still obligated in a reserve-type role.

There are unique cases when candidates' previous training or security clearance status could preclude their being able to live in certain countries, especially if they had specific knowledge of defense systems that could jeopardize their country's security if that information became available to a foreign government. These cases are rare, but early discovery could clarify if there are limitations on where candidates might be able to serve.

From time to time, a missionary candidate seeks to be sent by a sending church or agency from a country other than their passport country. Most U.S. organizations have limitations as to whom they can actually consider employees and therefore allow on their payroll. Those limitations generally include the possession of a residency permit (green card), which allows certain types of employment in the sending country. Exceptions will require careful research with legal experts to ensure employment laws are not violated.

Personal and Family Matters

A matter of concern to all missionary parents is the long-term educational needs of their children. Children learn, grow up, and successfully mature in a variety of living environments and educational systems. Not all children learn in the same speed or same manner, and there are those who can only progress appropriately in specific educational and developmental settings. One must consider the schooling options for children in the potential location of assignment, as well as the long-term goals for that child once they reach adulthood.

For example, educating them fully in the schools of the host country may not meet the educational requirements for the child to attend college in their country of origin. Other implications could include issues such as proficiency in the home language, academic achievement, and acceptable credits. Home-schooling is an option in many cross-cultural settings, but not all children adapt well to home-schooling in the teenage years, so missionary parents must be prepared for a variety of complicating scenarios.

With this many factors to be processed, it is important to have an informed professional assess the children and assist the parents in considering educational options to meet each child's needs. Of primary importance is identifying any learning or developmental challenges that will need to be addressed to help ensure the child will reach his or her potential. When these challenges are identified, proper placement is critical when the final job match decisions are made.

Some sending agencies will not accept families with teenage children. This may seem harsh and an unnecessary limitation on those families who feel called. We have seen teenagers and their families go to the field and have a successful term. However, there are many cases where teenagers were not able to deal with the normal challenges of growing up combined with the pressures of adjusting cross-culturally. The effect of these two elements together may be too much for most teenagers to navigate successfully.

Missionary applicants should be challenged to think through their obligations to care for aging parents, even though that need may be years away. They should clearly communicate with their family on these matters to avoid inaccurate assumptions about the future. In many cases, the applicant could be considered by the family as being the primary caregiver, which may even include financial obligations to provide for one's relatives during the declining years. In some cultures, this obligation could mean taking on the management of the family assets, including businesses. Anticipating these types of situations can prepare the missionary for the inevitable and help him or her manage the changing conditions that are sure to arise.

It also would be wise for the sending agency/church to carefully look at the work history of missionary applicants. There is no set rule for how long a candidate should normally remain in a particular position, but an ability to stay the course and carry out difficult tasks is a trait often observed in fruitful missionary personnel. When working in an unusual cultural setting, with a language one has only recently learned, the ability to continue in the assigned task in spite of difficulties will contribute to the longevity of the missionary family. The work history of young missionary applicants is often short and does not answer all of the questions one might desire, but looking for trends and indicators will help in assessing whether or not the candidate has the temperament to serve fruitfully over a longer period of time.

Interaction with the missionary candidates in the application process can help in the assessment of their readiness to move their family overseas. Missionaries are cautioned to expect the unexpected, and to be able to adjust their life and schedule to a local culture that is generally more relationship-oriented than time-oriented.

How do candidates respond to the application process and the assessment team? Do they have a positive attitude? Are they prompt in returning the information requested? Do they complete the materials appropriately or are their materials sloppy and incomplete? Most missionary application consultants see their job not merely as screening the applicants for service, but discipling them through the process and helping them prepare for missionary service. Observing how the candidates respond to this discipling process and their ability to become a "learner" is a noteworthy observation to be made as one leads them through the process.

References

One aspect of the missionary calling is a personal sense of the leadership of the Holy Spirit to live and work cross-culturally in a foreign setting. This calling should be investigated, as mentioned in other chapters. There also is a sense that missionaries are sent by the local church (Acts 13:1-3) and therefore those in the local church who know them well should confirm the personal call.

There are three levels of references that can provide a relatively comprehensive view of how others perceive the missionary candidate. The first is endorsement by the local church. It is imperative for the local church to be able to envision candidates working and serving as cross-cultural missionaries. Although the language and culture may be different, the basic missionary tasks of evangelizing and planting reproducing churches should be a part of the ministry wherever they might be currently serving.

There also is the need to hear from close, trusted friends (the second level of references) who can assess the appropriateness of the individual or family to serve in another location as cross-cultural missionaries. These references are asked to comment regarding church involvement and service, effectiveness in personal relationships, and their observations of family dynamics.

The third level of references is often the most revealing. The references listed by the applicants are asked to provide even more names of others who might know the candidate. This third level of references, chosen by their trusted friends rather than by the applicants themselves, sometimes reveals a broader picture of candidates.

The three levels of references are only as good as the honesty of those providing the information. In a safe, confidential environment, considering what is at stake in regard to the candidate's family and the work on the field, those completing the reference form generally desire to give a fair representation of the candidate.

Of special note will be any indications of how the candidate works with people, since the entire missionary enterprise is built on establishing productive relationships and working in team and community. When the information provided on the written form is unclear, a personal visit or phone call can clarify the comments or input provided to the assessment team.

Case Study

John and Mary Jones* arrived in an Asian city excited about their new assignment. They had identified a local church where they could be mentored by a capable local pastor, study the language, and adjust to life in their new culture. The Joneses had a great relationship with their local church back in the U.S. that provided a reasonable support sum each month, which was wired to their local bank account in their new country.

John and Mary had not anticipated how culture shock would impact their family, especially their two high school girls. Although they had been home-schooled before, the two girls had no idea how much they would miss their friends at church. It was hard to get to know the locals of the same age because Asian students spend so much time studying.

This challenge was in addition to Mary's frustration at not finding the normal things she used to prepare the family meals. Shopping and cooking took long hours, and the vegetables and meats had to be carefully washed and prepared. With no car and the inconvenience of carrying groceries on public transportation, the family found themselves eating a lot at Western restaurants where they could find familiar food. Many Western restaurants were available in their city, but these were at least double the cost in the U.S. For a family of four, this began to stress their budget.

Some unexpected things happened in the world economy that John and Mary did not understand, but these situations resulted in the U.S. dollar weakening significantly versus the local currency. At the same time, rent and other local costs went up by several percent and John and Mary found themselves short of enough money to cover their monthly needs. They were embarrassed to ask their home church for more money as they knew that a recent downturn in their home country's economy had negatively impacted the church's budget.

John considered getting a part-time job in his country of assignment, but that would violate the term of his visa and he felt that would not be a good witness, even if he were to work undetected by the local authorities. The problems seemed to keep stacking up to the point where the pressure was unbearable.

When John was finally introduced to a missionary from another organization and talked through his situation, he learned that in many ways his family was having normal cross-cultural stress. Yet he also realized that his family was already at a crisis point in terms of their ability to remain in this new country. This interaction was too late because no matter what they tried, workable solutions were not found. Unfortunately, the Jones family returned to the U.S. primarily due to two issues: a shortage of family support and the unanticipated hardship of cultural adjustment for the entire family, but especially the two teenagers.

Obviously, many of the practical, pragmatic issues were not considered during the Joneses' application to serve as cross-cultural missionaries. Had they thought through these issues ahead of time, they would have been better prepared for overseas service—and probably could have remained on the field. This is why an efficient assessment process must include even these minor details. All issues must be considered before launching a family into overseas ministry.

About the Author

Carlton Vandagriff and his wife Allison have a married son and a granddaughter. He has two degrees from East Texas State University, an Ed.D. from the University of North Texas, and studied at Southwestern Baptist Theological Seminary. Carlton was a high school coach and teacher before going overseas. He served two years in Brazil and 25 years in East Asia doing student work, church planting, and leadership training. He is currently the Associate Vice President in the Office of Global Engagement, IMB, leading those who process and deploy missionaries and networking with international partners.

13

Right Person, Right Place, Right Time, Right Assignment
by Brett Freemon

Having the right people in the right place, in the right type of job at the right time, continues to be the most important and strategic goal for both the individuals involved and the organization. For the potential missionary, you want to be in a situation where you can best be used by God to make the most strategic kingdom contribution, continue to learn and grow, and daily walk in the Word/Spirit.

These are not counter-productive in relation to the organizational goals; however, there is a different perspective. The organization wants to effectively prepare and continually equip people, make the best use of resources, address the needs and issues of ministry, and keep growing a depth of experience and leadership. Both want to make positive strides in carrying out the Great Commission (Matthew 28:18-20).

Individuals' skills, talents, spiritual gifting, passions, experience, personality type and how they have dealt with life are all factors that the Lord can and will use to fulfill His purposes. This chapter uses specific examples and anecdotes to address the "why?" and "how?" behind the many questions that need to be considered in selection and job matching, especially from the perspective of the persons who are going/being sent. The following is a list of some of those questions.

- What preparations should I undertake?
- How do I find the "right" assignment?
- How do I know the timing is right?
- How do I know this is the right organization?
- How do I choose among all the needs/opportunities?
- Am I ready? What else do I need to do?

- What do I do when I doubt or when doubts come?
- Why this assignment?
- What if I need a partner but don't know anyone, or what if I am "alone?"
- What do I do when things change or the assignment is not what I expected?

The Right People (Who am I?)

Miranda* is a young, single woman who began her journey to a crowded Muslim country asking herself the following questions. "What is God calling me to sacrifice? What is my theology and what do I think about contextualization? Can I work on the same team with/under supervisors who are more conservative/more liberal than I am theologically or missiologically? Can I marry and if I do, how do I feel about my role in that context?"

She continued to ask God, "Where do you want me to go? What group of people (age, gender, religion, economic status, etc.) do you want me to focus on?"

Miranda asked others to tell her what they saw as her passions/talents/gifts and what kinds of people they observed Miranda connecting with the best. She sought the Lord's face and direction through prayer and reading scripture. And God used a powerful encounter to move her heart.

> "I was sitting with a friend over brunch one day and this friend began speaking about her own life, telling me that she had become comfortable and was enjoying a job that was only meant to pay off her debts before she continued her education to become a Bible translator. As she spoke of God's ultimate call on her life, the Spirit was speaking to me, and I knew that it was time to pursue His call on my life."

When asked about being "ready" for the mission field, Miranda had the following words of wisdom.

"If you wait until you are ready, you will never go. If you even have the least calling in your life, pursue it with all your heart and let God open or close the door. God doesn't always give us all we want in advance. You may not be ready until you get there!"

As we've already seen, a missionary applicant's character and attitude are supremely important. Character is made up of several complex components. It is the fabric that comprises the distinct mental and moral qualities of a person. This fabric holds together the thoughts, feelings, and behaviors that govern what makes an individual's personality unique.

A key quality on the mission field is teachability. Applicants must be willing and able to learn and adapt, even if they are already experienced in ministry. Flexibility is paramount as change is inevitable on the mission field, but the primary goal of seeing lives changed with the good news remains the same.

James* and Millie* were professionals engaged in successful careers. Both were highly specialized: James as a software/systems engineer and Millie as a neonatal nurse. Their "call" to international missions came independently of each other, but simultaneously through a revival service at their local church.

This began a three-year process and journey toward their assignment in a mountainous Asian country. Their call was not to a specific people or place, but to a least reached and hard to access people. Both clearly understood that God wanted them to pursue a change in their service to Him. James began taking seminary classes while continuing to work full time. Millie, too, continued to work until the birth of their third child a few months into this new journey.

A great church family got behind them with prayer and encouragement as James and Millie sought God's direction. A combination of excitement, trepidation, some discouragement, and uncertainty became regular emotions throughout this exploration. No assignments directly fit James' professional skill set. As the long process continued, James and Millie prayed through the possibilities, asked questions, and communicated their passion to engage the least reached and to go where their backgrounds could open doors where others could not go.

After several other potential assignments had been rejected, James and Millie selected and were matched to an assignment in a megacity in Southeast Asia. However, they chose to remove their names from that assignment after concerted prayer led to a lack of peace. A few close friends were instrumental in this prayer effort and the subsequent decision.

One week later, a new job was presented to James and Millie in a small mountainous country in South Asia where there was only one other family working. This assignment required a highly technical background in order to secure a visa; it was a good match to James' education, work history, and skills. Both James and Millie knew this was the "right" assignment. Their prayer partners and the mission organization confirmed this with them as well. This same country had come across their path several times, but until now there had been no actual assignment that fit so well. They were on their way!

On the other end of the spectrum is another missionary's experience with a new applicant. His insights point out the importance of having the right person in an assignment. Craig had submitted a job request for two short-term personnel. He was working in a tough area by himself with little fruit from his labor.

"I received a call from the organization in the U.S. saying there was a single, older lady who was interested in taking the assignment. I spoke to Pat* on the phone, but I did not consider all the implications of a single woman serving on my team, since I was a single male.

"When Pat arrived she was very fearful. I had found a flat for her in a section of town not too far from where I lived among our people. She told me later that she was scared to leave her flat the first several weeks. From the beginning she was resistant to any advice or direction I tried to give her. Her typical response was, "I'm a single lady, I can't do that." Pat

171

was a widow who came from a dysfunctional family. She had a very bad attitude and lost her temper with literally everyone serving in the city.

"After she lost her temper with me during a meeting with national partners, I scheduled time with her to talk. Before we met, I sought advice from colleagues and accountability partners at the time. I began the meeting by praising Pat for the good things she was doing. Then I asked her what she thought her losing her temper in front of our national partners had done to our ministry.

"She responded, 'I'm sure I've ruined it.' Pat sat quietly as I talked to her and then asked if I was finished. When I said, 'yes,' she began to insult me, first telling me I was the most critical person she'd ever met and then degenerating into random insults. I told her this was not helpful and I felt like we needed to get counselors involved.

"Counseling did help and Pat's attitude was much improved in her second year though she did continue to lose her temper from time to time. I finally stopped trying to give Pat much direction because when I did she never took my advice. One of Pat's national partners told her she should not work with our people group because they are dangerous, so she stopped. She would disciple women and girls that others, including me, brought to her. She would not engage in outreach and evangelism. She never did the job she had accepted.

"One lesson I've learned from this experience is that I will never make a decision about a possible teammate based on just a short phone call. I realized that in our context, others do our recruiting for us based on job requests that we write. However, the more contact we can have prior to a commitment to accept a job, the better."

The Right Place (Can I Live There?)

What is it that makes a place "right" for a missionary? You may have never even heard of a place before, or perhaps all you have heard is the news that it is dangerous and different. But these factors don't matter. Psalms 112:7 says "he will not be afraid of evil tidings; His heart is steadfast, trusting in the Lord."

Mike* and Lindsay* were a young family. They had been working a number of years toward the goal of pursuing a call to international missions by studying at seminary, working in ministry, and doing short-term trips overseas. They had this to say:

> "The short story is that we planned to go to one place and were lined up to go there, but the Lord drastically shifted our plans. Looking back now, we are so thankful for His providence. The Lord used the organization's process to shift us to our new location due to a medical issue. Through all of it, we had a deep peace that the Lord was leading us overseas, and with a specific organization. This leading allowed us to accept (and still allows us to accept) more gracefully and more willingly any circumstances that are different from 'our' plans."

Rachel,* a young mother of three, said that when she was really struggling with her place of service, she would turn to God.

> "Go back to the Word. Go back to prayer. Fall prostrate before Him, beseeching Him and asking is this from Him, is it from my fears, or is it from the enemy? Do not move forward (or change how you are already serving) until He makes it crystal clear and you have been given that peace that surpasses all knowledge, which will guard your heart and mind in Christ Jesus.

> "Find verses in scripture that speak about not complaining, taming the tongue, living a quiet life, being content in all circumstances, not sinning in anger, forgiving as God forgives, endurance, and perseverance. Then get on your face and beg

God to help you obey what He has commanded through His Word, ask Him to reveal Himself to you in the midst of the storms of life and choice. Yield to Him and He will either calm the storm around you or calm you in the midst of the storm."

God can sometimes send you to a place you didn't expect or imagine. Holly,* a young single lady, had this to say about how she landed in Asia.

"Has God laid a certain nationality, country, or region on your heart? For me, I had never imagined working anywhere outside of Latin America (LA). I loved Spanish and had gotten pretty good at it and I had visited many LA countries. However, God began calling me to South Asia about a year before I went to my missions conference. I met and worked with local refugees from Asia, which opened up my heart to the possibility of South Asia. I met other refugees from the Middle East, which opened my eyes to needs of Muslims. At the conference, I looked at both Latin America and South Asia. To say that God worked out His perfect plan is an understatement. I am now working in South Asia, focusing on Muslim women. I never would have planned this huge blessing for myself!"

Holly did her homework as well, asking about the perspective of the team she would join, where she would live in relation to the others, whether there were families and other singles, whether she would have/need a partner, and how she would fit into the strategic plan.

"The experiences of my supervisor and his family have been crucial to success and happiness here. Sure, we could survive without them through God's provision. However, as we delve into ministry, we are realizing that their experience and vision for the country, as well as the fruit they are seeing, is encouraging, motivating, and invaluable."

You may be wired as an explorer or a trailblazer or you may make the best contributions as a part of a team. Knowing this about yourself will help you as you select the right location and all that comes with it.

Remember James and Millie from earlier in this chapter? They were struck with the meagerness of the drab, four-room, concrete apartment when they arrived at their new home halfway around the world. They looked at each other and thought, "What have we done?" God used their young daughter, saying "Wow! I actually have a bed instead of a straw mat on the floor," to help them with their perspectives. Knowing they were where the Lord wanted their family to be got them through tough bouts with sickness, a shortage of clean water and electricity, plus many frustrating days of language learning. The team that was there to help was a huge added blessing.

Another missionary couple whose story we heard earlier, Mike and Lindsay, went to their missions conference trying to keep open minds and hearts.

"Lindsay previously served in Africa and we both had a strong inclination toward rural work. We felt this kind of environment suited our particular gifts and family dynamic. As we prayed, we began to focus in on Africa and eventually listed a position in a very rural region. We had never sensed as a couple a specific 'call' to one region or place, simply a call to obediently work among the nations.

"The fact that the job had not been filled for seven years did play a part in our growing desire to work there. After receiving the notification after the conference to continue working toward an assignment, we did more research on that area and sensed confirmation from the Father in continuing to move forward. At the time, Lindsay was just days away from delivering our first child. We notified the Africa representative that we would like to take that position.

"After the birth of our son, we noticed a small spot on his eye. We went to a pediatric ophthalmologist to hear that it was not a concerning diagnosis and did not seem likely that it would ever cause a problem, other than a bi-annual visit to the doctor.

We notified [our sending organization] and moved forward. Several months passed, and we were planning to move to Africa the following summer. One day we received a call from the organization's doctors who, after reviewing the information about our son's eye, had concluded we would have to have access to a pediatric ophthalmologist while living overseas.

"They could not locate a suitable specialized doctor within any reasonable distance of the location where we would be living. In one phone call, the decision we had felt so affirmed in making, changed. We were confused and somewhat sad. Africa seemed to be fading out of our reach. They sent us two positions on the continent within reasonable distance to the type of care we needed. We looked into both and after researching both options, we decided we would not be a good fit for either.

"Our representative told us that the next step was usually to work in concentric circles outside of where we were originally positioned. Lindsay had publicly stated on multiple occasions that she had no desire at all to go to South Asia. It was at the bottom of our list. We were sent a list of 42 priority jobs, all in South Asia. God used this list to reset our priorities. We again went to our knees to wrestle with that area of the world. The Lord broke our hearts for the vast lostness in South Asia.

"Through research and more prayer, we narrowed it down to two positions. Then we contacted the supervisors in both regions. As we got details about the team arrangement, job description, and cities, we felt that we would be a better fit in one location. Of particular help to us in making that decision were the online meetings with both supervisors. We got more of a feel for their personalities and work, and this made our decision easier.

"Since this area had been on the bottom of 'our' list, our entry expectations were pretty low. With one exception, we were the only ones in our orientation group who did not like South

Asian food. The only thing Lindsay could honestly say she thought she would like was the clothing. We flew over expecting to find the living conditions difficult and the crowded, communal culture exhausting. In some ways it was, but not in the ways we really expected. We had served previously in remote regions. We were not used to ex-pat grocery stores and high-rise complexes. These simple conveniences surprised us.

"The apartment we chose was a great fit for us. We had the wisdom of supervisors who encouraged us to think more about our family's daily needs than immediate access. They scoured the city ahead of us and let us make the final decision about where to actually live. This put us in a place with parks and walking paths where our young children could play. Our expectation had been that we were giving those things up, so when they were handed back to us, it was a gift.

"We listened as seasoned workers told us how to set boundaries around our home and time so that we could maintain a place of rest and refreshment. It was a slow process, a time of listening and obeying, a process of being willing to train our eyes to see beauty, rather than focus on the difficulties. We have marveled at the mercy of God in redirecting us. We thought we knew where we were headed and how our gifts would fit best. What we thought would be a terrible fit actually is a good fit. The last place on earth we 'wanted' to go has become our first choice."

The Right Time (Why Now? Am I Ready?)

In a lot of ways, there is no "good" time to take the leap and move ahead. We can all come up with great reasons why later is better. If you are like me, you will be saying things like "not just yet," "I need more preparation," "my family needs me," etc. Abraham was 100 and Sarah 91 when they had Isaac (see Genesis 17:17). That wasn't convenient. I am pretty sure that the timing wasn't right for Joseph in Genesis 37:12-36 when his brothers sold him into slavery. Moses questioned the Lord's choice and timing when God spoke to him out of the burning bush (Exodus 3). God may not speak audibly to you or send you by force to a foreign land, but He will make it clear that now is the time for the next step.

Normally, the actual timing should just make sense in your heart. Do you have a peace about the decision on going now? Have you been praying, and have you asked others to pray with and for you? Are you willing to put all you have on the altar and trust the Holy Spirit? Miranda had this to say, reflecting back on the timing of her departure for the mission field.

"For me, God's timing was not my timing. I thought that I would either graduate from college and do a two-year assignment or go to seminary and then on to the field. I also thought that I would get married somewhere along the way. Well, none of these plans happened. I did begin seminary right after college, but after completing one year, my dad was diagnosed with cancer and I felt the need to go home and be with my family.

"This definitely left me questioning God about what in the world He was doing, as I never envisioned myself not being overseas. He taught me contentment in the unknown, and I became comfortable in a job and in several ministries in my hometown. In fact, I became so comfortable that after my dad passed away, I could have easily stayed home and kept doing what I was doing.

"But, the Lord convicted me through a conversation with a friend. The very next day, I contacted the organization with which I had decided to pursue an assignment and shared who I was and what my life circumstances were. The lady I spoke with encouraged me to wait a couple of more months before beginning the application process as my dad had just passed away. Even though I knew that I was not making an emotional decision, since the Father had been calling me to the field for many years, I wanted to respect the organization's advice, so I waited two more months and then began the application process."

On the other end of the career spectrum are Greg* and Felicia.* They were in their mid-50s when they felt the time was right.

"Our initial questions concerned our children and parents. We did not want to neglect or ignore them. We saw that our children had all finished college and were in careers and jobs that they liked. The four children had all moved out of our home and were young adults. My parents were deceased, and Felicia's father was deceased. Her mother was in great health and lived alone. Felicia also had a brother who visited and took care of her mother faithfully. I was becoming restless in my work as a campus director at a satellite campus. Most of the growth and expansion was done. I wanted to be used to the maximum in my work for the Lord.

"Felicia and I knew our health, age, experiences, ministry preferences, and family situation all told us, 'Go now.' We were eager and willing to do cross-cultural work. To meet the health standards, I lost 40 pounds.

"We had the counsel of many godly friends. Everyone confirmed their agreement with our call. Knowing we had been careful and wise, along with what we heard from mature people, helped us deal with any doubts. We prayed and sought His face and had peace with the decision. It was enough."

There are always things that you can do to better prepare yourself. What have you been doing in the area of spiritual disciplines (prayer, Bible study, discipleship, evangelism, ministry, etc.)? What about debt and education? It is never too late to get these in order. I met a 70-year-old grandmother when I was in the process of getting some seminary preparation, who also was preparing to go overseas for a first-term assignment. Her passion and excitement for being ready and able were inspiring and scary at the same time. The key is to never give up, to be as ready as possible for whatever God may want you to do. Take David* and Laura's* experiences as an example.

"When we began to pursue an assignment, we had been on a clear trajectory toward overseas service for several years. The time spent even before marriage included multiple trips as well as several longer stints serving overseas. The Father worked very specifically in our individual hearts to affirm calls to work among the nations. During seminary, we began to move forward with our application process.

There were a number of tales told on campus of poor experiences in interviewing, getting rejections, and wrestling with difficult questions. This was not the case for us. There was a new process that was straightforward and we began the journey of finding the right fit for us and with the organization God intended for us to join."

As you consider the timing for going overseas, it's important to ask whether or not you have counted the cost, because there is a price to pay. Your choices and decisions will mean having to say no to other things, many of them good and worthwhile. Are they in line with what God is telling you?

Again, James and Millie dealt with some of these when they were in the process of preparing and settling on which organization was right for them. James' engineering job gave him the opportunity to transfer to several different countries where his company was working. The company James worked for would require them to live on a "safe" compound and restrict how much involvement he could have in local religious matters. Also, their church was just starting a new local ministry with Hispanics that had moved into the community.

James already spoke Spanish, and there was a need for someone with Millie's professional background. Ultimately, it was embracing their call to the least reached and hard-to-get-to places that paved the way for them to go where God was already preparing the way. There were lots of yard sales, leaving a dream house, saying goodbye to family and friends, taking grandkids halfway around the world from their grandparents and being willing to step out into the unknown.

The young, single, career woman mentioned earlier, Miranda, struggled with the cost of being "alone."

> "I am alone, but I have the Father. Yes, I had Him in America, too, but what a hard, sweet, and sanctifying time this has been for me on the field. In my first year of service, I prayed that He would teach me to trust Him more, and was encouraged to stop believing the lie that I needed someone else. Yes, I want someone else to serve alongside, but all I need is God. I asked God, in His kindness—not because He was obligated to—to

prove Himself trustworthy to me and to do it in ways that I could not miss. He was faithful.

"Just after reaching the one-year mark on the field, I had a major gas explosion in my house that should have caused serious injury or death to people and a fire in my home. Ceilings, windows, and doors blew out, but no one in my house was harmed and nothing caught on fire. No partner or husband could have shielded me or my house in this situation. No partner or husband could have saved us from harm; no partner or husband could have kept my house from catching on fire.

"Now if this weren't enough, I continued to ask God to prove Himself trustworthy to me, to prove to me that He is all that I need. Several months later, I was on the way to a Bible study with a friend and we needed to cross the road. Now here in South Asia, to cross the road, you first need to somehow stop the traffic. I had grown very used to doing this for myself and didn't even realize how much stress it was causing me until on this day, when my friend stopped the traffic for me and I simply walked across the road. Now for whatever reason, this was a HUGE deal to me, and I literally couldn't stop thinking about how nice that was of my friend!

"The next day, I left my house to get a rickshaw and as I walked down my street, suddenly a motorcycle came around the corner and literally almost took me out (but it didn't). I then proceeded to get on a rickshaw and be on my way. Not more than five minutes after getting on the rickshaw, my rickshaw was hit and smashed by a bus, but I came through the accident unharmed. I suddenly heard the Father say to me, "Who stopped the traffic for you yesterday?" Once again, only the Father could have shielded and protected me in these events. He IS all that I need!"

Other costs that need to be turned over to the Lord include missing life events with extended family and friends, job aspirations, being more in control of general life and the life of your family. Are you willing to home-school or use national schools if required? Will you be able to trust that the Lord can and will use you even if you don't see eye to eye with your supervisor or when your job assignment changes? God consistently brings many of these "sacrifices" back around as unexpected gifts/blessings.

The Right Assignment (Are My Needs/Expectations in Alignment with the Job?)

To prepare for the place God wants you to serve, do your homework to find out what is required for missionary service and start working on those things that you do not already have in place. Get your "house in order" so when the Father says it is time, you are ready. Be proactive in getting experience where you are now, such as working among refugees. Consider all the possibilities for gaining cross-cultural experience. Perhaps you can take some courses at a local school that will open doors for you, or give you a better identity in an overseas setting. Even taking mission trips to other places can help you find the place where God wants you to serve.

Greg shared this experience about helping a couple make sure their assignment was the right one.

> "I met Brent* and Delia* when they had been in the application process for a first-term job for several years. He was a bank V.P. with a solid career. She was a nurse but had stopped working to be home with their three young children. They were at the point of choosing a job and were considering a student worker job on my team. In my first phone call to them, I detected fear and worry on Delia's part. I urged them to come visit and see what life is like here before committing to a job.
>
> "Delia wanted to bring her baby, aged 18 months. I suggested they not do that, so they could more easily travel. She also wanted to bring the associate pastor of their church as a 'support' for them while they were here. Because of Delia's insistence, both the baby and associate pastor came with them. It was a nerve-wracking trip for them and Delia

constantly fretted, worried, and spoke of her fears of the place, the food, the diseases, the filth, etc. She stayed in the guest apartment several days and refused to travel.

"The husband, Brent, had multiple good experiences overseas on volunteer trips and felt a strong call to the area. He and Delia had been to Asia and Europe on volunteer trips. He was eager to come. Yet she was terrified and dreaded it. Brent spoke of desires to do evangelism, teach and disciple students, and other work. He taught a few lessons with me and did well.

"Both Brent and Delia were trained in Evangelism Explosion and had led training groups. However, Delia refused to participate and never taught or helped in any ministry while here. She even refused to give a simple testimony of salvation to a group of poor women. Delia said her father was very worried about their volunteer trip as well, and he was very concerned that they might serve here. Delia clung to her baby while they were here and would not allow any company personnel to care for him so she could see more, travel the city, or participate in ministry here.

"In every way, Delia was resistant, fearful, and withdrawn while here. I gently, but firmly, told them at the end of their trip that they needed to face her fears. She would only tell me, "I need to pray about this." They were about to pick the job, sell their nice house, and Brent was preparing to quit his bank job. I urged him not to do anything yet. It was clear Delia would not live, function, or minister in this cross-cultural setting."

Alex* and Jennifer* were struggling as they moved through the hiring process. It was difficult choosing the right assignment. But they took advantage of the field supervisor's insights.

"We felt like we divulged so much about ourselves but struggled to get some info about the organization. We tried to be transparent about ourselves to our future supervisor. He wanted us in a good match and wanted to put all his players in the right positions. Supervisors know the field better than applicants, so trust their placement and care. If you hold back something you should have said, you may not be placed as well as you should have. I was pleased with the company's desire and effort to place us where there was a big need, where we could succeed, and be happy. There's always an element of sacrifice, but pursue needs and opportunities for ministry in places you can picture yourself living."

Here is Miranda's description of her own choices and what she felt the Lord had put on her heart about her eventual place of service.

"I felt that I could be happy in any hot climate telling women and children about Jesus. I am very type A, and I told God that I was not good at reading in between the lines, so I wanted a very clear, definite answer from Him. When I asked other missionaries how they knew where they were supposed to go, they told me that they just knew. I remember one lady in particular telling me that when she saw the cover to a mission's publication about Japan, she could just see herself there.

"This is kind of what happened to me as well, and then God continued to give further confirmation about the assignment He had planned for me. While at an initial missions conference, I decided to attend a session on South Asia. Now while I never envisioned myself going to Asia, I decided to attend this session merely based on the fact that there were more job openings for single women in this part of the world. And as I sat there and listened to the presenter, the same thing happened to me that had happened to my friend years before. Suddenly I could just see myself in South Asia.

"In looking further into the jobs available for single women, there was one that fit my passions, talents, and gifts just perfectly. Then the confirmation came. Earlier that year, I had led the children's/youth department at my church in praying for South Asia. We studied about and prayed for all different areas, but South Asia was the most recent, and one week after reading about the great darkness in South Asia, the Spirit led me to pray, "Lord, send me." I didn't really think He was going to send me, but I just thought that I needed to be willing. Then I actually forgot that I had prayed that prayer!

"The Father reminded me of that prayer, and I was in awe of His faithfulness. And if this wasn't enough confirmation, several days later, when reaching into the fridge, a magnet that I had picked up at a missions fair in college (seven-plus years earlier) caught my eye. Now this magnet had been on my fridge for a long time, and I had stopped paying attention to it. But on this day, what did the magnet say? 'South Asia Bound!' Again I stood in awe of the Father's faithfulness to this girl who isn't good at reading between the lines!"

Sometimes we're not even aware of what our needs and expectations are going to be when we arrive on the mission field. God's faithfulness in providing large and small victories, as well as support from leadership when times are not going well, were key needs that were not initially acknowledged by Alex:

"Nanda's and Dipti's faith have been such an encouragement. It is for Him and His glory and for them, but it was for us, too. God gave us the experience early on of leading them to faith. This and our opportunity to continue to disciple them was and continues to be a critical encouragement. As a result, we can continue to serve in the face of spiritual warfare and sickness."

There are some people who need to be in close proximity to a team whereas others don't need a team at all. The expectations of a leader can be either a help or a burden. It's important to consider what kind of leader you could work with and what type of leader you might potentially be. This was an important element for Steve* and his crew:

"As a family, we have adapted and adjusted well to the culture, but the struggles have come mostly because of the challenging and sometimes overwhelming expectations of the organization. Once we arrived, the requirements and control of the organization weighed heavily on us."

Dealing with an organization's strategy and expectations can carry with it unexpected surprises. Holly accepted an assignment and location and then was faced with change.

> "Always, always, always expect things to change. The job description that I had accepted ended up being very different practically from the job I am doing. How did I handle that? I thought, 'Well, I am not sufficient for either of these jobs and God knows what He wants me to be doing, so I will do it.' Trust that the organization is trying its best to be consistent and has your best in mind, but trust even more that God is orchestrating an even better plan. Expect change, expect unmet expectations, but also expect God to work in any and every situation."

As we've seen thus far, flexibility and commitment are two of the biggest field needs. Organizations that are trying to impact unreached people and places are prone to change. So you need to approach each assignment with an attitude of trying your best to work yourself out of a job and then be willing to consider another assignment. Sometimes the job changes even before you get to the field due to breakthroughs, personnel changes, and access issues. Listen to Rachel's thoughts about selecting the right assignment:

> "Is this about you, your preferences, your wants, your ways, etc.? If it is, then expect to pack up and leave early due to it not turning out the way you wanted. However, if it is truly about God Almighty, what He wants, and what He wills, then you will know that if change occurs or the assignment isn't what you expected, the Lord is allowing it for a purpose for your good and His glory. It will not be easy in any way, form, or fashion. But hold tightly to your Sovereign Father, do not quench the Spirit, and keep doing what you are doing until He clearly shows you differently. When you do this, you will come to the end of this season looking more like Him. He's the Potter. You are the clay. Welcome to the Potter's wheel.

> "Being a stay-at-home, home-school mom is a full-time job (several full-time jobs in one)! I knew that I was bringing all

of this on the plane with me and in many ways it was going to be more 'work' than what I was doing in the States (cooking takes longer, laundry takes longer, grocery shopping is different, accomplishing different tasks throughout the day takes much longer, etc.). I was prepared for this part of my life when I got on that plane.

"However, I was not prepared to have another full-time job outside my home. I expected to be a helpmate for my husband in the ministry but did not realize that I would be expected to have the same first-term requirements as my husband. This is extremely hard to do in this season of life when multiple small children demand so much of my time and attention.

"I'm not really sure what could have made a difference for me before coming except realizing ahead of time that I would be doing all the same first-term things as my husband and as the singles.

"I have grown to love this country, this culture, and these people. I enjoy living here and would love to watch our children grow up and call it home. The truth I have held on to for dear life in the midst of this has been that the Lord has brought us through enormous, impossible mountains and valleys to get us here. If He can bring us through all of that to get us to this place, then He can accomplish what He knows needs to be accomplished this first term. He will complete His good work in our family."

Speaking of flexibility and commitment, Greg had this to share about the importance of attitude:

"Seek a friendly, uninvolved, and totally honest third party who can weigh your complaints in an objective way. Ask them for a blunt, honest assessment of you. Assume goodwill, kindness, and good intentions from people with whom you disagree. Be frank, but be charitable in your discussions. You are dealing with Christians who deserve your courtesy. At times, (for example, in language learning matters) you may just have to put up with stuff you deeply dislike and/or disagree with. Your leaders and supervisors are 'over you' in the Lord. Doing as you are asked will bring leverage and depth to you in later years of service with these same people. Attitude is more important that actions."

Miranda shared about the inevitability of the assignment not being exactly what is expected, at least to some degree:

"After arriving on the field, I soon realized that the assignment that I had taken was not one that I would enjoy. My assignment was eight hours away from where my team lived, and my team used Arabic words in sharing with Muslims, even though there are non-Arabic words in the local language to convey the message of the gospel. I wrestled with feeling guilty for not wanting to make the sacrifices needed to travel several times a month to the village. I wrestled with my convictions about what words to use in sharing. I wrestled with how to talk to my supervisors about these things in a humble way. I wrestled with not wanting to let my supervisors down.

"Ultimately, I had to ask God what HE wanted of me, and knew that I must obey God first. I had also decided in my heart that I wanted to keep my word in taking this job assignment and complete this first term in that assignment if my supervisors saw that as best. In talking with my supervisors about my feelings, the Father gave me further confirmation that my feelings were from Him. My supervisors graciously listened to me and affirmed the desires that I had to change job assignments and to use the words that I felt the Father was leading me to use in my sharing.

"Counselors have been great in helping me deal with this and other issues, helping me understand that a lot of my unmet expectations have been the root of many of the frustrations that I have experienced. I wouldn't have said that I had issues with anger before I came to the field, but in being here, I have been pressed, and I have seen what has been in my heart all along."

Conclusion

The people who have contributed these stories continue to strive to serve the Lord to the best of their abilities. They are the right people in the right place, at the right time and in the right assignment. As a result, they are seeing God do amazing things through them and often in spite of them. These accounts are not the end of their discoveries and struggles but parts of the journey. After all, it is in the journey that we develop the strength of our character. Our reliance on the Father, our reputation in the work, and our solid relationships carry us through our low points. God goes before us and is with us as we go.

About the Author

Brett Freemon and his wife Donna have been living and working in South Asia for twenty years. He is currently the director of a leadership development company and a trainer of overseas workers. Brett holds a Bachelor's Degree in Applied Physics from the Georgia Institute of Technology. He has done masters work at New Orleans Baptist Theological Seminary and holds a Masters in Organizational Leader-ship from Regent University.

14

Interviews and Techniques
by Joel Sutton

An exhibit at the Georgia Aquarium in Atlanta is the largest aquatic habitat in the world. The *Ocean Voyager* is 284 feet long, 126 feet wide, and ranges in depth between 20 and 30 feet. It contains over 6 million gallons of water. That is a huge aquarium! Can you imagine how long it would take to explore the entirety of that tank, from end to end and from top to bottom? That is an adequate comparison to the difficulty encountered by an assessment team in trying to know and understand a new missionary applicant. There is so much territory to cover.

That has been the thrust of the preceding chapters. So how can an interviewer explore all the areas related to the Five Components? It would be easier if you had to only skim the surface, but problematic issues usually don't reside there. Those things that will cause a ministry or family unit to disintegrate on the mission field are generally located in the depths of a person's life. The interviewer must be able to dive to the bottom to see the entire picture of a candidate's spiritual, mental, emotional, and physical health.

The assessor of potential missionaries has two kinds of tools for getting below the surface and into the depths. The first is a variety of interviews, and we will discuss different types that yield distinct results. The second group of tools is a portfolio full of interviewing techniques that enable the interviewer to move from the shallow end to the deepest parts of an individual's personality.

Types of Interviews

1. Initial Interview

As the name implies, this session is the first opportunity an assessor has to talk with the candidate about the possibility of missionary service. Basic, surface information can be obtained during this interview, covering all five components. Here are some examples of what can be learned or discussed: age, marital status, size of family and ages of children, education background, work history, ministry experience, cross-cultural involvement, salvation and spiritual pilgrimage, spiritual gifts, sense of God's call, evangelism training, and recent examples of sharing the gospel.

This also is the time to determine if there are any hindrances or issues that indicate the candidate should not proceed further with the application. These are "red-flag" items that essentially make the candidate ineligible for consideration. Such issues can include children's developmental needs that can't be met on the mission field, pending litigation, ongoing lifestyle issues, serious medical conditions, significant debt, and miscellaneous areas that are important to the church or denomination.

Usually the applicant volunteers this information on a form that's been developed specifically for this purpose. Asking about such issues doesn't require significant probing into the private areas of a person's life. They are facts that are easily shared and discussed. If there are roadblocks to an application, it is best to know that as early as possible. This keeps candidates from getting their hopes up, only to find that it was all for naught.

This **initial interview** is usually not the moment to delve into the deeper, more personal areas of an applicant's life. In order for individuals to open up and share the secret fears and motivations of their heart, it takes time and the development of a relationship based on earned trust. Discussing matters that are emotionally sensitive— pornography use, past experience with abortion, instances of abuse or rape, eating disorders, roots of depression or anxiety, and lack of marital intimacy—should be delayed until such a time as the interviewer has established a good rapport with the applicant.

2. Update Interview

Depending on the needs of the sending group, an application for overseas service can take many months to complete. This is generally a desirable element in a well-designed process. Moving people too quickly through the approval stage allows them to go to the mission field based on a whim or a flash of spiritual zeal. But when there is time to reflect carefully, without the influence of emotions, the decisions are usually more solid and the commitment is deeper.

When there is a lengthy process, situations are likely to change for the applicants. They may start a family, discover a new direction for ministry, discern a new element in God's call on their lives, or encounter unexpected difficulties. Sometimes this new information can be simply communicated by phone or email. But there are times when the interviewer will want to discuss the change, along with its implications, with the missionary candidate. At times like this, an **update interview** is needed.

Following such an interim interview, there may be different plans needed for the future. The applicant's "green light" could turn to "yellow," meaning he or she needs to slow down and take more time before proceeding further. In some cases, the new information could even result in a "red light." If there's no option for the candidate to move forward, this interview may be his or her last one. Sometimes there's a "turn ahead" or a detour, showing the individual that plans for the mission field may have to wait until a later time.

3. Teen Interview

Teenagers and pre-teens are often at a difficult juncture in life. They are changing, growing, and maturing. That is a challenging experience even when they're in their home culture. But taking those same ordeals into a new culture can greatly magnify their impact. If a youngster is trying to establish his or her own identity, it can be quite complicated when living in an area where the language is unknown, the culture is unsettling, friends are scarce, and parents are floundering themselves.

The purpose of a **teen interview** (or pre-teen) is to determine a child's readiness for living in another culture. First of all, it should be ascertained whether or not the teen's identity is too deeply rooted in his or her home culture. Some teens can manage a transition out of their maternal language and familiar surroundings, but others cannot. Also, it's good to know youngsters' level of maturity. Those who are self-focused and still immature will generally not do well in adapting to another culture. But those who know how to put the needs and desires of others ahead of their own will be better equipped to handle culture shock. That's especially true if they have spiritual maturity.

In order to properly assess teens' identity and maturity, the following areas should be addressed:

- Home Life—How is their relationship with their parents and siblings?
- Spiritual Development—Are they a born-again believer? Are they growing spiritually?
- School Progress—Are they focused and able to achieve their goals?
- Missions—Have they been involved in the family's discussion about moving overseas? Are their feelings and opinions taken into consideration by their parents?
- Fears/Stress—What are their concerns about moving overseas?
- Friends—Do they have friends of other races? Is there a girlfriend or boyfriend they'd be leaving behind?
- Future—Will their time on the mission field interfere with their plans for college or career?

Answers to these questions can be gleaned by use of a questionnaire and a face-to-face interview. It is recommended that parents allow the teen to be interviewed in such a way that his or her answers can be confidential. The parents can be in an adjoining room or at a sufficient distance so that the teen can talk freely and confidentially with the interviewer.

In addition to dialoguing with the teen, the interviewer may also want to provide some questions to the parents, to make sure they're thinking about all the issues that their teen may be confronting.

A. Living and relating cross-culturally

- Has our teen had cross-cultural experience in the U.S.?
- Does our teenager have friendships with peers of other ethnic groups?
- Has our teenager been involved in an inner-city ministry?
- Has our teenager been on cross-cultural mission trips?

B. Our teenager's perspective on this potential move

- How much input has our teen had in making the decision for overseas service?
- How has our teenager responded to the possibility of uprooting and moving overseas?
- Have we sensed resistance, fear, reluctance, openness, or excitement?
- Does our teen have any emotional, physical, or spiritual need that would prohibit him (her) from meaningful life overseas? What about a known learning disability?

C. Personal and social issues

- What are our expectations for our teen's support/social network overseas?
- What are our teen's expectations for support/social network overseas?
- Do we have expectations of returning home to the U.S. at personal expense for typical teenage needs such as driver training and licensing, visiting colleges, etc.?

D. School options in the overseas setting

- If home schooling is our choice as parents, are we capable of doing this overseas?
- What are our expectations for schooling our teen on the field?
- In the overseas environment where missionary kid (MK) boarding school would be the best option we and our teen would choose, should our teen live at home with us for at least the first year overseas?
- If we choose not to home school our teen overseas, can we afford out-of-pocket educational expenses above what the agency/church can pay for MK education?
- Does our teenager have a life goal for specific college education requiring specific courses that can best be gained in the U.S.? If so, will going overseas jeopardize this goal? Example: Our teen wants to pursue a profession that requires specialized courses, labs, and languages that may not be obtainable overseas.
- Does our teen have a strong investment in a specific extracurricular activity such as athletics, music, dance, etc.? If so, should this investment be broken to go overseas?

E. College planning

- Do we already have a plan engaged for financing our teen's college education?
- Where would home base be in the U.S. when our teen returns home for college?
- Where would our college-age MK spend holiday/summer times during college?
- What if our teen chooses not to enter college? What might this require of us as parents? Would we plan for our teen to remain on the field with us?
- Does our teen have aspirations for college scholarship in one of these areas that might require continued training and performance in the U.S.?

F. Questions for parents

- Have we considered delaying the application process until our teen finishes high school in the U.S. and enters college?
- If a delay is best, is this a time for us as parents to complete any needed or additional education?
- Do we have other children younger than our teen who will become teens while on the field? Have the same questions been anticipated and asked for them?

4. In-depth Interview

By this point in the application process, the interviewer should already have gleaned as much information as possible in order to construct a fairly accurate picture of the applicant's past experiences and present mindset. The **in-depth interview** allows the interviewer to go beyond the printed page or obvious facts and become familiar with the most hidden areas of a person's life, including inner wounds, struggles, motives, values, and spiritual growth. It is obvious that all five components need to be examined fully. To have an idea of what that would look like, here is a list of areas that may need to be explored.

- Debt level (credit card, secured debts, student loans)
- Past bankruptcy
- Financial decision-making
- Evangelism training
- Witnessing focus
- Success in soul-winning
- Formative years
  - Effects of divorce
  - Social development
  - Family dynamics
  - Personality development
  - Abuses (emotional, verbal, sexual, physical)
- Spiritual health
  - Spiritual pilgrimage
  - Victory over sin
  - Devotional practices

- o Ministry experience
- o Sense of personal call to missions
- o Doctrinal beliefs
- Emotional health
  - o History of depression
  - o Anxiety
- Lifestyle issues (pornography, eating disorders, etc.)
- Physical health (substance abuse, weight, medical conditions)
- Marital health/contentment as a single
- Communication skills and transparency
- Care for aging parents
- Job history
- Educational background
- College transcripts
- Background check
- Educational assessments for all children
- Evaluation of previous overseas service
- Military obligations
- Attitudes expressed through the process (e.g. worry, impatience, procrastination, rigidity)

5. Job-Match Interview

Even though applicants may be healthy in all ways and ready to engage in cross-cultural stress and ministry, that doesn't mean they can fill just any assignment on the mission field. There are several issues to consider when determining if a candidate is a good fit for a specific need in a specific area.

Living conditions

- Consider the type of housing that will be available. Some people don't mind living in mud huts, but those same personnel wouldn't want to be in a concrete high-rise.
- There are those who can live in cold climates and others who cannot. Some actually prefer extreme heat and can handle it well.

- Do your personnel expect to have a car, or will they be content with a bus pass, a metro ticket, a bicycle, or walking?

Medical conditions

- Some roads are so rough that a person with a sensitive back wouldn't last long. Back problems often help determine where someone should or should not serve.
- Breathing problems such as asthma and allergies should be taken into account. Sensitivities to mold, spores, or pollen can limit an applicant's ability to survive and thrive in some areas.
- There are those who are physically capable of climbing 10 flights of stairs, with their groceries, to reach their apartment. But if someone is not that fit, they should consider carefully where they'll be located.

Security risks

- In some countries, it's safe to be identified as a missionary, yet it's extremely dangerous for anyone to live there. This is especially true in areas where there are drug wars. Some candidates can handle that daily threat while others would be constantly paralyzed by fear.
- Religious extremists are more of a danger in certain countries. Personnel who live there must be willing to lose their lives, should they be attacked.
- Even if a city doesn't have problems with drug lords or terrorists, there still could be significant risk due to other crimes. New personnel must determine what level of risk they can handle.

Third-Culture Kid schooling options

- Can the available schooling options meet the educational needs of the children?
- Some parents insist on home-schooling, whereas others feel that is not a good option for them. It's important to know if

home-schooling is possible or legal in the country being considered.
- If a boarding school is the primary solution, can the family handle that separation between the adults and children?

World religions

- God has placed a specific burden on some people's hearts. They feel called to minister to Muslims, Hindus, Buddhists, or post-modern atheists. Sending them to an assignment that doesn't match their passion will likely result in frustration and burnout.

Open or creative access

- In many areas of the world, personnel cannot identify with the traditional missionary role. In order to have a valid ministry and presence in the country, they need to have a specific skill, fill a secular job, or exercise caution in how they share their faith. Some people seem to be uniquely gifted for such places.
- Other applicants don't feel comfortable being so cautious and guarded. They have a need to be outward and vocal, with no hindrances. They should serve in places that allow an open access to missionaries.

Language difficulty

- Not all languages are created equal, nor are missionaries. There are dialects that are simple and relatively easy to learn. But then you have languages that are highly complicated with lots of rules and exceptions to rules. A person's aptitude for learning a new language is a factor in where he or she should serve.
- A few languages are tonal. If individuals are not able to hear the nuances, they should not attempt to minister in those languages.
- There are some assignments where multiple languages are used. There may be a trade language that everyone uses in

conducting business and then another language for familiar life. In addition, if the people being reached are immigrants from a completely different area of the world, there could be a third language to learn. Not all applicants will have that kind of aptitude.

In order to demonstrate the usefulness of all these interviews, let's consider the case of Jeff* and Laura.* During their initial interview, they presented themselves as the ideal candidates for missionary service. However, as the application process unfolded, several issues came to light.

During one update interview, we learned that they had a home that had not sold. They were finally able to get a rental contract on the house. The next update interview was complicated. A church member from a former congregation leveled accusations against Jeff that seemed to be quite serious. After an extensive interview, asking about specific incidents in the church, we then turned to references from that same congregation. We finally gained a full picture of the situation. The accuser was vindictive, negative and had skewed the picture of Jeff's ministry. It turned out that Jeff had behaved in a godly manner.

Jeff and Laura had a teen daughter, Ashley.* We conducted a teen interview with her and found that she was quite mature for her age and had experienced for herself a call to missions. Ashley's zeal and depth of commitment were having a positive impact on her younger sister. As a consequence, the family would be more prone to thrive in another culture because these two girls were completely in agreement with this major move.

The in-depth interview for this couple confirmed the degree of their spiritual health. They had been through several trials including church conflict, difficult family members, and the threat of infertility. These challenges revealed their faith and heart attitudes, and taught them valuable life lessons. God had worked in their lives and brought healing so they could bear children.

The job-match interview was fascinating. As the couple considered the needs of the world, they found their hearts resonating with unreached peoples spread across a large European country. Everything about the job assignment aligned with their gifting, passions, and preferences. The family is now enjoying a successful ministry in their chosen field of service.

Using these five types of interviews, an assessment team has all the opportunities it needs to develop a full picture of the applicant. Not only do these interviews provide a broad scope of knowledge, but they also include options for going as deeply as needed in the five different components.

Interview Techniques

As mentioned earlier, the issues in a person's life that would be problematic under cross-cultural stress usually lie in the depths of a person's soul. Getting to those nuggets of information is similar to mining for gold.

Prospectors will go to a location that perhaps has already been known to be a source of gold and that's where they'll begin their work. They'll take several soil samples from areas where the rainwater has drained and left deposits. When they find some gold flakes or tiny chunks of the ore, they'll move upslope and take more samples. As they get closer to the source, the amount of gold they find will increase. Then it's time to dig and blast. As they get deeper, they're looking not simply for isolated specks of gold, but for the source of the nuggets. They're hoping to locate an entire vein of ore.

Those who are tasked with assessing missionary applicants must also look for patterns and frequency of actions or attitudes. And often it is necessary to dig deeper in order to locate the source of someone's inappropriate reaction to stress. Thankfully, there's a full set of tools at the interviewer's disposal that can help pinpoint and uncover those hidden wounds and motives.

Connecting the Dots—In order to get a full picture of an applicant's health, both inward and outward, multiple documents are often used to ask for information: personal testimony, autobiography, health questionnaire, transcripts, statement of beliefs, biographical information form, etc. It is important that the assessor not treat these materials separately. There may be one detail revealed in a document that is directly linked to another piece of information in a separate form. By connecting the dots, you may discover an important fact that would otherwise be overlooked.

For example, a transcript could show that an applicant earned poor grades during a specific year of college. By itself, that could call into question the applicant's ability to persevere in learning a new language. However, the autobiography may include the events that happened during that time frame. Perhaps the applicant's mother was going through surgery and ensuing treatment, and he or she was the primary care provider. During an interview, the assessor could verify the link between these two pieces of information instead of jumping to inaccurate conclusions.

Looking for Patterns and Trends—It's not unusual for someone to hold a job for only a year or two. But if you noticed that a missionary candidate regularly hopped from job to job every couple of years, you'd want to discern if this was going to be a continuing trend while on the mission field. There are many more types of patterns that we can look for such as:

- inappropriate reactions to stress
- unbroken cycles of addiction
- impulsive decision-making
- poor handling of finances
- immature communication styles

Probing Questions—Medical doctors are usually not satisfied to address simply the symptoms of an illness. They want to find the root cause and make sure that healing takes place. Similarly, the missionary interviewer does not want to only address the external evidences of deeper problems. It is important that we ask questions that will take us deeper and enable us to determine root causes of the symptoms. These probing questions are driven by the Five W's: who, what, when, where, why.

As a first example of using these investigative questions, let's use the case of Dana,* who had never been on a date with a man (which in itself is not a problem.)

    a. Why have you not been on any dates? [I've been asked, but I tend not to trust men.]

    b. When did you start not trusting men? [I think I was probably 13 or 14 years old.]

    c. What happened to you that caused you to mistrust men? [I was touched inappropriately by someone who was staying in our home.]

    d. Who was this person? Did you know them well? [It was my cousin who was 18 years old.]

    e. Could you please share with me what happened? Did you share this experience with anyone else?

    f. Have you worked through these feelings in your relationship with God? Have you allowed the Lord to bring healing to this area of your life?

Here was one aspect of an applicant's life story that was not a problem in and of itself, but there were root issues that needed to be addressed.

Another technique for using probing questions is to ask the question "why" five times. You can drill down deeply into an issue by using this method.

    a. Why do you struggle with pornography? [Answer: I mainly am tempted when I'm bored and/or curious.]

    b. Why do you turn to pornography and not some other activity? [It seems to my default preference, ever since I saw some magazines as a young teen.]

    c. Why did you see those magazines? [I was alone with a friend at his dad's house.]

    d. Why did you choose to stay and keep looking, instead of leaving? [I was not yet born again so I didn't fully realize it was wrong.]

    e. Why are you having the same struggles now that you are saved?

Dealing with Conflicting Information—Since most assessment teams depend on multiple ways of gathering information, it is possible that the missionary candidate will provide one version of a life event in one document, yet present a completely different picture in a separate form. For example, Corey* indicated he had not been in trouble with the law. Yet in his autobiography, he shared about his time of rebellion when he was charged with reckless driving and later with possession of a weapon.

Why did he answer differently? Because his criminal record had been expunged. The court had provided a way for his unwise decisions to be rectified through a time of public service. So in one document, Corey was sharing the personal side of his experiences, but in the other he was relating the non-existent legal ramifications.

Indirect Questions—If you ask someone a direct question, you will often receive the answer he or she thinks you want to hear. "How is your relationship with your in-laws?" "Oh, we get along well. We see them every three weeks and talk on the phone."

An indirect route, however, can often yield more accurate replies. For example, you could ask the following questions in order to glean insights about family dynamics.

a. "Describe your father (mother) using the three best adjectives you can think of." During the response, it's helpful to watch the spouse's body language. You may only hear chuckles and observe grins. But there are times when you'll notice tension, grimaces, or a rolling of the eyes.

b. Addressing the spouse: "Who is your husband/wife most like in personality: the father or the mother?" "Why do you say that?" "What qualities do you see in your spouse's parents that you also observe in your spouse?"

By observing non-verbal cues and casual comments, you can usually learn quite a bit about what a spouse really thinks and feels about the in-laws.

Another example of indirect questions is in regard to the marital relationship. Instead of asking if they're pleased with the quality of their marriage, you might ask them:

a. What is the strongest element in your marriage? (They may have different answers)
b. If you could change anything in order to improve your relationship, what would that be? The responses can be quite revealing. If both of them view one partner as being to blame, instead of sharing the responsibility, you've learned about the quality of their marriage. Other replies could show that a spouse is clueless about the issues they're confronting as a couple, or they could be in agreement that there is much still to address and change.

Open-ended questions (vs. yes/no answers)—Here are some examples of close-ended questions that prevent you from going deeper in understanding applicants:

a. Do you both feel called to serve as missionaries? <Yes>
b. Do you have any concerns about taking your children overseas? <No>
c. Will your debt be under control by the time you're appointed as missionaries? <Yes>
d. Is your family supportive of your call to missions? <Yes>

This type of question will keep you at only a shallow understanding of your applicants. But perhaps even worse, these questions encourage the applicant to give you the answer that will be most pleasing. They can tell what the "correct" answer is to these questions and that's the reply they'll provide.

Better questions will always demand a detailed answer that requires some thought. You can even take yes/no queries and turn them around to become effective probes for deeper information.

a. Please share with me what you consider to be the root, the starting point of God's call on your life to serve overseas. Why did you feel that God was speaking directly to your heart?

b. What are your top three concerns about taking your children overseas?
c. How much debt do you currently have? What are your plans for reducing the debt to a manageable amount?
d. You'll be taking the grandchildren to another part of the world. How does that make your parents feel? What hesitations do they have about your decision to pack and move abroad?

Objective, Broad Questions—If we ask specific questions, we'll receive specific answers. But that doesn't mean we get to see the whole picture. We may miss some important details, simply because we're not asking the right questions. It's like taking pictures of a sporting event or a family reunion. With the snapshots, you only see isolated moments. But if you shoot a video, you capture all the interesting details that would otherwise be missed.

The way to obtain this long view of a person's life and character is through stories. For example, the interviewer can ask, "Describe for me what it was like growing up in your family." That kind of broad question will likely yield more information than simply asking pointed questions.

Another example of a panoramic question deals with a person's spiritual life. "Trace for me a line that shows how you have grown in your level of spiritual maturity. Share with me what contributed to your growth and the incidents that appear to have hindered you or caused you to plateau spiritually." This line of questioning invites the applicant to think more deeply about his or her life experiences.

Future-Focused Questions—The bulk of application materials and interview questions deals with the past or the present. We look to a person's childhood, teen years, and early adulthood to understand who they are in their character and personality. We also consider who they are currently in their beliefs, ministry, work, and family. But if we're not careful, we can forget to ask about the future. When we ask candidates to look forward into the near future and share with us their fears and expectations, we can gain insights into their spiritual and emotional states that we otherwise might not obtain by focusing uniquely on their application materials.

Addressing Sensitive Issues—When an assessment team conducts a thorough evaluation of an applicant, they are going to naturally address some areas that can be sensitive. Examples of such issues include emotional abuse, verbal abuse, sexual abuse, abortion, eating disorders, sexual identity confusion, pornography addiction, sexual intimacy issues, etc. Asking pointed questions can be uncomfortable to applicants, and they may hesitate to share freely. Therefore, it is best to use broad questions. They'll enable you to probe into the areas where you need more insights, yet in a compassionate manner.

The approach used in addressing sensitive matters also is important. Above all, the interviewer needs to demonstrate great respect and love for the applicant. The following steps are a healthy pattern for making a difficult interview a bit easier for the applicant.

1. Empathize with the applicant
2. Acknowledge the sensitivity of the issue
3. Request permission to enter that area of his or her life
4. Seek their internal perspective on the event or issue
   a. What actually occurred
   b. Impact on their soul
   c. Residual effects today
5. Ask how God has brought truth and healing

The following example is a glimpse of how easily these five steps can be folded into an interviewer's approach when getting ready to discuss a sensitive matter with an applicant.

"I noticed in reading your materials that you had a traumatic experience in college in which you were raped by a male friend. I'm so sorry you had that experience. I'm sure that affected you deeply, and in many ways. Would you be willing to share with me what happened at that time and how it impacted you? How has the Lord empowered you to work through those wounds? To what degree do you feel that you've been healed from that experience?"

Reading Non-Verbal Clues—There are multiple signs that people provide in the ways their body moves, or doesn't move, during an interview. Paying attention to those can give you hints about the person's feelings and personality. Here's a partial list of those clues: squirming, rigidity, gulping, fidgeting, playing with hair, diverting eyes, frowning, and smiling. When there's a couple, it's also helpful to observe the ways they look at each other and whether or not they give touches of affection or reassurance during the interview. Take care, however, not to assume what those non-verbal clues mean. Fidgeting, for example, can mean that they're uneasy about your question, or they may simply be fatigued from sitting in the same position.

Summary

Interviewing potential missionaries is a spiritual art. Through time and experience, an interviewer can learn how to wisely blend the types of interviews and the variety of interview techniques in order to create an environment that allows missionary candidates to share the deepest parts of their lives, all while feeling secure and respected.

About the Author

Joel Sutton earned a BA in Music Education from Southern Ark. Univ., an M.Div. from Southwestern Baptist Seminary, and a doctoral research degree from Evangel Christian University of America. He has served the Lord as a music minister, bivocational pastor, missionary to France, missions supervisor for Western Europe, and consultant for missionary applicants (16 years). He is now the Lead Consultant for the Personnel Selection Team, IMB. He and his wife, Rhonda, are blessed by their three adult children and their families.

15

Not Now—What Now?
Personnel Assessment as a Tool in God's Hands
by Larry and Susan Gay

Ron* and Rhonda* approached the application process with extra enthusiasm. Although Ron had not completed all the education requirements, they felt confident he could complete the minimum required degree in plenty of time before their son would be a teenager and over the age limit for new appointees with their prospective sending organization. The family even spent a semester overseas in an internship as Ron was completing his degree and felt certain they were on a trajectory to move forward as long-term missionaries.

When they finally completed their medical exams, however, Ron was discovered to have a condition that would disqualify them from long-term service. Although his condition was not life-threatening and could be managed easily in his home country, the medication and necessary medical facilities would not be accessible in most countries overseas where missionaries were needed.

After all the family's effort to prepare for overseas service, they now were faced with the devastating news that this would not be possible because of Ron's condition. Ron, Rhonda, and their children were all crushed by the decision.

Ron's first reaction was one of shock. He was almost speechless for several minutes. Later the same day he called to ask how he could appeal the decision. Who could he convince to let them go? He managed to control his temper, but it was obvious that he was feeling both anger and hurt. He promised that he would take very good care of himself and follow all the medical advice to manage his condition. After all, he was doing very well with it at the time, so he felt he could also manage it overseas.

After several conversations, Ron and Rhonda finally began to see that this was not something that could be negotiated and reluctantly accepted the decision as final. For several months afterward, they questioned how they could have misunderstood God's will for their family, thinking they were called to a career as international missionaries. For the previous two years, the central focus of their lives had been preparing to live and work overseas. Now they were confronted with the need to re-evaluate their sense of call and determine how to interpret this to their friends and family along with the news that the future would not be as they had envisioned.

Not everyone who feels called to go can be sent. Good stewardship of resources both in the U.S. and on the field can sometimes require difficult decisions. To be effective on the field, missionaries need to be healthy in body, mind, and spirit.

The selection consultant or committee must ensure that there are no hindrances that can impede the potential missionary from realizing an effective and fruitful ministry. If the applicant is not found to be physically, emotionally, and spiritually healthy and mature, the only loving thing to do is to delay the process or, if there are insurmountable barriers, bring it to a halt. Saying "no" or "not now" if the timing is not right can be the most loving thing for all concerned including the applicant, the sending church and the team on the field.

Whether the answer is "no" or "not now," the missionary applicant will experience disappointment and some degree of grief. It might also be painful for you as the selection consultant or committee member, especially if you have worked with this applicant for any length of time and built a personal relationship. As painful as the decision might be, you can frame this as an opportunity to hear and learn from God. It is not simply a matter of putting a positive spin on a negative message. With assurance that God is in control, this can be a teachable moment to explore what it means for each individual or family unit to be obedient to the call of God, wherever He leads.

Barriers

Any number of barriers can slow the process or bring it to an end. The components mentioned in Chapter 3 provide a framework for examining each applicant's health and readiness to serve overseas. The list below is representative of the types of issues that could cause a delay or a non-negotiable closing of the application.

1. Maturity	
a. Spiritual maturity	See Chapter 4
b. Overall maturity	
2. Lack of adequate education or other qualifications	See Chapter 6
3. Medical deal breakers	See Chapter 8
4. Unresolved emotional wellness issues	See Chapter 9
a. Depression	
b. Emotional trauma	
c. Anxiety	
d. Anger	
e. Grief	
f. Personality disorders	
5. Lifestyle issues	See Chapter 9
a. Pornography	
b. Homosexuality	
1) Homosexual attraction or emotional entanglement	
2) Homosexual lifestyle or experience	
c. Abuse (as offender)	
d. Sexual offenses	
e. Substance abuse	
f. Divorce	
g. Adultery (including emotional affairs)	
h. Premarital sex	
i. Multiple sexual partners (whether while married or single)	

j. Masturbation (if habitual, associated with pornography or part of an unhealthy sexual mindset or lifestyle)	
k. Substance abuse (drug, alcohol, tobacco)	
l. Confused sexual identity	
m. Gambling addiction	
n. Debt	
6. Marital wellness issues	See Chapter 10
7. Children's issues	See Chapter 11
a. Teens or preteens	
b. Developmental or educational issues	
c. Custody issues	
d. Adoption/foster care issues	
8. Unresolved life experience issues	See Chapter 9
a. Unresolved family of origin issues	
1) Dysfunctional home	
2) Parents divorced	
3) Unhealthy relationship with parents/siblings	
b. Abortion	
c. Abuse	
1) Emotional	
2) Verbal	
3) Sexual (including rape or molestation)	
4) Physical	
d. Unresolved interpersonal issues	
1) Interpersonal conflict	
2) Unresolved hurt/anger/bitterness	
9. Expression of call	See Chapter 5
a. Unclear expressions of call	
b. Spouses not on the same page	
10. Lack of appropriate job match	See Chapters 7, 13

Often the problem will not be one single issue, but a constellation of issues that, when taken together, indicate the need to delay or close down the application. Some of these issues can be resolved with time and effort while others will be automatic deal breakers as determined by the policies of the sending church or agency. The interviewer should clearly communicate with the applicant if the issue is considered a permanent obstacle or something that can be corrected.

If it is not a permanent deal breaker, the applicant will need to know precisely what action to take, what specific changes must take place, and whether there is a clearly defined time limit. Even then, the interviewer must be very careful not to make promises. Instead, the applicant needs to understand that after any identified barriers have been addressed, it will be *possible* to re-engage the application process—barring any other unforeseen obstacles.

Involve the Team in the Decision

Sue Ann* appeared ready to move forward. She had met all the education requirements and was involved in a local, cross-cultural ministry. As the consultant learned more about her life history, however, he felt he should share the details of her application with the team of consultants. Sue Ann had only been a believer for three years. Before her dramatic conversion she had several life experiences that included alcohol, drugs, and a brief homosexual relationship as a college freshman. Sue Ann's consultant saw evidence that she was continuing to grow as a believer and felt that she was ready to go. She had been sober and drug free for three years, and it had been five years since her last sexual encounter.

Although all this was clearly in Sue Ann's past, when the team reviewed her application, there were concerns as to whether enough time had passed for her to develop the necessary emotional, spiritual, and character strength to withstand the stresses of cross-cultural adjustment. The team felt that more time would allow her to grow stronger and ultimately have a more effective ministry. The team agreed that Sue Ann should visit with a counselor to further assess her emotional and spiritual readiness and to ensure that there were no unresolved issues from her past.

After the counseling assessment and a year of intensive discipleship with a mentor, Sue Ann was able to move forward and had a fruitful first term on the field. Although she had been disappointed at having to delay going to the field, she later affirmed that the extra year of counseling and mentoring made a huge difference in her successful adjustment overseas.

Throughout the process it is important to maintain impartiality. It is always best that the decision to shut down or slow down an application be affirmed by a team, if possible. When communicating the decision, letting the applicant know that this was a team decision can help prevent accusations of bias and help the consultant or interviewer avoid becoming enmeshed in the individual's life.

Document, Document, Document

It is extremely important to document all conversations and correspondence with every applicant. You will want to keep an accurate record in case leadership requests a report on how the application was handled. If for any reason another consultant or team deals with this applicant in the future, having a record will help the selection team avoid having to cover the same ground again and ensure that any issues have been resolved in the intervening time.

How to Say "No" or "Not Now"

When possible, communicate the news in the most personal way possible. If a personal visit can be arranged on short notice, in most cases that is preferable. Skype video or telephone calls make it possible to share important non-verbal communication such as tone of voice and also allow for the immediate beginning stages of processing the shock of the unwelcomed news through dialogue. For married couples, make every effort to have both spouses present to receive the news together.

After the initial conversation, always follow up with an email confirming the conversation. In both the verbal and written communication, it is extremely important to be clear about the reasons the applicant cannot proceed in the selection process at this time. Consider writing the email before initiating the personal conversation. This will allow you to follow a script and stay on subject while talking and answering any initial questions. The email message can be tweaked or edited after the personal conversation and sent immediately afterward.

If possible, let the applicant know that "not now" does not necessarily mean "not ever." Give encouragement if there is any to be given. If there is hope for a possible reconsideration in the future, explain specifically what must change (such as gain more ministry experience, complete education requirements, address wellness issues, or make other changes) and define time frames if applicable.

At the same time, be clear that completing these assignments is no guarantee or promise of future appointment. Instead, let the applicant know that completing these assignments or meeting these conditions will open the door for re-engaging the application process. There could still be other barriers that are presently unforeseen.

Before communicating the "not now" message, consider all the known factors to help the applicant understand the requirements and conditions. In some cases, there might be mutually exclusive conditions that will prevent the applicant from moving forward in the future. For example, if the church or sending agency requires a certain number of years with no evidence of disease after a diagnosis of cancer, consider the ages that the applicants and their children will have reached by that time and also calculate the time for processing the application. If it will not be realistic to reapply at that time because of age limits having been passed, then say so.

Frame this as an opportunity to hear and learn from God. Emphasize the fact that God is still in control. Sometimes it is a matter of timing, as was the case for Abraham, Joseph, and Moses, each of whom had a call from God that was not fully realized for many years.

When the answer is a definite "no go" with the church or sending agency, provide assurance that other types of ministry might be open and the applicant should pursue these as God leads. Encourage the applicant to continue with active involvement in volunteer missions and mobilizing others to pray, give, and go. At the same time, be careful not to offer hope where there is none. Be clear if there is no possibility for future deployment.

Be sure to always close the interview with prayer. Ask God to continue to give peace and comfort as He shows this applicant what next steps He has in mind for him or her.

Recognize and Affirm the Stages of Grief and Disappointment

In the secular business world, job applicants often do not receive any notification of rejection. They simply are not invited to continue in the application process. In the application process for missionary service, however, the selection team has a responsibility as representatives of the body of Christ to help the applicant discern how God is leading in this unanticipated new direction.

When the answer is "no," the applicant will experience what amounts to the death of a dream or ambition. As in the experience of any loss by death, the stages of grief are likely to be felt:

1. Denial
2. Anger
3. Bargaining
4. Depression
5. Acceptance (Kübler-Ross)

Don't expect the applicant to go through these stages in a clean-cut, orderly fashion. Even a year or more after closing an application, emotions can resurface at any stage.

Do not allow a negative reaction to provoke a similar reaction in you as the consultant or representative of the church or sending agency. This might be the first time you are observing the individual under this level of stress, which often produces negative behaviors. Always respond with love, firmness, clarity, and acceptance. Sometimes a simple affirming statement such as, "I know this was not the news you were hoping to hear," can be helpful.

At the same time, *do not* say or even imply that you know exactly how they are feeling. Usually that is not of much help. Allow the applicants to express themselves without interrupting. Often a sympathetic listening ear can be the most effective tool to promote the beginning of a healing process.

In some cases there is an almost audible sigh of relief when the applicant receives the news that the process must come to an end. Some applicants take delight in telling family and friends that they are in the process of applying to go overseas as missionaries, but when the time seems to be drawing close, they "get cold feet" and almost seem to sabotage their own application. If you suspect this to be the case, however, it is better not to say anything like, "I have a feeling this is not such bad news to you." It might still be difficult for them to receive the news that this process is coming to a close and they will have to share the news with their family and friends. These people also need help framing how they will tell their story.

Communicating the News to Family, Friends and Church Leaders

As you coach applicants through the closing of the application, keep in mind the importance of future relationships with the applicant, the local church, and others who make up their support network. Assure the applicants that it is their responsibility to tell their own story. Encourage them to be truthful in their communication. In all cases, be sure to coach the applicants who are leaving the process to determine what and how they want to share with their family and friends. It is helpful to have the applicants identify a few people with whom they can share their most intimate thoughts and feelings. If they share with these people first, they are likely to receive wise counsel and to defuse some of the emotion of the initial communication.

When "No" or "Not Now" is Not Well-Received

The way a missionary applicant receives a delay can give valuable insight. Some applicants will not accept the news with grace. Some of these will exhaust every means possible exploring every avenue in their attempt to reverse the decision. If an applicant has a difficult time receiving "not now" for an answer beyond a reasonable point, there may be underlying emotional wellness issues that should be considered and dealt with before the applicant is allowed to resubmit his or her application.

While a normal grief response is to be expected, applicants who make threats, argue incessantly, or repeatedly try to call in "bigger guns" to defend their applications are giving evidence of deeper issues that need to be addressed, including the possibility of a personality disorder.

"If the applicant is so convinced of his call that he is not teachable or willing to submit to authority, there may be psychological or cultural agendas masquerading as call" (Andrews, Miller and Schubert, p. 231). A professional counseling assessment might be indicated in these cases before proceeding with the application.

These types of reaction are more common when the answer is a definite "no," requiring a firm and loving response. When following up with such individuals, always stay on topic and reiterate the original decision in a calm and loving manner, no matter what the reaction may be. The person will likely appeal the decision to other levels of leadership. You should be familiar with your church or organization's policies regarding appeals so that, if asked, you can inform the applicant of the appropriate persons to contact. The appropriate leaders should be well-informed and understand the nature of the decision so they can reiterate the same message to the applicant.

As a representative of the sending church or agency, you will be bound to maintain a high level of confidentiality, even if the rejected applicants do not tell the truth about why they were not able to move forward in the application process. Do not succumb to the temptation to "set the record straight" when an applicant appears to have distorted the truth about why he or she is leaving the application process.

When well-meaning friends or church leaders attempt to intervene on the applicant's behalf, keep in mind that maintaining confidentiality is not simply a legal responsibility. If the confidences that were shared in the interview process are broken or violated, word will soon spread and future applicants will not trust the confidentiality of the interviewers, undermining your ability to effectively assess any future applicants.

Responses to Common Questions or Reactions

The following are a few common reactions from applicants who have received the news that they will not be moving forward in the process toward appointment as missionaries. Below each question or statement are some suggested responses that might be helpful, although by no means are these intended to be formulaic.

"Why would God lead me down this path just to shut the door in my face?"

Assure the applicant that God is in control. Nothing ever catches Him by surprise. He has always had a plan from the past to the present that also includes the future. Sometimes He gets us moving in a direction so He can show us something we could not have seen or understood from our previous vantage point.

"Why didn't you tell me this sooner?"

Affirm that you could not have addressed the issue until you became aware of it. The nature of the application process does not allow everything to be covered all at once. That is the reason we gather as much information as we can through multiple means and over a period of time. As soon as we became aware of this issue we addressed it. If something was missed earlier, then apologize appropriately, but the facts that led to the decision remain.

"Is there anything I can do to change your mind?"

Let the applicant know that the decision was not made by one person and was not made in a vacuum. The team has already prayerfully reviewed the information and is united in this decision.

"But I heard about another applicant with the same situation who is on the field now."

Just as you regard this applicant's information as confidential, insist that there might be more to the other person's story as well. If the other person was already on the field, then that could also be different than sending a new missionary with the same unresolved issues. Do not allow yourself to be drawn into an argument or discussion about another case. You might say, "I don't know about that case" or simply, "I really can't discuss that situation. Given the reality of *this* situation, we will not be able to move forward with your application at this time." Stay focused on the decision and where the applicant goes from here.

"I am sorry now that I was honest on my application. If I had not shared this we would be moving forward and no one would know the difference."

Remind the applicant that he or she would know and God would know. It is far better for this to come out now than for it to surface under stressful conditions overseas.

"Everyone we have talked to is in agreement that we are absolutely called to be missionaries. We met the leaders of your organization at a missions conference, and they told us we were the kind of folks you are looking for. How can you now tell us no?"

Emphasize that the missionary call is a call to obedience. Affirm the applicant's willingness to be obedient to the call. For some to go, others must be willing to stay. Familiarity with the selection process will help this applicant to be a more effective mobilizer, calling others to pray, give, and go.

Consider also the fact that the world today is much more mobile. It is not difficult to identify and engage people from other cultures, languages, and ethnicities without moving overseas. This does not excuse all of us from going. It does, however, provide an opportunity for those who cannot go to be involved in sharing the gospel with individuals from every language, people, tribe, and nation wherever we encounter them. Help this applicant to focus on the broader picture to discover how God might use this circumstance to reveal other means of obeying the Great Commission.

"Perhaps we should try going with another agency."

Assure the applicant that your desire is to help applicants and their families discern and follow the will of God. Although your team is convinced that the timing is not right for this applicant to go with this agency at this time, the sending agency or church you represent certainly is not the exclusive agent of the Holy Spirit. Affirm that if the applicant is convinced this is the irrevocable will of God, then he or she should pursue that.

Conclusion

Regardless of the reasons leading to the decision, when the answer is anything other than "Yes, you are ready to go," missionary applicants often need help to discover how God wants to grow them through this experience. As a representative of the sending church or agency, you can help applicants who are not ready to go to hear and learn from God as they seek to be obedient wherever He leads—even if it is not overseas at this time.

Suggested Resources

Resources for applicants as they complete requirements or consider the need to pursue a new and different career path:

Alan, Hillary (2013). *Sent: How One Ordinary Family Traded the American Dream for God's Greater Purpose.* Colorado Springs: WaterBrook Press.

International Centre for Excellence in Leadership (2004). *Explore,* http://www.icelonline.com/Explore Richmond, VA: International Mission Board.

Sills, M. David (2008). *The Missionary Call: Find Your Place in God's Plan For the World.* Chicago: Moody Press.

Resources for the selection team:

Powell, John R. and Joyce M. Bowers (1999). *Enhancing Missionary Vitality: Mental Health Professionals Serving Global Mission*. Minneapolis: Mission Training International.

Works cited

Leslie Andrews, Carl Miller, and Esther Schubert (1999). "The Call: Psychological, Cultural and Spiritual" in John R. Powell and Joyce M. Bowers, Enhancing Missionary Vitality. Minneapolis: Mission Training International.

Elisabeth Kübler-Ross (1969), *On Death and Dying*. New York: Scribner.

About the Authors

Larry and Susan Gay have served as IMB missionaries for 24 years in Latin America, five years in Asia and five years with the personnel selection team. Susan is currently the Member Care Consultant for the Personnel Selection Team. Larry is Personnel Development Consultant and Coach in the Office of Global Personnel.

Larry received the Doctor of Educational Ministry from New Orleans Baptist Theological Seminary, the Master of Arts in Missiology from Southwestern Baptist Theological Seminary, and the Bachelor of Music Education from Samford University. Susan received the Master of Arts in Marriage and Family Counseling from New Orleans Baptist Theological Seminary and the Bachelor of Arts in Psychology and Sociology from Samford University.

Larry and Susan have been married since 1973 and have three grown sons, one daughter-by-marriage and three grandchildren.

16

Discipling a Congregation to be "Missionary Material"
by Caleb Crider

One thing is clear from Jesus' final words on earth before He ascended into heaven: God's people are to make disciples of all nations (Matthew 28:18-20). Disciple-making is more than just one of several important tasks for us to complete; it is the very mission of the church.

A disciple is a learner. Jesus modeled discipleship for us by calling a ragtag bunch of roughnecks from around Galilee to follow Him. He taught them by sharing life with them. Discipleship didn't happen all at once, but as they walked, talked, fellowshipped, and ministered alongside Him, the disciples learned how to think and act like Jesus. Clearly, "making disciples" is a process. We meet people where they are—hopeless, sinful, and rebellious—and encourage them toward maturity in Christ.

This process can be messy at times. When we share the good news of justification through faith (Romans 3:22) with others, we share news that is at once both supremely good and very bad. The Son of God doesn't just call us to accept the gift of salvation, He calls us to suffer and die for His sake (Matthew 16:24-26). This isn't an easy sell. This gospel offends people at every level and insults our pride (1 Corinthians 1:18). Most of those who hear our message do not believe it (Matthew 7:13). Those who do are often subject to ridicule, isolation, or worse. Making disciples is no easy task.

We recognize that discipleship includes much more than evangelism. In many ways, a person coming to faith in Christ is only the beginning of the discipleship process. And so we develop plans and systems to help us accomplish that second part of the Great Commission, "teaching them to observe everything I have commanded you" (Matthew 28:20a). But what is the goal? When can a person be considered a disciple? When is our work as disciple-makers complete?

Many seem to answer these questions with a vague notion of spiritual maturity. They consider a person discipled once he or she reaches a certain level of personal holiness, religious discipline, or biblical knowledge. Certainly there are benchmarks in the process of becoming a disciple that serve as indicators of the inward change that Jesus brings, but a biblical perspective on discipleship must consider Christ's example with the Twelve: the goal of discipleship is to produce earthly ambassadors for the kingdom of God.

After life among His disciples for three years, the resurrected Jesus ascended into heaven. But He left them with clear instructions: "But you shall receive power when the Holy Spirit has come upon you; and you shall be witnesses to Me in Jerusalem, and in all Judea and Samaria, and to the end of the earth" (Acts 1:8). This commissioning revealed the purpose for the instruction the Teacher had given to His students. The reason Jesus made these disciples was to prepare them for His mission.

Christ calls us to a salvation that isn't very safe at all. He doesn't just gather us to worship Him. He sends us like lambs among wolves. Just like the Original Twelve, it is only when we surrender our very lives to follow Him on His mission that we truly have fellowship with God. The mission of God is to redeem all of creation to its rightful place of worshipping Him, and the church is God's mechanism for accomplishing that mission. It is the factory that makes missionaries who are equipped for and devoted to the work of making disciples across social, geographic, and linguistic barriers. The church cannot, therefore, be content to raise up two or three "missionaries" to send to the nations. It must disciple the entire body to be a pool of candidates, qualified and equipped for God's mission.

Missionary Material

Surely diverse types of service in different parts of the world require unique skills, qualifications, and commitments. But since the goal of discipleship is preparation for mission, there is a general level of knowledge and experience that serves as the foundation for service anywhere. For disciple-makers, these are the benchmarks, the indicators of readiness for kingdom service. These foundational concepts prepare sent ones for the challenges they face at home and abroad, as they go into spiritually dangerous places and take the gospel to people who do not know it.

A church made up of believers who are "missionary material" provides a foundation that prepares its people for service. This training gives them the courage to face the challenges of ministry and the faith to obey God every step of the way. But what does this foundation consist of? What are the essential elements of discipleship that will ultimately result in a body of believers who are equipped and prepared for God's mission, regardless of where He may send?

In order to disciple our churches into missionary material, we need to focus our efforts toward the development of these characteristics: sound doctrine, good stewardship, and devotion to a missional lifestyle.

Sound Doctrine

The first mark of a disciple who is equipped for mission is right doctrine. Knowledge of the scriptures provides the foundation of belief that informs our words and deeds. Our understanding of the Bible serves as the lens through which we view the world. This is true of entire congregations as well. Doctrine is the "knowledge of the Son of God" that prevents our churches from being "tossed to and fro and carried about with every wind of doctrine, by the trickery of men, in the cunning craftiness of deceitful plotting" (Ephesians 4:13-14).

In his second letter to Timothy, Paul reminds the young pastor to "hold fast the pattern of sound words which you have heard from me" (2 Timothy 1:13a). This was the readily reproducible foundation of sound biblical doctrine with which Paul had discipled Timothy. This set of basic doctrines was what had prepared Timothy for ministry, and it was all that he needed to sustain him throughout that work. Right doctrine ensures that sent ones know the King and represent Him well.

God has revealed Himself through the scriptures, and as missionary people, we must commit ourselves to knowing and doing the Word of God. Sound doctrine is a system of belief that is firmly rooted in scripture. It includes the basic understanding that God is holy and just, that we are sinful and hopeless, and that Jesus died on behalf of the nations so that we all can be reconciled to God. Our foundation for these teachings is not human wisdom or tradition but the true Word of God. In order to ensure that our people are missionary material, four beliefs are of particular importance: the gospel, salvation in Christ alone, salvation by grace alone, and the doctrine of the church.

The Gospel

At the heart of sound doctrine is the gospel, the good news that God has made provision for humanity though the substitutionary sacrifice of his Son, Jesus. And this earth-shattering news was designed to be shared. It is God's counter-intuitive strategy for making His glory known among all the peoples of the earth. And yet many Christians— people who have professed faith in Christ—are unable to articulate this simple truth.

God's people must understand and be able to communicate the basic tenets of the Christian faith in order to make disciples. The gospel message is, by its very nature, offensive to those who hear it. People take issue with its insistence that we are slaves to sin and enemies of God. They are put off by its declaration that we are powerless to change our spiritual condition. Many don't like its exclusive focus on the life, death, and resurrection of Jesus. They're offended by a message that insists that the center of all things is the Creator and not us.

Yet how many people never have the opportunity even to be offended by the gospel? How will they call on Jesus if they've never heard of Him (Romans 10:13-17)? As God's people, we have been sent to proclaim and live out the good news among the nations.

Christians need to be trained to share their faith well. But in attempts to make it easier to share and more palatable to the world, the message is often reduced to propositional bullet points. The professionalization of ministry saw people raised up as experts in preaching the gospel, and believers everywhere gave up even trying to share the good news. They instead exchanged it for a kinder, gentler message of God's love divorced from God's wrath. Somewhere along the way, "come to Jesus" became "come to church," and a generation of people was indirectly taught that as long as they were good people who went to church, they would be OK with God.

"Come to church," (along with "be a good person" and "stop sinning") is, of course, a false gospel. Rather than glorifying God as the only means of our salvation, it points to outward human behavior as somehow being able to make us right with God. Yet for many church-going people, these have replaced the bold and offensive message of the gospel.

The responsibility for teaching the gospel to God's people falls squarely upon church leadership. The church that does not regularly hear the gospel proclaimed through teaching will quickly forget it. In order to make missionary material of God's people, the gospel must be taught and taught again: people are estranged from God due to their sin and they need the Savior to pay for their transgressions and reunite them with the Father. This is done through child-like faith and a turning away from sin (repentance).

Exclusivity of Christ

If the gospel is the center of our theological understanding, the exclusivity claims of Christ are the columns that support it. This refers to those biblical assertions that make the way of Jesus incompatible with other systems of faith. Specifically, these claims assume that salvation comes 1) in Christ alone, 2) by grace alone, and 3) through faith alone.

In order to make disciples across cultures, a missionary must understand and believe that salvation is only in Christ. The scriptures declare that "there is no other name under heaven given among men by which we must be saved" (Acts 4:12b). If this point is lost, the result is syncretism, the blending of Christ and His teachings into existing religious systems. If anyone is to follow Jesus, he must forsake all other gods and orient his life around the Most High God. If there were hope for others outside of the righteousness of Jesus, the missionary would have no reason to leave his home to carry the message to others.

A great way to transmit this teaching to a church body is by routinely identifying the idols we tend to worship. While the word "idol" may typically bring to mind carved statues for primitive people, an idol is actually anything other than God that we might be tempted to orient our lives around. What are those things—the people, systems, and structures—that we turn to in our search for salvation, righteousness, or comfort? These are our idols and they are powerless to save us. Identifying these things as idols allows us to contrast these finite, powerless, created things with the infinite, all-powerful Creator. Making this a regular practice helps equip our people to do the same regardless of their mission field.

By Grace Alone

Another key doctrine for mission work is that of salvation by grace alone. Humans can never be good enough to deserve God's forgiveness and all of the benefits it brings. This truth stands in direct opposition to the teachings of most world religions, which tend to emphasize the value of good deeds in determining one's standing with God (or, in some cases, with the universe). An equipped ambassador of the kingdom understands that there is nothing a person can do to be made right with the Creator and that there is hope in Jesus alone. Despite our hopeless condition, Christ is the way sin-filled humans can be justified before God. This is made possible through repentance and faith, the sincere act of placing complete trust in Jesus as Savior.

The reason this doctrine is of particular importance for the missionary is that it clearly distinguishes our faith from the self-righteousness pursued by adherents of the world's religious systems. Salvation by grace is very good news, but it's a foreign concept to most people. We naturally want to work to earn (or at least pay for) our salvation. When missionaries lose the doctrine of salvation by grace alone, the gospel they plant will be a false one.

In order to extend this truth across an entire church, we must fight the pattern of performance. When a church measures the commitment of its people by clocking the hours spent doing church activities, we inadvertently communicate that our behavior does anything to secure our salvation. The church that makes missionary material is the church that celebrates what Christ has done more than it celebrates what His people do.

The Church

The fourth vital doctrine for the missionary has to do with sound ecclesiology. A missionary makes disciples across cultural boundaries. This should result in churches being planted. In order to plant new churches, the missionary must know what a church is and how it should function.

Christian missionaries have a tendency to evaluate churches according to their own experience. This makes sense because most of those we send out grew up in our churches. Being products of the environments in which they were discipled, the missionaries we send tend to plant churches that look a lot like the churches they were used to back home. The result is Western-style churches in non-Western contexts.

So today you can find people on every continent who worship in dedicated buildings on Sunday morning, sitting in rows facing a pulpit, and singing 18th-century European songs accompanied by a piano and organ. These stylistic choices were made by the Western missionaries who started these churches and do a great deal of harm to the indigeneity of the local church.

We see this in local churches in the West: Christians whose previous experiences (both good and bad) shape their expectations for their church today. This problem is only made worse by the church that caters to the comforts and preferences of its people. You can't treat people like consumers and spectators and expect them to act like ministers and ambassadors.

What is a healthy theology of church? As outlined in scripture, a New Testament church is a local congregation (1 Corinthians 1:2) of baptized believers who covenant together for fellowship (Acts 2:41-42), teaching (2 Timothy 3:16), worship and prayer (Ephesians 5:19), service, and mission (Hebrews 10:24). It has identifiable leaders; it administers baptism and the Lord's Supper; the members meet regularly. These are the universal functions of a local church. They are practiced by all Christian churches everywhere.

What a church should *look like*, however, depends largely upon the culture in which it's been planted. It is vital that people of every tribe, tongue, and nation have in their midst a church that models for them what their lives would look like if they were in Christ. So we see that a church must meet regularly, but how, when, and where they meet should reflect the rhythms of the local culture. Churches must worship, but we do this in a way that redeems the customs of cultures that have been used to worship lesser things than the Most High God.

A church can teach its people to hold loosely to its cultural expression of church by exploring various other cultural practices. A primarily white congregation could learn much by a visit to a predominantly black church on a Sunday morning. Worshipping with an underground house church in East Asia will quickly reveal the cultural influences in our own worship. When we're able to see fellowship, teaching, worship and prayer, service, and mission in an environment that is quite different from our own, we can begin to distinguish between the biblical marks of a healthy church and our cultural versions of it.

Stewardship

A second mark of a disciple prepared for mission is stewardship. Simply put, stewardship is the right management of things, relationships, roles, and responsibilities. In the life of a believer on mission, stewardship can make the difference between an effective gospel witness and an ineffective one. When outsiders look at our lives, they should see that we hold things in a correct order that glorifies God by putting Him first. It is the responsibility of the church to lead its people to be good stewards of all that they have.

From the world's perspective, a person is the owner of all his possessions. If someone were to receive the gift of a sweater from a friend, the person would be considered the owner of that sweater. But in God's economy, people aren't owners of material goods, but merely stewards. Our treasures are stored up in heaven, not on this earth (Matthew 6:19-21). Seen in this light, the things we have are not our own. They have only been entrusted to us for a while. We must therefore glorify the Giver by stewarding them well.

Everything we have comes from God (Psalm 24:1). We know that He is the Creator, Sustainer, and Owner of all things (Acts 17:24-28). So our relationship with things reflects our utter dependence upon God to provide all that we need (2 Peter 1:3). By acknowledging the temporal nature of physical things, we point the world to the One who sustains us.

When we see ourselves as merely stewards, we open ourselves up to accountability in how we manage all that we've been given. It would be terribly rude for someone to accuse you of mismanaging your own car, for example. But from one borrower of a car to another, we might accept helpful advice for how to best take care of that car. So it is with God's people. We encourage one another toward good stewardship of all that has been entrusted to us, and we hold each other accountable to maintain a right relationship with all we have.

Because of their importance to daily life on mission, the challenges of stewardship in three key areas are especially significant for God's people: finances, family, and time.

1. Finances

Good stewardship of finances entails staying out of debt, living within our means, saving responsibly, and giving generously. When we as God's people manage our money in this way, we can approach even major financial decisions (such as raising funds or moving abroad) with confidence, knowing that our stewardship won't negatively impact our freedom to pick up and go. Good money management is all the more important when it comes to dealing with money that others have sacrificially given in support of our ministries.

A church can lead its people into good financial stewardship by providing regular practical workshops to teach the skill. There are a number of good books on the subject, and often the best way to teach good financial stewardship is to invite those who are particularly good at handling money to advise those who may not be (Titus 2:1-15). A pastor must not shy away from speaking about the importance of tithes and offerings, and must practice transparency with the church's financial dealings. Such an environment is fertile soil for raising up missionary people who are empowered, not encumbered, by financial stewardship.

2. Family

Of course, stewardship extends beyond finances. God's people have been blessed with families that we've likewise been told to manage well. If we're making mission-ready people, we must lead them to manage their households well (1 Timothy 3:4). Scripture is full of commands for the Christian family: married people must be faithful to their spouses, children should obey their parents, and all are to give themselves to purity and personal holiness. But all of these relationships are guided by a single overarching principle: that we love one another (John 13:34-35).

If you want to see whether a family is ready for missionary service, observe how they interact with one another. A family that is constantly bickering and arguing with one another in the comforts of their own home culture will be far worse in a foreign one.

3. Time

Perhaps the most neglected area for instruction in stewardship is that of time. Due to cultural differences in time orientation, time management can be especially difficult on the mission field. A family should be equipped to use time wisely and to live in the knowledge that we never know how much time we will have (Ephesians 5:15). In mission, this fact is usually expressed in the desire for an "exit strategy." This means simply that upon arrival on the mission field, we say "hello" with "goodbye" in mind.

As with finances and family stewardship, time management is best taught by walking alongside a wise and godly friend. We recommend that any church desiring to disciple its people to be missionary material provide ample opportunity for younger disciples to spend time with more mature believers.

A Missional Lifestyle

The old adage is true: if a person doesn't live on mission at home, he will not live on mission elsewhere, no matter where he goes. Moving into a tiny apartment in a global mega-city filled with unbelieving people of a distant culture will not make one suddenly change into a selfless, gospel proclaiming, cross-cultural missionary. In fact, we've seen the opposite to be true: someone who is not committed to thinking and acting like a missionary at home will be a poorer missionary outside his comfort zone. "Past behavior," my friend and colleague, Larry McCrary is fond of saying, "is the best indicator of future performance."

If you want to raise up a church that is equipped and ready for mission among the nations, you simply must foster an environment where a missional lifestyle is valued and celebrated, where being on mission is the measure of Christian obedience. When your people know the gospel and hold firmly to it, when they study culture and become familiar with the bridges and barriers to the gospel, when they make it a matter of habit to make disciples, then they are truly ready for service anywhere the Spirit leads.

You probably already know who the missional members of your church are. They're the ones who know their neighbors. They sometimes miss a church event in order to accept an invitation to a friend's birthday party or to help plant community gardens. They intentionally live where change is happening in order to represent Jesus in the process.

The funny thing is that our process for reproducing this sort of missional mentality often undermines our efforts. We tend to take people off the "front lines" of ministry in order to have them teach seminars, write books, and lead groups. A better way to make more missional people is to send people to spend time with the practitioners in real life. It's the teacher/learner partnership model that Paul practiced when he took Silas, Timothy, and others along on his missionary endeavors. There is no better way to teach someone to be on mission than to have them spend significant time with a missionary. And as people develop this missional lifestyle, they'll grow in the areas of evangelism, social skills, initiative, and holiness.

Witness in Word and Deed

Scripture shows us that there are two parts to being a witness: presence and proclamation. On one side, we understand that an absent witness is no witness at all. Jesus set the example of gospel presence when He humbled Himself and took on the likeness of man (Philippians 2:5-11). It was this act of incarnation—putting on flesh—that brought a distant God near to us. In assuming the frailty of humanity, Jesus showed us a side of God that we could relate to. This is the place of the missionary: living among those who don't know God in order that they might know Him and worship Him as Lord. Right doctrine and right living places God's people in a position to be scrutinized by those outside the kingdom.

The other side of our witness is proclamation: what we say to others about Jesus. Actions alone will not bring others to saving knowledge of Christ. It isn't enough for us to have witnessed the glory of God. We must point others to it. This requires that we verbally communicate the good news in order for people to be saved (Romans 10:14-17).

A church can develop both presence and proclamation among members by intentionally living among unbelievers. Christians in the West often find themselves living in seclusion from non-Christians. When the majority of social time is spent with believers, Christ-followers can fall out of practice when it comes to being a witness. But when God's people deliberately live among those who do not know Him, we quickly become accustomed to the challenges of living differently and boldly proclaiming the gospel. The best way to do this is in groups. The scriptures say that the world will know us by the love we have for one another (John 13:35), and there's no better way for them to see that love than by sharing life with God's people.

People Skills

We also need to look beyond the strategic skills of gospel communication and biblical instruction and consider the role of interpersonal skills. The church's task in God's mission is to make disciples, and discipleship is a relationship. As God's sent ones, we must be able to interact in meaningful ways, and often with people who are very different from us. We must, therefore, equip our people to be good at relating to others.

Some churches have recognized the need to teach their people basic social skills, like looking people in the eye, remembering someone's name, or using good manners. Being a good guest or a thoughtful host is at the heart of our interaction with those who do not know Christ; yet, churches rarely teach these things as a part of basic discipleship. In an age when we're more comfortable tapping out messages on our phones, it may be wise to spend time teaching people how to make small talk, ask probing questions, and focus in conversation.

Initiative

Another key indicator of mission-readiness is the ability to start something. A good missionary is an initiator, someone who takes the gospel where it isn't, starts conversations, and takes it upon himself to make disciples who form churches. Someone who has no experience initiating outreach in his own culture will find it even more difficult to do across great cultural barriers.

We shouldn't all expect to be "church planters" in the popular sense of the term, but at the very least, our response to the gospel should be to proclaim it where it isn't being proclaimed. Often our initiative is nothing more than responding to what God is already doing. In order to equip God's people to be movement-starters, churches must press them into the practice of beginning things: conversations, relationships, discipleship, and churches.

A great way to teach people to start something is to have them actually start something. The key is to begin with something simple: asking a question that gets people thinking, praying for someone, inviting someone for coffee. Jesus modeled this for us when He asked the woman at the well for a cup of water (John 4:7), or when He invited Himself over to Zacchaeus' house for dinner (Luke 19:5). For a sent one, these are the rhythms that become second nature. For a church trying to prepare sent ones, they are the baby steps that build runners' legs.

Holiness

Perhaps the most important area for a mission mentality is that of personal holiness. When a believer is on mission, his holiness can support or undermine his message. The world, as they say, is watching us, and unrepentant and persisting sin will disqualify one from ministry by dishonoring the One who sent us.

To be holy means to be "set apart" for a purpose. God's people are to be a holy people (1 Peter 1:16), different from the rest in order to represent Him (Leviticus 20:26). Mission-ready people are holy people: not perfect, but set apart by their justification in Christ. Spiritually, we are covered by Christ's death and resurrection, which atone for our sins and make us holy. But we live as already-but-not-yet-saved people, free from sin but nevertheless wrestling with it.

Most churches have some plan to move people toward holiness. Many teach spiritual disciplines. Others set up accountability groups in order for their people to spur one another on in personal holiness. No matter how this is done, a church that sets out to make missionary material of its people must actively seek to raise the level of spiritual maturity and holiness of the entire church body.

On a practical level, spiritual discipline provides a sent one with the tools necessary for "life and godliness" along the way (2 Peter 1:3). For example, a believer who is devoted to reading scripture will know the source of truth when sent to live among those who do not know truth. The one who has memorized scripture will be especially equipped to discern good from evil and avoid sin (Matthew 4:1-11), having hidden God's Word in his heart (Psalm 119:11). A disciplined Christ-follower knows to flee temptation (2 Timothy 2:22) and to avoid the appearance of evil (whatever that may be in the various cultures in which we may find ourselves) (1 Thessalonians 5:22). These patterns of personal holiness put God's ambassadors in a position to represent Him well.

Conclusion

The church is God's mechanism for making ambassadors for Christ. We typically call this process "discipleship," but churches sometimes stop short in equipping people for mission. A church that takes seriously its role in God's global mission won't be content to wait until God calls out two or three from its midst. It will disciple an entire congregation to be prepared for missionary service wherever God leads them.

Acts 13 is known for the account of Paul and Barnabas being sent out from the church at Antioch. We may be tempted to overlook the way the passage begins.

> Now in the church that was at Antioch there were certain prophets and teachers: Barnabas, Simeon who was called Niger, Lucius of Cyrene, Manaen who had been brought up with Herod the tetrarch, and Saul. As they ministered to the Lord and fasted, the Holy Spirit said, "Now separate to Me Barnabas and Saul for the work to which I have called them." Then, having fasted and prayed, and laid hands on them, they sent them away (Acts 13:1-3).

To set the scene for the sending of these missionaries, Luke, the author of the book of Acts, lists the members of the church who were qualified and spiritually mature ("prophets and teachers"). The picture here is of a group of prepared, equipped disciples, ready to serve at the bidding of the Holy Spirit. This should inspire those of us who lead our churches on mission to be proactive and intentional about discipling our people to be a ready reserve of missionary material.

When we are faithful to train the saints in the work of ministry, to build up the body of Christ (Ephesians 4:12), we follow Jesus' model of teaching fishermen to fish for men (Matthew 4:19). Missionary skills should not be reserved for only the few who are called out from among us. They should be part of basic discipleship for all of God's people everywhere.

About the Author

Caleb has an MA in Intercultural Studies from Golden Gate Baptist Theological Seminary. The Criders served with the IMB for seven years as church planting missionaries in Spain. They then returned to the U.S. to found The Upstream Collective, a network of missional churches. He also co-authored *Tradecraft: For The Church On Mission*. He is now IMB's Director of Church Training, where he teaches and develops curriculum for church-based missions education. Caleb is married to Lindsey and has two children, Jonas and Meredith.

17

Developing a Sending Church
by Eric King

I was heading to a small city whose name I couldn't pronounce, much less tell you where it was. We were going to an interior location to help plant a church where there were very few Christians. As happens with traveling internationally, we had already had a tiring day with delayed flights, special attention from airport security, several connections, and immigration. We were finally boarding our last flight to take us to our final destination. That was the good news.

The bad news was that as I looked out on the tarmac, I saw our awaiting chariot. Our next ride was a tiny turbo prop plane being flown by a guy who looked too young to drive, much less fly a plane. We reluctantly loaded the plane and prayed we would survive. The flight was unnervingly bumpy and felt like a kite on the end of the string swaying back and forth in the wind. My greatest attention, however, was given to the great view of the spinning prop, which I unceasingly prayed would stay attached, and not come directly toward my head.

After what seemed like an intercontinental flight, the pilot's voiced announced something in Portuguese that I obviously didn't understand, and we instantly began to descend—which I assumed meant we were soon landing. To say the landing erased all of my previous apprehensions about this flight would be an outright lie. We rocked to and fro until the wheels finally hit, and I do mean *hit*, the ground. We had survived!

I think we ran out to escape the tiny plane as we headed toward the airport that looked more like a bus stop. Immediately small kids rushed around us, excitedly telling us of things we totally didn't understand. As we waited for the workers to hand carry our luggage to us, a young man approached us and repeatedly asked, "Right place? ... right place? ... right place?" We were sure we had to be in the "right place" because it's where the airplane took us.

After we tried our best to tell him where we thought we were heading, he finally said, "No, you wrong place!" Fear, nothing but fear, totally overtook us. Where were we? How were we going to get to where we were supposed to be? I'm not sure I've ever felt more lost! We looked out in terror to see if our plane was still on the tarmac and sure enough, not only was it there but the pilot was out of the plane waving us back. No one had told us that this plane made multiple stops like a city bus! We had mistakenly thought that we were at the right destination.

A Church on Mission—A Sending Church

Knowing your final destination is an important element for any trip. Without knowing where you are and where you are heading, you'll never have clarity on next steps in the journey. So what is the final destination of a church on mission with God? How will you know when you have gotten there? What will be celebrated?

In this chapter we will define the final destination for a church on mission with God as a sending church. We will discuss both the end vision of a church and pathways for getting there. Having traveled over much of the U.S. helping pastors and church leaders engage in global missions, I have discovered there are many misconceived ideas about the end destination. It might be easier to define a sending church by first dispelling some commonly believed myths.

Myth #1: Missions is a Department of the Church

In many churches today you find missions relegated to a cold, dark, boring Sunday School room down in the dungeon of the church facility, filled with a group of mission junkies who "do" missions for the church. They decide where the money will be sent and try to come up with some ideas to get others in the church off of their seats and into the community to do something good.

I remember a conversation I had about global missions with a pastor in Alabama. As I expressed God's desire for every church to engage in global missions, his response was "Yeah, we have a team that does that."

If missions is a department or committee of the church, then what would you call the other activities of the church?

Myth Busted: Missions is the reason local churches exist.

Every church activity should be for the sake of making disciples who will then in turn make disciples until the gospel has been proclaimed to all nations. Scripture clearly defines Jesus' expectations of His church as He has called us to make disciples among all nations. This includes both sharing the gospel with those who haven't heard and teaching them to follow after Jesus, becoming more like Him. This is our one and only mission. It includes making disciples in our immediate context to sending members out to make disciples among the nations (Matthew 28:18-20). Missions is the mission of church. It is the very reason Jesus established His church.

Myth #2: Missions Isn't for Everyone

"What a relief that only those feeling a unique call have to do the mission thing." I even heard a pastor say one time that he didn't like another pastor and he hoped God would make that pastor's kids go to the mission field. It's almost as if we view those being called to missions like outcasts who've been banished to a remote land. This myth states that some do missions while the others stay home, do church, and join in local ministries.

Myth Busted: Every believer has a role in global missions.

Let's look at God's Word for the truth that busts this myth.
- All of us as Christians are not at home in this world. We are no longer of this world but are citizens of a heavenly kingdom (John 15:19, Philippians 3:20, Hebrews 11:13-16, 1 Peter 2:11).

- All followers of Jesus have been sent and commissioned by Jesus (John 20:21, John 17:18, Acts 1:8, Matthew 28:18-20).
- Missions is part of our new identity in Christ (2 Corinthians 5:14-21, 2 Corinthians 4:7-12).
- Making disciples is the mission and every Christian has been called to make disciples (Matthew 28:18-20).

Every regenerate member of every local church has been sent to this world to proclaim the gospel and to make disciples who make disciples. A sending church will disciple, equip, and commission each believer to live out this identity, no matter where God might send him or her. This is the reason for which God created us and saved us. Allowing believers to live outside of this truth is to rob them of the joy found in living out God's mission.

Myth #3: Missions Starts Local before Going Global

"There are so many in our own city who are lost and haven't heard the gospel. How can we fly to the other side of the world and ignore the thousands all around us?" "Our country used to be a Christian nation; we have to win it back for the hope of global evangelization. Let's get our act together locally. Then we can figure out how to go to other countries."

Myth Busted: The mission of every local church is a global mission.

It is true that every local church should be passionately pursuing local and national mission. It would be disobedient to do otherwise. But this vision is way too small in light of God's global mission. From the beginning, scripture makes it clear that God desires His glory to be made known to all nations (Genesis 12:1-3, Psalm 96, Acts 1:8, Revelation 7:9). So often, churches use Acts 1:8 as a framework for their mission strategy, aligning their activities into local, national, and international categories. While this is not inappropriate, we may miss without further examination the intended message of this passage.

Using Acts 1:8 as a lens through which to view the rest of the book of Acts, we will see it as a synopsis of how God intended to use His church, empowered by His Spirit to proclaim the gospel to all nations. Acts 1:8 simply restated the eternal purpose of God to make His name known and to redeem a people for Himself among all nations. His mission remains unchanged. Every local church is to join God in this mission globally.

Myth #4: Missions Can Be Performed by Osmosis

I've never actually heard this myth stated, but I've seen so many live as if it is their belief. "Surely, if we can make people like us, then they will want to come to Jesus. So let's smile and be kind to everyone we encounter. Let's be positive and encouraging. If we can do enough good deeds then the lost will want to join us. We enjoy helping people so let's work together to end poverty, address social ills, and share all the blessings that God has given us."

Myth Busted: The message of the gospel is the only hope for the broken.

Yes, of course we should be kind, generous, and care for the marginalized, but missions is much more than this. So often we attempt to separate gospel proclamation and demonstration. The thought is that some can proclaim while others lean more toward demonstration. Let's be honest; this is not even biblically logical. As followers of Jesus who are being conformed to His image, caring for others is an outflow, a natural result. It's an example of works fueled by our faith (James 2:14-26), an expression of who we are in Christ (Galatians 5:22-23). It is assumed. But once again, missions requires more than that. Paul tells us in Romans 10 that the gospel is the hope of all who are lost, but they can believe only if someone proclaims and they HEAR. He goes on to tell us that "faith comes by hearing" (Romans 10:17). As a sending church, we must understand that outside of the transformative power of the gospel, people are destined to current and eternal separation from God (Ephesians 2:1-10, Colossians 1:21-22).

Myth #5: Missions is Only an Obligation or a Duty

"Thank God for those who make the sacrifice to be missionaries. It's a tough calling and requires them to give up so much! Even those of us who stay behind are obligated to live out missions because God commanded it and so many are lost. Mission is a drag, but surely God will reward us one day in heaven."

Myth Busted: Joy is found in a life on mission.

While we are obligated to Christ's mission because He has commanded us to go, there is no greater joy that can be found than in a life obediently on mission with God. There are no promises of comfort or safety, but we can be sure that as we take steps of obedience, Jesus is walking right beside us. He told us in context of His mission that "I am with you always" (Matthew 28:20). A life on mission is a life in step with our Creator, Redeemer, and Lord.

Paul tells us in Ephesians 3:1 that he was made a minister of the gospel in an act of grace. Think about it: God has not only saved us, but He has also given us a new purpose. That is an act of grace! In 2 Corinthians 5:20 we are called ambassadors of Christ. That is not a position of drudgery but of incredible esteem. We have been made representatives of the one true, good, sovereign King of kings. Mission is duty? Absolutely not. Delight? Most definitely!

The End in View

Seeing the end destination helps us understand the pathways so we can lead our churches in getting there. By dispelling some commonly believed myths, we can begin to unveil what a true church on mission looks like. In a snapshot, a sending church:

- Understands that the mission of making disciples among all nations is the purpose for which the church exists and, therefore, utilizes all activities, resources, and time in the fulfillment of this mission.
- Finds the greatest motivation based on the supreme worth of God and His worship among all nations.

- Operates under the belief that all believers have been sent as God's missionary people to this broken world. The pastors and church leaders see their roles as equipping, training, and commissioning every member to live out missions wherever God may send them.
- Prioritizes the transformative message of the gospel and its proclamation by those whose lives are worthy of the calling of God.
- Celebrates the lives of those members who are joyfully and faithfully living out Christ's commission.

Steps on the Journey

So, the first step in the journey toward being a sending church is to assess the current realities of your church. What can you celebrate? What are areas of needed change or prioritization? With a better understanding of a sending church, let's discuss some marks that will help you identify potential areas to celebrate and other areas for growth. Below we will discuss three overall marks of a sending church. Don't view these as chronological steps but rather key marks that should be evident in the life of a sending church.

1. Support the Mission

First, a sending church is a church that is leading its people to support the fulfillment of Christ's commission. As we discuss this, think of support in three primary areas: praying, giving, and discipling.

Praying—Prayer is truly a work of mission. We know that we can do absolutely nothing without Christ and He has commanded us to pray to the Lord of the harvest to send out laborers into the harvest. There can be no mission outside of our consistent and intentional prayer. Consider how your church:

- Leads and equips members to pray specifically
  - For specific peoples and places not currently being transformed by the gospel both locally and globally

- o For missionaries, that their lives and work will be led by the Holy Spirit
- o For the whole church to live faithfully as God's sent people
- Provides avenues for intentional prayer
  - o Scheduled time within corporate gatherings
  - o Focused attention within small group ministries
  - o Members discipled to engage in daily, personal prayer
- Celebrates answered prayer

Giving—Giving is likely one of the topics we as church leaders like to talk about the least. We are sensitive to how it will be perceived by the members. Yet as we address giving from a perspective of missions, we should not be timid. Sacrificial giving enables and facilitates the steps of obedience in both making disciples and in sending them out among the nations. We give to enable the work of the church in fulfilling Christ's commission. This is why we must strive to be sure the resources given to us from God are being utilized for that purpose and our budget should be organized and communicated from that understanding. Questions to consider:

- Are we effectively utilizing our resources in our local context for the sake of making disciples?
  - o Priority should be given to disciple-making communities and processes.
  - o Investments should be in systems and processes for equipping and training members to live out their biblical purpose of being sent on mission.
  - o We should fight the urge to make this world our home, focusing on inward comfort, preferences, and desires. Everything here is temporal. Therefore, spending should be focused on things that impact eternity.
  - o Financial decisions should be made in light of Christ's commission.
- Does our budget reflect a passion for God's glory made known among all nations?
  - o What percentage of gifts is used to help send messengers of the gospel to the nations?

- How does your budget reflect the readiness of your church to help send out members to the nations?
- Are personnel/staff expenses due to the focus on equipping members to be intentionally discipled and sent out?

Discipling—Far too often, pastors and church leaders are surprised when they have a member express an interest in being sent out. Not only should this *not* be a shock, but it should rather be a regular expectation of every pastor within the natural rhythms of his congregation. A sending church focuses on intentional discipleship that prepares and expects every member to live out missions wherever God sends. Below are some areas of focus as you intentionally disciple your people to live as sent ones.

- **Theology**—Disciples must continually grow in their knowledge of who God is and how He has revealed Himself in scripture. This is of utmost importance as members are sent out into a hostile world that has been blinded by the lies of the enemy, false religions, and pluralism. If God is the message of our mission, then it stands to reason that disciples being sent out should be on a pathway of increased, intimate knowledge of who He is.
- **Gospel**—The message of the gospel is the only hope for the brokenness of mankind. It is through this message that the dead become alive, that enemies of God become children of God, and those who are wicked become righteous. Disciples should understand the message of the gospel as well as ways to share it effectively in different contexts.
- **Community**—God has established His church to be the context for members being discipled and then being sent out. Because of this, members need to be discipled to embrace the commitment to a local church and the establishment of churches among all nations.
- **Holy Spirit**—We as believers are not left to devise our own plans and strategies but are rather led by the indwelling work of the Holy Spirit. As sending churches prepare their members to be sent out, an ongoing dependence on and empowerment

by the Holy Spirit will guide them to the where's and how's of fulfilling Christ's commission.

- **Culture**—While some elements of culture may be good and others may be bad, the reality is that culture is the lens through which people understand and respond to information and experience. Culture shapes the worldview of those with whom we hope to share the gospel. Teaching members how to observe and interpret culture will enable them to find ways to communicate the unchanging message of the gospel more effectively.

- **Discipleship**—As given to us through Christ's commission, our mission is to make disciples of all nations who are becoming more and more like Christ. Teaching members the rhythms of a life that conforms to the image of Christ enables them to help others grow in Christ.

- **Readiness**—Understanding that this world is not our home empowers us to view our lives here as only temporal, leading us to maintain shallow roots wherever God might send us at any given time. This understanding transforms our perspective on finances, property, relationships, health, etc. Members of sending churches realize that although their identity of "sentness" does not change, the location in which to live that out is dependent on the leading of the Holy Spirit.

2. Join the Mission

Strong, supportive leadership provides the church with a solid foundation for actively joining God in His mission. Believers have a role in God's global mission, and it is the responsibility of church leaders to equip and train them to be sent out. A sending church also provides avenues and pathways for members to join in His mission while keeping the big picture of God's heart for nations in view. As you look for ways to create pathways, consider the following principles.

- **Focus on the purpose of the pathways, not just the accessibility for members.** Often times, I hear well-meaning church leaders wanting to provide easy opportunities for those just beginning to step into missions activity. Yet the avenues of service are not truly effective and/or helpful. Providing accessible opportunities is crucial—but don't sacrifice the importance of gospel proclamation, disciple-making, and church planting.

- **Consider the nations next door.** God's plan from the beginning has been to redeem people from every nation, tribe, and tongue. The exciting reality of our day is that God has brought so many nations within proximity of our churches. Our cities are becoming more and more diverse, and many of the ethnic groups have very few disciples among them.
- **Explore relationships God has already provided.** As you seek pathways to join in God's mission, look for connections God has already provided to you. For example, seek ways to partner with those your church has already sent out. Or explore the possibility of establishing relationships with other missionaries who are already serving cross-culturally. You can seek out partnership opportunities with an end vision and methodology that fits both the mission field and your church.
- **Learn to assess members.** Although every believer does have a role in God's mission, not every member is best equipped for every opportunity or context. Some members will be best equipped to engage their neighbors, their community, and city, while some will be effective in moving to another culture. Some members will be able to pastor a church or even plant new churches while others will make incredible team members for church planting. Learning to assess others' readiness and skillsets will help your church send and shepherd your members more effectively.
- **Seek ways to take the message of Christ to where He is not yet known.** While gospel proclamation is needed all over the world, there are still many places among the nations where the gospel is not known. Since God wants to be worshipped among all nations, we should strive to find ways to proclaim the gospel to those who are still unreached. Once again, the commission Jesus gave us was to make disciples of all nations.

Thus far we have examined two marks of a sending church: supporting the mission and joining the mission. The third and final mark of a sending church is that of owning the mission.

3. Own the Mission

God's mission began long before you and I came on the scene, but now He has entrusted to us, His church, both the message and the ministry of reconciliation (2 Corinthians 5:18-19). Therefore, as Jesus' disciples, we must own the mission as having been stewarded to us for this season. So what would it look like for a sending church to own the mission? Below are a few potential characteristics. A church that takes ownership of God's mission:

- Develops and maintains a long-term mission strategy that guides its activities, use of resources, and the sending out of its members. This strategy …
  o is led by the Holy Spirit
  o is guided by global realities and needs
  o leads toward planting churches where no or insufficient disciple-making churches exist
  o strengthens existing churches for the sake of making disciples who make even more disciples
  o partners with the global church for the sake of disciples being made and churches being planted among all nations.
- Creates processes and systems to intentionally disciple, call out, and train members to be sent on mission. It finds ways to send church members out regularly, generously, and globally through …
  o intentional assessment processes that will determine locations, contexts, and roles for those being sent
  o creative thinking in sending, looking for ways to include businessmen, students, families, craftsmen, teachers, healthcare professionals, etc.
  o rhythms of celebratory grieving as members are being sent out regularly to live out missions in new contexts and locations.

- Ensures healthy sending and shepherding processes for the long term by providing ...
  - pastoring and shepherding even from a distance
  - partnership in the work
  - ongoing member care
  - tangible demonstrations of love, ensuring that those sent out are not forgotten
  - financial needs that are both personal and ministry based
  - support for sent ones when they return.

Summary

In review, we have discussed three primary marks of a sending church: supporting, joining, and owning the mission. How would you assess your church? If your first impulse is to think that your church has arrived and needs no further change, be careful. It's likely your church still has much growth to experience and an incomplete assessment will only hamper your church's spiritual development. On the other hand, if despair is your response, then take heart. God majors in grace and new beginnings. This is a new day, and God will provide ways and opportunities to take the next steps in leading your church toward becoming a sending church. Gather together a few leaders in your church with whom you can brainstorm, pray, and dream. Ponder together these questions:

- What immediate steps do we need to take to lead our church to become a sending church?
- What do we currently celebrate that needs to take a backseat?
- Who else can help lead our church in its next steps?
- What priorities need to shift in our church?
- Have we lowered the bar of expectation for our church members?
- Has God broken our hearts for His mission? Will we pray that He'll do so?
- As individuals, are we personally living out God's mission?

With most journeys, there is a point of completion or arrival. But as you strive to lead your church to become a sending church, there must be a realization that there is no completion of the mission until the return of Christ. In recent days, there have been many conversations and debates on what it means to complete the mission. Actually this is not our concern because we don't know when Jesus will come again. Instead, we can trust our sovereign God to complete His mission in His own timing and manner. Our job is simply to be about the task of making disciples among all nations. Our work will never end until the day that Jesus comes back to take home His bride. So until that time comes, let's be about the Father's business.

About the Author

Eric King has served as a church coach and strategist for over 9 years and currently leads a team of coaches with IMB. Prior to IMB, Eric served almost 9 years as a mission pastor in Florida. His education includes a Bachelor of Science degree and a Masters of Public Administration from the University of West Florida. Eric, Mariah and their 3 kids are part of Movement Church in Richmond, VA where Eric also serves as an Elder.

18

Ongoing Relationships on the Mission Field
by Carlton Vandagriff

All cross-cultural missionaries hope to see their work result in kingdom fruit, whatever the focus or scope of their ministry. Assessment (sending the right people), job matching (sending the right people to the right place), and timing (sending the right people to the right place in the right time) are all critical elements in helping new missionaries see their work bear the fruit they envision.

But beyond this initial phase, mission-sending churches and agencies too often give little time and effort to consider how the missionary is to function once on the field, specifically in regard to decision making, strategy planning, field supervision, and many other issues that must be addressed. At times, missionaries find themselves relating to a U.S. agency or church that does not understand the complex cultural context of the mission setting. In other settings, the missionary is functioning totally independent of the sending agency or church, and ministry focus can get sidelined by local pressures or circumstances for which the missionary is not equipped to address. In many situations, the missionary is cooperating with personnel from other groups or national partners and doesn't have the final word in all matters of concern.

There needs to be a delicate balance between all of the entities involved—the sending church, the agency, the field structure, and the missionary. Defining these relationships beforehand will help clarify how each entity speaks into the issues faced by missionaries on the field, plus establish the avenues for the on-the-field support they need to maintain healthy families and sustain effective ministry.

Included in this chapter are four models of how these relationships might be structured. These models are not ends in themselves but starting points for discussions between the parties involved. Having already had this discussion in many contexts, I've observed that the models not only clarify the thinking of each party involved, but also serve to demonstrate the advantages and disadvantages of each model.

No one model is perfect, and each can be utilized effectively. However, if one party expects matters to function in one way, but another party has different expectations, then each faces a disparity in understanding that can lead to conflict, hurt feelings, and dysfunction, and usually in times when all parties need to be working together to address the needs of the missionaries on the field. Moreover, it allows the parties to develop a fifth model, the model under which they choose to function.

The models provided at the end of this chapter include the four entities that are basic to the sending of most missionaries—the missionary, the sending church, the agency, and the missionary enterprise on the field. A solid line indicates where the primary decision-making authority lies, with the primary decision-maker highlighted in capital letters. The dotted line represents a functional relationship that is advisory in nature. They might have a part in the decision-making process, or provide pertinent information, but they do not have the final say in the decision or the development of a plan.

Stakeholders should discuss the appropriateness of each model for their context. It is important that the advantages and disadvantages of each model are discussed and a plan made regarding how the relationships are to be structured. A fifth model might be developed with additional circles that indicate other significant stakeholders, varied lines of relationships, and different arrangements of the circles.

In some cases, organizations may choose to operate under a set of multiple structures, depending on the nature of the work, the strengths of the missionary, and the desires of the sending church. In these instances, the organizational model must be clearly discussed and defined early in the process so that clear lines of authority and decision-making are identified. There may be certain instances where one model is utilized in specific settings, while another is utilized in other settings, all within the same missions location and strategy.

In **Model A** (diagram at end of chapter), the missionary is the primary decision-maker in the structure. This individual relates to a sending church and agency on an advisory basis, gaining input from each entity as deemed necessary. Often the sending church is primarily responsible in the raising of funds and sending the support. The agency provides training and logistical support, and helps to manage crisis and coordination on a macro level. The missionary relates to the work on the field as the primary decision-maker and planner, and calls upon the church and the agency to assist on an as-needed basis.

There are many examples of this model around the world, especially with missionaries who raise their support from a variety of sources. This method is quite popular among missionaries with a bent toward independence, desiring to be empowered to make quick decisions to capitalize on unique opportunities as they arise.

Model B has the church as the primary decision-maker in the structure. The agency provides services and logistical support, often on a fee basis, and possibly some coordination on the field. However, the church is the primary decision-maker in field matters and the primary contact for the missionary in seeking answers to questions they have not been empowered to address.

Many large churches that have the resources to be the primary funding source for missionaries utilize Model B. They are proactive in assisting missionaries to identify an agency that appropriately relates to their structure and intended mode of operation. This model is popular as it maintains an intimate relationship between the missionary and the sending church.

Model C pictures the agency as the primary decision-maker in the structure. This model is quite common with large denominational agencies and allows for the maximum utilization of cooperative resources. With a large agency, there are often expert resources that can be made available in times of need, and there can be a broader approach to strategy planning and visioning for the future. The church has a role in the process, but once the missionary is selected and the job identified, the agency becomes the primary voice in the life of the missionary.

Model D is one in which each entity has an equal say in the decision-making process. Before major decisions are made, there is a consultation and verification with each entity. Although this model is not widely used, it can be the default choice when the lines of authority, responsibility, and decision-making are not clearly identified in the beginning. It is interesting to note that in the utilization of this discussion method in many countries and in many settings, those in the early stages of establishing their organizational structure often choose Model D. The strength is that it provides the maximum input before major decisions are made. This can bring a measure of comfort to everyone involved, plus it ensures that the missionary is not forgotten in the process of forging plans for the future.

Case Study Number 1

John and Mary Doe* were hard-working missionaries. Once on the field, John became heavily involved in the ministry, learning language and mentoring young national leaders, thus spending many nights away from home. Mary began to struggle with the children, especially Charlie*, who was approaching the rebellious teenage years. Mary found herself arguing constantly with Charlie about mundane matters.

When John came home, he had little time to give Charlie and told Mary just to deal with it, effectively ignoring these family relationships. Mary complained to anyone who might hear, but there were no close missionary co-workers in the area with the authority to intervene. The sending church in the U.S. had little cross-cultural experience and just told Mary they would pray for the family. They did not want to get involved in personal matters of their marriage and assured her that this was a natural culture shock phase and all teenagers go through rebellion.

Mary became frustrated and began to share her heart with a national brother who had a listening ear. The agency connection was a country away and not attentive to Mary's cries for help. Moreover, agency leadership was interested in the progress John was making in the work, and probably encouraged his approach by giving many positive kudos about the results he was seeing.

This national brother spent time with Charlie and helped to relieve some of the parenting pressure from Mary. Mary began to share more and more with him as he would listen. He would visit frequently and Mary enjoyed his company, but she did not recognize that she was approaching a slippery slope of temptation.

One day it happened. Charlie stormed out of the house in a rebellious spirit, and Mary called this man for help. He came over, and before they knew it, the sympathy and comforting became physical, and the line of sin was crossed. Ultimately, John and Mary left the field and returned to the U.S.

How did this happen? Where were the accountability structures on the field for John and Mary? Who was there to hear Mary when she initially called out for help? Who was helping John maintain the proper balance between work and ministry? In many cases, when all are responsible, no one is actually responsible.

Case Study Number 2

First Baptist Church adopted the Mallakani people of a Southeast Asian country. Little information was available on the people group, but all indications were they had only a few believers and no churches or mission-sending agencies seeking to plant churches among them. The church began to pray for this people group and even sent a few teams to the area to learn about the local needs.

Bob and Jean Smith* were a part of the church's missions effort and after a vision trip to the country, they felt called to plant their lives among the Mallakani as cross-cultural church planters. Bob and Jean shared this calling with the church, and after a period of prayer and assessment, the church agreed to send and support them as their missionaries to this unreached people. The church had little experience in that area so they connected with a missions-sending agency that could provide a logistics infrastructure, strategy planning, and field support for the Smith family.

The Smiths learned the language well, then deployed to the area working on a tourism platform visa provided by the mission-sending agency, living in the heart of the Mallakani people. Bob gave about eight hours a week to platform management in return for the visa. Things went slowly during their first year on the field, and just about the time they began to gain momentum in the work among the Mallakani people, the agency lost some key personnel in a nearby country who were attached to the same platform.

The agency saw no solution but to inform the Smiths they would have to move to the nearby country so they could manage the platform. Many missionaries in the region depended on this platform for their visas. Due to Bob's knowledge of platform operations gained through experience plus his business background, he was the only one who could fill this role.

Needless to say, the Smiths were disillusioned with this abrupt change because their people group did not live in the neighboring country. The home church felt betrayed because they were not involved in this decision and were not given any opportunities to offer other remedies to the problem. The agency's view was that the Smiths have to consider the greater good of the work, which sometimes means sacrifice.

The Smiths found themselves in the middle of a major disagreement between their sending church, which provided their financial support, and the field agency that provided the local infrastructure and visa. The church questioned whether or not they could continue supporting a missionary who was not focused on the church's adopted people.

In the excitement of initially establishing this relationship, the church, the agency, and the missionary never worked out the structures and decision-making process in the event this sort of situation should arise. In the midst of the crisis, emotions were intense, time was short, and it was difficult to appropriately process the issues 5,000 miles away from church leadership.

Conclusion

It is imperative that as new structures and plans are discussed and adopted, the vision of establishing the church in places where there is no church is not forgotten and remains the centerpiece of the entire endeavor. The challenge for U.S. entities is our independent approach to much of what we do. We believe we can do it better, whatever it is, and that the involvement of others in that process is a sign of weakness and a lack of total surrender to the Lord. All four entities must be challenged in this regard.

Missionaries also are independent spirits, a trait that is sometimes necessary to function in challenging environments. They require empowerment and leadership, yet with appropriate accountability and training.

The Lord established the local church as His organization, His chosen structure for the fulfillment of the Great Commission. However, local churches cannot be an expert in everything, so they have to figure out how to cooperate and trust the expertise of agencies and organizations that do missions full time and have developed expertise in the many unique security and cultural settings around the world.

It also is important for the church to realize that kingdom resources should be channeled to take the gospel to those who have never heard, and agencies are often the only advocate for the vast populations of the unreached existing to this day.

Agencies must recognize that without the local church, there is no missions effort; both missionaries and missionary support come from the local church. In this day of social media and instant communication, the church is able to have an even more direct influence in the missions effort. Today's missionaries look to the church for vision, encouragement, prayer support, and personal engagement in the task.

Field realities do not fit into any one structure and can change over time as the work develops and matures. What might have begun as the ministry of one couple could end up as a combined effort of several mission organizations from a number of countries and a growing national church. The decision-making and responsibility for that work will change with each step toward maturity and will hopefully end with the national church taking on the full spectrum of responsibilities.

That does not prevent missionary involvement, but it does indicate a foundational point: the establishment of indigenous churches hinges on the potential for fully independent local bodies of believers. There is no defined time period for this to happen, but it is generally accepted that the role of missionaries is to "work themselves out of a job."

North Americans can learn much from our brothers and sisters in other countries. The survival and maximization of our efforts means we have to develop structures of mutual accountability and interdependence. This will require significant work from the outset but will reap much kingdom fruit as we determine how to walk forward, hand in hand, under the leadership of the Holy Spirit. In reality, the Great Commission belongs to the Lord; He simply allows us to participate.

Four Models for Missionary-Church-Agency-Field Relationships

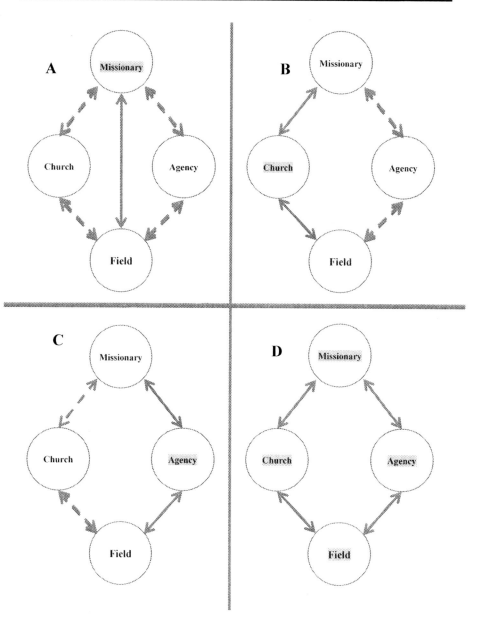

About the Author

Carlton Vandagriff and his wife Allison have a married son and a granddaughter. He has two degrees from East Texas State University, an Ed.D. from the University of North Texas, and studied at Southwestern Baptist Theological Seminary. Carlton was a high school coach and teacher before going overseas. He served two years in Brazil and 25 years in East Asia doing student work, church planting, and leadership training. He is currently the Associate Vice President in the Office of Global Engagement, IMB, leading those who process and deploy missionaries and networking with international partners.